LA MALINCHE IN MEXICAN LITERATURE

T0327016

La Malinche
in Mexican Literature
From History to Myth

by Sandra Messinger Cypess

UNIVERSITY OF TEXAS PRESS, AUSTIN

Fourth paperback printing, 2000

Requests for permission to reproduce material from this work should be sent to Permissions, University of Texas Press, Box 7819, Austin, Texas 78713-7819.

⊗ The paper used in this publication meets the minimum requirements of American National Standard for Information Sciences— Permanence of Paper for Printed Library materials, ANSI Z39.48-1984.

Library of Congress Cataloging-in-Publication Data
Cypess, Sandra Messinger.
  La Malinche in Mexican literature from history to myth / Sandra Messinger Cypess.—1st ed.
    p.   cm—(The Texas Pan American series)
  Includes bibliographical references and index.
  ISBN 0-292-75131-1 (alk. paper).—ISBN 0-292-75134-6 (pbk. : alk. paper)
  1. Mexican literature—History and criticism. 2. Marina, ca. 1505-ca. 1530, in fiction, drama, and poetry. 3. Mexico—History—Conquest, 1519–1540—Literature and the conquest. I. Title. II. Series.
PQ7125.M37C97   1991
860.9'972—dc20   91-15702

For Ray
Everyone knows why

Contents

Preface

THE FIGURE of La Malinche has fascinated me for a long time. On the surface we have very little in common, this sixteenth-century Amerindian woman I prefer to call La Malinche and I, a teacher and critic working in the United States, dedicated to the study of Latin American culture. She is a symbol for me of women in patriarchal culture, just as the reactions to her also bring into discourse the debate on ethnicity and identity as well as the gender issue that unites us. She appears to have had so many characteristics valued by our society, combining beauty and intelligence, motherhood and a career. Yet during most periods of history she has been maligned and mistreated, an exile in her own land. The contrast between my perceptions of her and the changing interpretations that successive generations have produced shows clearly how ideology is encoded within each text, as part of each interpretation. Just as I have tried to evaluate the ideological agenda of each writer, I acknowledge my own feminist perspective tempered by cultural biases. Recognizing that the interpretive process involves issues of ethnicity, class, sex, and culture does not mean, however, that the reader or critic must mirror the writer's identity or sociohistorical situation in order to read the text. A positive resolution to this difficulty is based on the critic's recognition of difference as a starting point, whence I proceeded with my inquiry into the Malinche paradigm.

Some technical points need to be clarified with regard to translations and the transcription of Amerindian names. Unless otherwise noted, I am responsible for the translated passages. My aim was not to create a literary version but to convey for the reader a sense of the literal text for purposes of my analyses. As for the rendering of Amerindian names, I have tried to be consistent by following the English custom of no accent on the Nahuatl words while using the accent in the Spanish texts according to Spanish usage. Thus I have endeavored with the help of the editors to assure that the reader will see Cuauhtemoc or Cuauhtémoc, Quetzalcoatl or Quetzalcóatl, etc., in the appropriate contexts. Since there are many variants of the spellings of some names, from La Malinche's Indian name (Malinal, Malinalli, Malintzin—even Malitzin, according to Rodolfo Usigli's play *Corona de fuego*) to the names for Moctezuma and Cortés, I would like to prepare the reader in advance for any apparent discrepancies.

Since one of the assumptions of this book is the dependency of a given discourse on other discourses, I want to acknowledge some of the sources that have helped to shape this text. I have sought the advice and suggestions of colleagues and friends in my attempt to offer a comprehensive and thoughtful discussion of the theme. First to be remembered are the early influences of Luis Leal, Merlin Forster, and Frank Dauster; their work and dedication have always been an inspiration. A number of people read drafts of different chapters, providing commentary and observations that have enriched the manuscript; I am particularly grateful to Edward Sisson, Guillermo Schmidhuber de la Mora, and Inés Hernández. Maureen Ahern especially was always ready to provide encouragement and good criticism. Sharon Magnarelli should also be singled out for suggesting insightful recommendations with her usual generosity and style. Rachelle Moore, the Latin American bibliographer at SUNY Binghamton and a dear friend, assisted in many ways, from gathering sources to listening to ideas. Their contributions along with those of the readers and dedicated editorial staff at the University of Texas Press have enabled me to avoid errors of fact and interpretation, yet I accept the ultimate responsibility for the final text. On the technical side, the staff of the SUNY Binghamton Computer Center offered their help and facilities during the long hours I spent at the computer.

It is important to recognize with thanks the many friends and colleagues who offered suggestions of additional texts that either mention La Malinche or appear to use the paradigm as a subtext. The temptation to continue adding more material to this book was finally tempered by considerations of time and space as well as by the resolve to carry on this project with further studies on aspects of the theme not covered in this initial monograph. I also want to express appreciation to Dr. Michael Carter, Dean of the College of Nursing at the University of Tennessee, Memphis, where I served as a research professor in gender and culture during the 1990 spring semester, putting into practice the ideas on gender and ethnicity that were generated from the preparation of this study.

I am also grateful to the National Endowment for the Humanities for its support; through my participation in the NEH–University of Maryland Summer Institute held in Mexico in 1989 on "The Encounter of Cultures in Sixteenth-Century Mexico," I was able to increase the scope of the study and share ideas with many new and old friends with similar interests. In Mexico I am proud to have had such distinguished personal guides to the literature and culture as Emilio Carballido, Sabina Berman, and Margo Glantz.

Most important has been the Messinger-Cypess consortium which I have been a part of for many years. The unfailing support and constant encouragement of my husband, Ray, a Renaissance scientist-educator whose critical comments brought focus and continuity to the project, need to be singled out for special recognition. My sons, Aaron Martin and Joshua Neil, have shared me with my books and students all the years of their lives, and their presence is a part of everything I do.

Acknowledgments

I AM grateful to the following publishers for allowing me to quote from material previously published in their texts: *Theatre Journal* for "From Colonial Constructs to Feminist Figures: Re/Visions by Mexican Women Dramatists," in *Theatre Journal* 41.4 (December 1989): 492–504; Anita K. Stoll, editor, and Bucknell University Press for "The Figure of La Malinche in the Narratives of Elena Garro," pp. 117–35 in *A Different Reality: Studies in the Works of Elena Garro* (1989); *Cincinnati Romance Review* for "Shades of the Past: Revenants on the Mexican Stage," in *Cincinnati Romance Review* 9 (1990): 154–64; *Alba de América* for "Dramaturgia femenina y transposición histórica," in *Alba de América* 7.12–13 (1989): 283–304.

The "Marina" poems, © 1976 by Lucha Corpi, translation © 1976 by Catherine Rodríguez-Nieto, were first published in *Fireflight* (Berkeley: Oyez, 1976) and are reprinted here with permission from the author and the translator. Gabriel Guerra Castellanos, Maureen Ahern, and the University of Texas Press granted permission to reproduce the translation to the poem "Malinche" by Rosario Castellanos. The Archer M. Huntington Art Gallery of the University of Texas gave its permission for the reproduction of slides from the Lienzo de Tlaxcala. *Cortes and Malinche*, by José Clemente Orozco, is reproduced courtesy of the Instituto de Investigaciones Estéticas, UNAM, Mexico.

LA MALINCHE IN MEXICAN LITERATURE

CHAPTER ONE

La Malinche as Palimpsest

THE CONQUEST of Mexico begun in 1519 by the Spanish conquistadors is a pervasive subtext for Mexican culture. The invasion constituted a clash of cultures involving archetypal patterns that have formed a myth more consequential than the historical reality. The historical event has been described, interpreted, and converted into a symbolic construct that is reinterpreted by each successive generation. The conquest remains a reverberating presence in the Mexican and Latin American psyche, and the characters of the dramatic spectacle sustain both Mexican and world literature.

The participants themselves differed in their views of the circumstances, as a comparison of the existing documents reveals. Hernán Cortés, leader of the Spanish expedition that conquered the Aztec empire and brought the several Indian nations of Mexico under Spanish control, wrote ongoing reports to his king, Charles V, and his *Cartas de relación* (*Letters*) offers his point of view. His secretary and biographer, López de Gómara, also published a version of the conquest, which was considered sufficiently controversial that one of Cortés's foot soldiers, Bernal Díaz del Castillo, was motivated to "set the record straight." Accounts of indigenous reactions to the conflict can be found in the collection compiled by Miguel León-Portilla, *La visión de los vencidos*, translated in 1962 as *The Broken Spears*. Moreover, key literary texts in subsequent historical periods have provided alternatives to the traditional telling of the conquest. Each narrator focuses on different elements of the event, reflecting the distinct historical and political needs of that period.

The opinions of all participating groups have been represented in the formation of the tradition, except for the voice of one major figure whose role is considered crucial and consequential but whose discourse does not appear in a first-hand account: La Malinche, the Indian woman who became the interpreter, guide, mistress, and confidante of Cortés during the time of the conquest. Although her voice may have been silenced, her presence and functions are documented in the chronicles. For that reason she may be considered the first woman of Mexican literature, just as she is considered the first mother of the Mexican nation and the Mexican Eve, symbol of national betrayal.[1]

She is also known by different names, a characteristic she shares with another prominent historicoliterary woman, Queen Boadicea.[2] La Malinche is called Malinal, Malintzin, Malinche, or Doña Marina. Malintzin is formed from her Nahuatl birth name, Malinal, and Marina was given to her at her Christian baptism; La Malinche is the syncretic, mestizo form by which I shall call her, employing the others according to their use in the literary texts.[3] La Malinche has been transformed from a historical figure to a major Mexican and Latin American feminine archetype, a polysemous sign whose signifieds, for all their ambiguity, are generally negative. Like Don Quixote or Don Juan, La Malinche has become an international figure whose story has enriched the literature of other cultures and a variety of artistic forms.[4]

Despite the many controversies concerning other participants in the conquest, no figure is as ambiguous and abstract as La Malinche. Disputes abound concerning the formation of her very name, her birthplace, her early life before her encounter with Cortés and recorded history. The events of her life after the military phase of the conquest are also shrouded in mystery, and the date and causes of her death remain unknown. Very few Mexicans before the modern period were willing to accept her as anything other than a prostitute or a traitor. I must agree with the Mexican psychologist Juana Armanda Alegría that "La Malinche was the only important woman during the conquest of Mexico, and in that role, she deserves to be reconsidered. History has not been just to Doña Marina."[5]

The surviving image of La Malinche is a product of interpretations by both popular culture and the writers who have formulated the literary tradition in Mexico. Since the conquest, La Malinche has been the subject of biographical, fictional, pictorial, and symbolic interpretation, but this study is the first to delineate the transformation of the historical figure into a literary sign with multiple manifestations. It is also the first study to identify the formation of a Malinche paradigm, characterize its features, and show the changes that have occurred in the use of the sign through the impact of sociopolitical events on the literary expression.

The image we have of La Malinche has been produced largely through fiction and therefore can be studied as a literary construct. Based on the idea that literature is a social institution that has pro-

Anonymous, Lienzo de Tlaxcala Manuscript (courtesy Archer M. Huntington Art Gallery, The University of Texas at Austin, Archer M. Huntington Museum Fund, 1964)

vided role models and set patterns of acceptable and unacceptable behavior, the following chapters chronicle the presentation of La Malinche in Mexican literary texts: her historical significance, her evolving literary representations, and the changing interpretations of her role from the historians of the conquest to contemporary Mexican American/Chicana and Mexican women writers who consider La Malinche a symbol of the tensions, contradictions, and oppression inherent in their own sexual, racial, and ethnic identity. (Although I have just mentioned "Mexican American" and "Chicana" as apparently equivalent terms, their use may involve misconceptions and requires further explanation. Both may refer to the same individual, that is, one who lives in the United States but whose cultural roots are Mexican, yet the political and social implications differ depending on the context of use, the speaker, and the audience to whom the terms are addressed. In the 1970s, more conservative people considered themselves "Mexican Americans" and identified the term "Chicano" with politically radical attitudes or with social position rather than ethnic origin. Some writers still use the terms interchangeably, focusing on the common ethnic elements and overlooking the possibly different political perspectives. I use "Chicana" henceforth to refer to the women writers working in the United States whose cultural roots are Mexican in recognition of their acceptance of the term to describe themselves.)

By implying that "Mexican American" and "Chicana" may refer to the same individual yet may refer to two different concepts, I am making explicit the arbitrary signifying processes inherent in sign systems. In the following chapters I shall follow the semiotic definition of the linguistic sign as an arbitrary combination of a signifier and a signified. As the science dedicated to the study of the production of meaning, semiotics recognizes that each element we call a word is a sign, composed of two aspects, the expression plane, or the signifier, and the content plane, or the signified.[6] Within this semiotic framework, the construction of meaning is seen as an active process rather than something intrinsic in the sign. The following chapters explore how literary texts configure the sign "La Malinche." I have evaluated the ways in which the signifier, "La Malinche," enters into mobile correlations with the content plane, or the signified. The same signifier has come to stand for varying signifieds that have changed to meet the ideological requirements of a given sociocultural moment. The signifying elements include the way in which La Malinche is presented to the reader, the name by which she is known, what characteristics of personality and motivating psychological factors are attributed to her, the activities assigned to her, and the reactions of other characters.

The concept of intertextuality—that texts are continually being incorporated into other texts—is another guiding principle in my reading of "La Malinche." Intertextuality suggests that a text is not a self-contained unit and obliges one to consider the special referentiality of literary works; it is thus an appropriate theoretical framework for analyzing a historical figure and a historical event that have entered the discursive space of a culture, where the texts of the past coexist within the present, while the present image becomes intelligible only in terms of prior discourse. Thus the sign "La Malinche" functions as a continually enlarging palimpsest of Mexican cultural identity whose layers of meaning have accrued through the years. With each generation the sign "La Malinche" has added diverse interpretations of her identity, role, and significance for individuals and for Mexico.

Intertextuality offers a way of reading that places a text or sign in a discursive space, relating it to other texts and to the codes that operate in that space.[7] This book attempts to describe the intertextual space of the Malinche figure and the other discourses that affect it, refer to it, build from it, and grow within it. As Jonathan Culler reminds us, intertextuality "involves many things: explicit conventions of a genre, specific presuppositions about what is already known and unknown, more general expectations and interpretations, and broad assumptions about the preoccupation and goals of a type of discourse."[8] The importance of presupposition for literary analysis is that it modifies the way a text must be read by offering implicit references to prior discourse, to a tradition and conventions that the reader must decode. Following Edward Keenan,[9] Culler defines the notion of presupposition and its importance to intertextuality: presuppositions, distinguished as either logical or pragmatic, "relate sentences of a text to another set of sentences which they presuppose."[10] He uses as one example William Blake's poem "The Tyger," which begins with a series of questions: "What immortal hand or eye / Could frame thy fearful symmetry?" He comments that the poem identifies as implicit such sentences as "An immortal hand framed the fearful symmetry." These presuppositions of the sentences of the text are part of a discourse or mode of discourse already in place, "a text or set of attitudes prior to the poem itself."[11] Similarly, for each reader "La Malinche" is a textual sign loaded with presuppositions that influence the reader's relationship with the sign and its text.

When La Malinche was transformed into a sign, she became part of her culture's myth system. From an anthropological perspective, the dramatic stories that become myths authorize the continuance of ancient institutions, customs, rites, and beliefs.[12] Myths provide examples to be emulated, precedents to be repeated, and in light of that function their study enables us to decode a culture's attitudes toward its members. Because La Malinche, as an archetypal female figure in Latin America, plays such a vital role in Mexican and Latin American myths, it is imperative that the role she is traditionally assigned be evaluated and reevaluated. Such a study may contribute to cultural revisionism in Mexico, a society deeply involved in the process of change.[13]

For too long, false myths have distorted the images of women; and especially in Mexico, the myth of La Malinche has been one of the most restrictive. It is not, however, the only myth to generate images of women. As Luis Leal points out, La Malinche constitutes one of the two major female archetypes in Mexico, along with the Virgin of Guadalupe.[14] The Virgin of Guadalupe embodies the most virtuous feminine attributes: forgiveness, succor, piety, virginity, saintly submissiveness. La Malinche is the Mexican Eve, the tainted sex "who is selfish and rejecting, while Guadalupe is giving and nurturant. . . . A polarized perspective of women emerges whereby only La Malinche as supreme evil and La Virgen as supreme good are possible."[15]

Rosario Castellanos adds the seventeenth-century nun Sor Juana Inés de la Cruz, in "Once Again Sor Juana," her 1963 essay on the archetypes of Mexican culture: "There are three figures in Mexican history that embody the most extreme and diverse possibilities of femininity. Each one of them represents a symbol, exercises a vast and profound influence on very wide sectors of the nation, and arouses passionate reactions. These figures are the Virgin of Guadalupe, La Malinche and Sor Juana."[16] As a feminist, Castellanos sees the figure of Sor Juana as an enigma because of her dual configuration as genius and female. The lonely, oxymoronic stance of female genius, implied by the appellation "the Tenth Muse," as Sor Juana was called, has symbolized for Mexican culture not what women in their plurality were capable of achieving, but what only an idealized Woman, the *rara avis*, could attain. For Castellanos, the Virgin of Guadalupe and La Malinche are less ambiguous figures. She agrees that only positive elements are associated with the figure of the Virgin, an observation supported by specialized studies by literary critics, historians, and sociologists.[17] Veneration of the Virgin transcends pure religiosity and has become equated with a sense of unselfish motherhood and positive national identity. La Malinche, at the opposite pole, embodies both negative national identity and sexuality in its most irrational form, a sexuality without regard to moral laws or cultural values.

Although Castellanos is more intent on focusing on the controversial views relating to Sor Juana, she tacitly acknowledges that La Malinche is fundamentally a polemical figure who influences contemporary behavior patterns: "Some call her a traitor, others consider her the foundress of our nationality, according to whatever perspectives they choose to judge her from."[18] La Malinche comes to signify the traitor to national goals; the one who conforms to her paradigm is labeled *malinchista*, the individual who sells out to the foreigner, who devalues national identity in favor of imported benefits. Castellanos compares the power of La Malinche to that of the Greek mythological figure Antaeus, who was always revived when he came into contact with the earth. Similarly, La Malinche has not died but remains in contact with Mexico, and her power to influence behavior has not diminished with time.

In the same way that the lexical term *malinchista* was derived from her experiences, so have the figures of La Chingada and La Llorona become involved with her paradigm. La Malinche's sexual involvement with Cortés led to her designation as the first "*chingada*," a term charged with severe negative connotations for Mexicans, conjuring up personal violation and submission to rape, as will be discussed in chapter 5. The image of La Llorona, or weeping woman, at one point became conflated with the image of La Malinche because they share a sadness relating to lost children.[19] In popular mythology La Malinche serves as a synecdoche for all Indian women who lament the fate of their progeny born to the Spanish conquistadors.[20]

Textual analyses of the figure of La Malinche demonstrate how the cultural myth has evolved through time and how it continues to serve as a paradigm for female images in Mexico, for the ways men and women relate to each other. Paradigms serve as guidelines for ethical, esthetic, or conventional actions. I consider La Malinche to be a root paradigm in the way Victor Turner uses the term. According to Turner, a cultural root paradigm goes beyond the cognitive and the moral to the existential domain; in so doing, it becomes "clothed with allusiveness, implications, and metaphor."[21] A root paradigm is a cultural model that is continually reinvested with vitality within the social drama. Turner defines social drama as a period in which conflicting groups and personages attempt to assert their own paradigms; he includes the Mexican Revolution of Independence in 1810 as an illustration of "a root paradigm at work in a series of social dramas."[22] For Turner, the years between 1810 and 1821 comprise a complex and dramatic liminal period in which those being moved in accordance with a cultural script were liberated from normative demands. The period of transition from colonial rule to Mexican nationhood generated "new myths, symbols, paradigms, and political structures."[23]

The time of the conquest, from 1521 to 1528, was similarly a complex and dramatic liminal period that generated new myths, symbols, paradigms, and social structures. This was the period during which the political and cultural consequences of European dominance in the Americas were set. The conquest was the crucial event in the formation of male-female relations. Succinctly described by Elu de Leñero, the traditional image influencing male-female relationships is derived from Cortés being served by La Malinche. In the way a Mexican man enjoys dominating a woman, wants service from her, and expects to impose his will and body on her and then dispose of her, he repeats the pattern Cortés established with La Malinche.[24]

In the literary texts that employ the Malinche image, the popularly known characteristics of the paradigm have been added to the legendary character because of past literary interpretations rather than the actual deeds of the historic figure. Although folkloric narratives and popular poetry make use of the conquest theme and La Malinche, I have analyzed in this work only those elements of the popular expression that have been successfully incorporated into literary texts. Future studies will attempt to cover the many variations of the paradigm that are found in expressions of popular culture as well as in the texts of other cultures.[25]

In following the development of the sign "La Malinche" from a diachronic perspective, the relevant presuppositions that have been deeply embedded within the palimpsest need to be uncovered. The palimpsest is an important archaeological image in Mexico and describes the way the Aztecs, Mayans, and other tribes built one pyramid atop another, or how the Catholic church constructed its religious sites on pre-Hispanic foundations. Chapter 2 presents the Aztec environment in which La Malinche was reared as Malinal and the attitudes toward women in that society as well as the sociopolitical alliances of the tribes in the region and the conventions at work that affected the behavior of the protagonists of the conquest. Contemporary mythologies, including the belief in the return of Quetzalcoatl, one of the important gods in the Amerindian pantheon, are additional factors considered in analyzing the cultural environment entered by the Spaniards.

As the Spanish texts of the conquest show, the Amerindian woman called Malinal was quickly transformed into a Hispanic lady and baptized with the name of Doña Marina. As Doña Marina, she was seen as a positive figure, and her actions and behavior were equated with those of chivalric heroes from the Spanish literary tradition and biblical figures such as Joseph in Genesis.[26] The debt the Spaniards owed her for their victory over the Aztecs was clearly expressed by a number of chroniclers. Protector of the foreigner, she was also the Great Mother; the child she bore Cortés, Don Martín, was considered the first mestizo, origin of the Mexican nation, the union of the Amerindian and European.

During the colonial period, Doña Marina was largely ignored in the literary texts of the colony, including those by the major writer of the period, Sor Juana Inés de la Cruz.[27] After the War of Independence, the identity of Doña Marina was subsequently transformed from its Spanish cultural form to a version circumscribed by the patriarchal culture developing in a newly independent Mexico. The Spanish conquistadors had read La Malinche as Doña Marina, an object of desire—of male dominance of the female, of desire for the land newly conquered. The Mexicans, in contrast, as a way of declaring their political independence, invented new interpretations for the signs of the colonizers; they required a construction of the signs that would serve as a signal of the new sociopolitical agenda.

To wrest control of the land from Spain meant dominating the images formed within a Spanish context. The new reading of the mother figure projected the resentment of the children for their progenitors and the system they had created. As the texts of newly independent Mexico show, many of the characteristics of Doña Marina considered positive by the Spaniards are reelaborated as negative elements. Disrobed of her accoutrements as the biblical heroine, Doña Marina is reincarnated as Desirable Whore/Terrible Mother, and the biblical image used to describe her at this stage is the serpent of Eden. This transformation signals a protest rejecting Spain and all associations with *"la patria."*

From the feminine version of the biblical Joseph, then, La Malinche becomes in the works of the postindependence period both the snake and the Mexican Eve, the traitor and temptress, the rationalization for the Amerindian failure to overcome the Europeans. From great lady to Terrible Mother, La Malinche serves the particular historical needs of a complex society in change.[28] The transformation can be found in *Jicoténcal* (1826?), also known as *Xicoténcatl,* one of the first known novels to deal with the events of the conquest. Published anonymously in Philadelphia, it is one of the first texts to present a negative view of La Malinche,[29] according to Luis Leal. Calling her Doña Marina, the unknown author paints a literary portrait of her as the evil temptress and betrayer of *la patria.* This text made an impact in Mexico. By 1870, the phrase "seller of her nation" had become integrally associated with Marina in the portrait developed by Eligio Ancona in *Los mártires del Anáhuac* (The martyrs of Anahuac).

Ireneo Paz, the grandfather of the well-known contemporary literary figure Octavio Paz, contributed a more tempered picture to the formation of the legend of La Malinche in his romantic novels *Amor y suplicio* (1873; Love and torment) and *Doña Marina* (1883). His work is representative of the postreform period of Mexican history, and his texts attribute to the literary Malinche and to other Amerindian women the characteristics associated with the historical Malinche: willingness to consort with the newcomers, betrayal of her people in favor of the Spaniards, rejection of Amerindian culture, and acceptance of the Catholic religion. Paz uses the Cortés-Malinche paradigm as the emblematic encounter between Europeans and Amerindians. By rewriting the military and political exploits of the conquest in terms of a sexual encounter, he follows the patriarchal view of women as objects of exchange; but instead of considering the woman an inferior social being, he romanticizes her as a noble being whose actions were dictated by destiny and the gods. He offers a positive interpretation of Mexican *mestizaje,* providing his readers with a positive conception of themselves and their history. He rewrites history in a way that fits the social and political ideologies of his time: a nationalism that strives to incorporate the Indian within the paradigm of Mexican identity.

From the time of Ireneo Paz to that of his grandson, Mexico underwent a major liminal experience: the Mexican Revolution. The literary explosion of works dealing with Mexican national themes concentrated on the revolution, while the Conquest of Mexico as a literary motif was slighted by most writers. Esthetic expressions of the theme of the conquest were created within the context of the indigenism of the great muralists of the twenties and thirties, José Clemente Orozco and Diego Rivera. In *The Aztec Image in Western Thought* Benjamin Keen describes the presentation of both Cortés and La Malinche in these murals.

The written text that synthesizes the most representative aspects of the modern attitude toward the Malinche legend is *El laberinto de la soledad* (1950; *The Labyrinth of Solitude*) by Octavio Paz. The section "Los hijos de la Malinche" defines La Malinche for the mid-twentieth century. Paz shows La Malinche's relationships with the biblical Eve and with Mexican figures such as La Chingada and La Llorona. He sees La Malinche as representative of the "cruel incarnation of the feminine condition." For Paz, the Conquest of Mexico was a violation, and Doña Marina represents the violated mother, the passive figure in the event—La Chingada. This study emphasizes the intense negativity with which La Malinche is regarded and shows the polarized perspective with regard to women in Mexican society. The successful dissemination of Paz's portrayal in the modern period can be gauged by its use in popular books destined for foreign consumption, such as Irene Nicholson's *The X in Mexico.* Nicholson uses Paz's essay to substantiate her view that modern Mexicans consider themselves the sons of Malinche and, therefore, "they are traitors in their own minds."[30]

Although Paz did not invent the negative role for La Malinche, the synthesis found in his essay serves as a norm for most of the texts written during this period. In the interest of being instructive rather than exhaustive, I have selected for analysis some representative texts that portray the traditional negative image of La Malinche in their presentation of female figures. While during the nineteenth century narrative form was popular for addressing the theme of the conquest and its role in the building of the Mexican nation, in the aftermath of the Mexican Revolution the theme of the conquest was displayed on the Mexican stage; narrative was employed instead to record the experiences of the more recent bloody and violent conflict that was the Mexican Revolution. *Corona de fuego* (1960; Crown of fire) by Rodolfo Usigli and *Cuauhtémoc* (1962) by Salvador Novo provide examples of attempts to offer enthusiastic support of the Amerindian contribution to modern mestizo Mexico, to the detriment of the reputation of La Malinche.

La Malinche o La leña está verde (1958; Malinche or The firewood is green) by Celestino Gorostiza re-creates an image of La Malinche that is meant to be more positive and supportive of her role as First Mother. Nevertheless, Gorostiza betrays his heroine on the sacrificial stone of patriarchal patterns of behavior. *Todos los gatos son pardos* (1970; All cats are gray) by Carlos Fuentes also attempts a positive portrayal, or at least one that breaks the traditional configuration; yet this Marina, too, is restricted by the paradigms of patriarchy. While Gorostiza was writing at a time in which positive Mexican nationalism was strong, Fuentes's play reads the events of the conquest within the context of the Tlatelolco massacre of 1968.

His recall of the contemporary political scene is similar to the double readings offered by the authors of *Xicoténcatl* and *Los mártires del Anáhuac,* who were writing during earlier complex and dramatic liminal periods. The deadly clash between the Mexican armed forces and university students on the same site that witnessed the conflict between Amerindians and Spaniards during the conquest leads Fuentes to conclude that the repetitive patterns in the social drama of Mexico remain intact. Although he calls his character Malintzin/Marina/Malinche in an effort to reflect his all-inclusive agenda, the character fails in the attempt to organize a new social structure.

One positive response to the dramatic nature of interactions occurring during the liminal period of the Mexican social scene after the Tlatelolco Massacre is that the theater has become a site where cultural change is not simply reflected but also enacted.[31] Theatrical representations not only make use of the iconic value of La Malinche as a sign but also change the signified elements. The project of creating new readings of Mexico's past indicates a rejection of the belief that the past is predictor of the future. This new perspective is reflected in the plays of Rosario Castellanos, Willebaldo López, and Sabina Berman. They accept the idea that the past is not a closed system but "a dialectical field of forces whose artifacts can be actively engaged through theory, interpretation, transformation, parody, subversion, whatever."[32]

The traditional image of La Malinche continues to be transformed by writers who question past interpretations of the sign and judge them as no longer appropriate for today's perspective on female-male relations. Rosario Castellanos's poem "La Malinche" re/views the paradigm from a point in the history of the figure itself, initiating an approach developed by Chicana women. La Malinche is a part of the cultural heritage of today's Chicanas, who see the need to place her contributions to history within a sociopolitical context corrected for distortions. Many are feminist writers, whose representations of La Malinche have radically altered the configuration of the image. The revisionist works of these Chicana writers are significant because they react to the negative presentations of La Malinche as a direct defamation of themselves. Representative of this attitude is the comment of Adelaida Del Castillo: "Any denigrations made against her indirectly defame the character of the Mexicana/Chicana female. If there is shame for her, there is shame for us; we suffer the effects of these implications."[33] For many of the Chicanas, La Malinche stands at the base of *la mexicanidad* and *el mestizaje*—the origin of the mestizo nation. Her body becomes the locus of origin of the contemporary Chicana and her offspring are symbolic daughters and sons. The Mexicana/Chicana writers point out that the use of La Malinche as a scapegoat figure can be interpreted as an effort to sustain male power by treating women as sexual objects and inferior moral entities. Her participation in the conquest as an active and vital figure needs to be re/viewed as a way to reject the destructive implications of previous interpretations and to recover the positive attributes brought forth by feminist and nationalist perspectives.

Several writers who challenge the accepted conventions offer in their texts a different reading of the historical record. They begin with the old presuppositions but critique the traditional assumptions of the patriarchal culture. Two texts by Elena Garro, *Los recuerdos del porvenir* (*Recollections of Things to Come*) and "La culpa es de los tlaxcaltecas" (The Tlaxcalans are to blame), fit into this new agenda, as do two recent plays by Emilio Carballido: *Ceremonia en el templo del tigre* (1986; Ceremony in the Temple of the Tiger) and *Tiempo de ladrones: La historia de Chucho el Roto* (1983; Time for thieves, the history of Poor Chucho). Although these texts do not deal ostensibly with the conquest, the figure of Marina and the events of that historical period serve as a subtext, thereby inserting aspects of the paradigm into a consideration of male-female relations and into the theme of nationalism. These works that use the Malinche paradigm as a subtext prove the continuing impact of the image in Mexican culture and point to the need for a revision of the paradigm. The traditional image presented a script that determined male-female behavior patterns according to a patriarchal model. Yet the tightly bound image of a patriarchal Malinche that once crystallized the thoughts and emotions of a nation has been refashioned as an icon with new signification that reflects a new cultural agenda. Re/formations and re/visions of the meaning inherent in the sign of La Malinche signal the development of real structural changes in social relationships.

CHAPTER TWO

Aztec Society before the Conquest

MOST STUDIES of the Spanish conquest of Mexico agree that Hernán Cortés and fewer than six hundred Spaniards conquered the Aztec empire, whose subjects numbered millions.[1] How could such a tiny handful of men prevail? The routine explanations refer to the importance of a number of factors that have to do with the skills of the Spaniards in exploiting the political situation they encountered and the cultural factors at play in the Amerindian world. The popular view that La Malinche's actions caused the downfall of the Aztec nation is not supported by the sociopolitical conditions at the time of the conquest, although it is easier to denounce her than to ascribe the ignominious defeat to a series of complex cultural and military confrontations. The irony of her portrayal as a force powerful enough to bring down an empire can be appreciated after an overview of pertinent customs and institutions of Amerindian civilization, which will also help to explain the successes of the Spaniards.

Any attempt to re-create the nature of Amerindian culture before the arrival of the Europeans is handicapped by the sources of information. The Amerindian documents were composed after the reality they wished to re-create was in the process of disappearing or no longer existed.[2] *The Broken Spears* is a useful recompilation of the versions of the conquered people, transcribed in their own languages or translated into Spanish, but written from their own perspective. As Miguel León-Portilla informs us, some native accounts were generated as early as 1528, only seven years after the fall of Tenochtitlan, capital of the Aztec empire, yet they were largely ignored by subsequent historians.[3] Not only were the disseminated versions of the conquest those of the conquerors, but the European writers also tried to explain American peoples, customs, and culture in terms of their own vocabulary and needs, a Eurocentrist mentality that the Spanish chroniclers were not even conscious of applying, as noted so carefully by Enrique Pupo-Walker in *La vocación literaria del pen-*

samiento histórico en América (The literary vocation of historical thought in America). Our knowledge of preconquest indigenous society has largely been filtered through the minds of the conquering Spaniards.

Franciscan friars were the first of the Europeans to record the indigenous civilizations. The Franciscan Toribio de Benavente, referred to by the indigenous people as "Motolinía" (poor man) because of his threadbare garments, wrote *Historia de los indios de Nueva España* (*Motolinía's History of the Indians of New Spain*) in 1541 and is considered the first writer of a history of the Indians of Mexico. Father Bernardino de Sahagún is the most illustrious early historian of Mexico and has been called the progenitor of modern ethnography.[4] His *Historia general de las cosas de la Nueva España*, written between 1558 and 1569 and translated as *General History of the Things of New Spain*, is an encyclopedia of ancient Mexico. His initial compilations were based on oral interviews and a study of the documentary records available—the codices and pictoglyphic books transcribed after the conquest. Sahagún's records have been corroborated so far by the most recent works on Mexican archaeology, history, and mythology and provide much of what is known about the native reactions to the arrival of the Spaniards.

When the Spaniards first entered the city of the Aztecs on November 8, 1519, the confrontation was more than a meeting of two expanding nation-states. As León-Portilla describes it, "It was the meeting of two radically dissimilar cultures, two radically different modes of interpreting existence."[5] Spain had recently proven victorious in its long battle of reconquest against the Moors and had gathered its political forces under a united crown.[6] Although Cortés had been sent on his Mexican expedition by Diego de Velázquez, governor of Cuba, he served as the agent of the Spanish king and therefore the single representative of European power facing the Aztec empire, another rich and complex civilization. Because many studies are available to provide detailed discussions of the sociopolitical history of Spain and pre-Spanish Mexico, only a brief history of the Amerindian nations in the fifteenth century is necessary for this discussion.[7]

The Nahuatl-speaking Aztecs dominated much of Mesoamerica at the time of the conquest and were the prevailing imperial power to be subdued by the Spaniards. They had originally migrated from the north in the early thirteenth century into the central valley of Mexico, conquering highly advanced city-states in their path. In the valley of Anahuac, they founded Tenochtitlan in 1325, the religious and political center of their empire. The Aztecs continued to con-

Anonymous, Lienzo de Tlaxcala Manuscript (courtesy Archer M. Huntington Art Gallery, The University of Texas at Austin, Archer M. Huntington Museum Fund, 1964)

quer other tribes and absorb other cultures until they dominated all of central Mexico.

Although the Aztecs overshadow other indigenous groups in popular legend, the pre-Columbian Amerindian world was not homogeneous but composed of many nations. The pre-Hispanic sociopolitical system was composed of tribal groups with complicated alliances. The Aztecs joined forces with Texcoco and Tlacopán as members of the Triple Alliance that successfully dominated various tributary towns. Notable among the independent states were those of the Tarascans and the Tlaxcalans. Rivalry among the groups, a significant motif that reappears in many contexts, was exacerbated by the heavy tribute that conquered cities were required to pay. Cortés took advantage of the hostility and resentment of many of the peoples who had been subjugated by the Aztecs. They helped Cortés as a way to find salvation for themselves from the tyranny and economic ties of Moctezuma.[8]

Aztec society was a stratified enterprise with five major classes organized in pyramidal fashion: the nobles, the priests, the merchants, the mass of the common free people, and—the major group at the bottom rung—slaves. (La Malinche was a slave at the time of her meeting with Cortés, but she is said to have been born into the noble class.) Slaves were usually victims taken in warfare but might also be people who could not pay debts or were guilty of crimes that required forced labor for expiation.[9] They had certain rights; bondage was not considered a hereditary position, and even slaves could be released from servitude after fulfilling their obligatory work. Slavery was so deeply ingrained in Aztec society, according to María Rodríguez, that there were special merchants dedicated to this type of commerce. The women were used for manual labor and sexual service.[10]

Another large group at the lower end of the socioeconomic scale were called *mayeques,* those who rented their labor as agricultural workers or did other labor for wages. Above them were the ordinary citizens or *macehualtin,* who were divided into clans living in specific localities. They worked the land communally and were trained in warfare and agriculture at the schools they attended, but they were not taught the special subjects reserved for the noble class: reading, writing, astrology, and theology. The upper divisions, consisting of nobles or lords, were called the *tecuhtli.* At the pinnacle was the emperor or ruling leader, selected by rotation from candidates among the noble families; once chosen, he was considered a descendant of the sun and a deity who could not be touched or looked upon by the common people.

Because of the Aztecs' constant involvement in battles and conquest, the warrior gained prominence in Aztec society, and with him the divinity of war, Huitzilopochtli. Associated with the sun, he is the great god of Mexico-Tenochtitlan.[11] Military success was one way to become a *tecuhtli*, a status that was part civil and part military. War was sanctioned by religion; the religious goal and purpose of war was to obtain sufficient victims to feed Huitzilopochtli the food he required: human blood. Many European historians have focused on what they considered the barbaric aspects of these customs, not placing the military practices within the context of the religious rites. León-Portilla stresses that beyond the apparent motivations "to conquer new territory, punish a rebellious vassal state, or repel an aggressor," the cause of their constant involvement in battles and conquest was their religious conception of warfare.[12] John Manchip White suggests that the elite depended on aggressive warfare to keep them in their luxurious lifestyle.[13] As Edward Sisson suggests, this view has become increasingly prominent because it makes Aztec society seem less aberrant.[14] After every campaign, the captured victims were sacrificed to Huitzilopochtli, but the booty was divided among the elite, and the tribute from conquered states maintained their wealthy status. The warriors secured the empire and procured wealth as well. The riches and military power of the Aztecs were results of conquering other states as they advanced from their northern homeland to the south.

León-Portilla indicates that the chieftain Itzcoatl, elected king around 1426, rewrote the past record of the Aztecs with the help of his royal counselor, his nephew Tlacaelel, in order to strengthen their future activities as conquerors.[15] The new version asserted their descendance from the Toltec nobility, and "most important of all is the exalted praise given to what can only be called a mystical conception of warfare, dedicating the Aztec people, the 'people of the sun,' to the conquest of all other nations."[16] It was then that the sun god, Huitzilopochtli, gained in prominence over all other gods. León-Portilla believes that Tlacaelel was responsible for convincing the subsequent rulers after Itzcoatl's death—Moctezuma I and Axayacatl—"that their mission was to extend the dominions of Huitzilopochtli so that there would be a constant supply of captives to be sacrificed."[17] Thus, war was legitimized on religious grounds, while at the same time serving economic and political goals.

The Aztecs were so successful in conquering other city-states that some groups elected to sign treaties and deliver tribute rather than risk war. The Cempoalans on the Gulf Coast agreed to pay tribute, but their ready compliance with the Spanish conquistadors proved their enmity to the Aztecs.[18] The Tlaxcalan state was a confederation of four republics with whom the Aztecs had been allies at various times. In the mid-fifteenth century, however, the two nations were in an almost perpetual state of military battle, referred to ironically as *Xochiyaoyotl,* or the Flowery Wars, which have been described as carefully ritualized war games in which both groups engaged in limited battles as a means of providing the sacrificial victims needed to propitiate their gods.[19] Recent interpretations of the Flowery Wars suggest that the Aztecs may have been unable to conquer the Tlaxcalans easily and were unwilling to pay the high price of an all-out war.

When the Spaniards arrived in 1519, the Tlaxcalans were involved in the Flowery Wars. As an independent nation, they were surrounded by Aztec-dominated states and were receptive to allying themselves with the Spanish against their enemy. The Spaniards came from across the seas and spoke a different language, but so had previous foreign invaders. The Aztecs also had come from "across the waters" (a lake) and spoke a different language from those used by many of their subjugated peoples.

The rivalry caused by the bellicose attitude of the Aztecs was used by the Spaniards to their advantage. Ironically, the way the Aztecs waged war was another element that led to their defeat. The Aztecs had a religious conception of warfare that motivated their aggressive expansion into neighboring territories. Elaborate rituals were followed at the commencement of a battle: "shields, arrows and cloaks of a special kind were sent to the enemy leaders as a formal declaration that they would soon be attacked. This explains the Aztecs' surprise when the Spaniards, their guests, suddenly turned on them without any apparent motive and—more important—without the customary ritual warning."[20] León-Portilla believes the cultural differences in waging war were a major reason for the Spanish victory over the Aztecs: "On several occasions the Aztecs probably could have wiped out the Spaniards to the last man—their best chance of all was on the Night of Sorrows—but the ceremonial elements in their attitude toward war prevented them from taking full advantage of their opportunities" (p. xxv).

Two other factors played a crucial role in preventing the Aztecs from capitalizing on the advantages they possessed, and both had to do with semiotics, or the reading of signs in a highly structured society. One factor was communication practices, the other the communicable diseases that the Spaniards brought with them. Although cultural differences led to a communication impasse in the verbal sphere, the pathogens of smallpox, typhus, and other diseases easily transferred themselves to the new populations. Interpretation of the signs of these communicable diseases could not have been based on an understanding of the underlying immunological causes. Instead, the obvious outer signs of disease were interpreted within the context of the Aztecs' previous experience and their conception of signs.

War and the religious calendar dominated daily activities. Just as special schools educated the young men of the noble class for war, other schools trained the priests in their complicated rituals. The Aztecs followed a religious calendar composed of thirteen months of twenty days, each day possessed of its own character, either lucky or unlucky. The nature of the day influenced all activity, from the fate of the child born on that day to the actions one was required to perform. The idea that one's birth on a given day influenced subsequent events meant that "free will and individual initiative held little promise, since all lives and destinies are in the hands of the gods."[21]

This belief in predestination was basic to the Aztec vision of time. The Aztecs believed they were living in the time of the Fifth Sun, four previous suns or ages having already been destroyed. The Spaniards arrived at the end of the Fifth Sun, when once again "there was the ever-present fear that the fifth sun would also be destroyed."[22] The Aztec belief in cyclical destructions marked their philosophical outlook with a "resigned fatalism" and a "foreboding of impending disaster."[23] Because the past could foretell the future, astrologers and soothsayers were important in the culture and were consulted before any major activity could be performed. It was a society in which a preestablished and systematic method of interpretation overrode any possibility of accidental happenings.

In the *Conquest of America*, Tzvetan Todorov, known for his semiotic studies of literature with their particular focus on symbolism and interpretation, studied the communicative strategies that were brought into conflict by the European encounter with America. For Todorov, the European discovery and conquest have paradigmatic value for us today: "it is in fact the conquest of America that heralds and establishes our present identity."[24] Although his own reading of the signs of the enterprise has been challenged, his insistence on the importance of the different ways the Indians and the Spaniards practiced communication can be accepted.[25] Basing his reading on documents provided by Motolinía and the Dominican Diego de Durán, another chronicler of the pre-Columbian world, Todorov emphasizes the importance of the prophet-priest class, who were regularly consulted by Aztec leaders before undertaking any important activity; "an overdetermined world will necessarily be an overinterpreted world" is his conclusion.[26]

The divine, the natural, and the social were known through indices and omens, with the help of the priests or soothsayers. Because everything was foreseeable, everything was foreseen, and in a sense the history of events became a realization of past prophecies, or as Todorov explains: "The whole history of the Aztecs, as it is narrated in their own chronicles, consists of realizations of anterior prophecies, as if the event could not occur unless it has been previously announced. . . . Here only what has already been Word can become Act."[27] A further development of this attitude was the collapsing of past and future. The very nature of events obeyed a cyclical principle, for time was thought to repeat itself. The Aztec calendar in the form of a circle provides a graphic illustration. They conceived of time not as a linear progression, as Western European thought has envisioned it, but as a series of repetitive actions frozen in an unalterable sequence, so that knowledge of the past led to that of the future, the two being the same thing. This characterization of Aztec relationships among the past, prophecy, and future action is important in the determination of the events of the conquest, because the chroniclers and historians tell us that the Aztec leaders had been told through omens and their own calendar that a great change was about to take place in the year Ce-Acatl. Theirs was a past-oriented, tradition-dominated world that could not easily accept the idea that an event could be entirely unprecedented; the conquest was an event foretold in the prophecies even before the arrival of Cortés and his men in 1519.

Many important prophecies featured Quetzalcoatl, the Feathered Serpent. His cult was one of the most consequential aspects of the Mexican belief system; its presence is traced to the third century C.E., to the Teotihuacan civilization on the central plateau. First conceived as an earth and water deity associated with the rain god Tlaloc, by the sixteenth century the Aztecs identified Quetzalcoatl with the planet Venus. As the morning and the evening star, the god was the symbol of death and resurrection.

Of the many legends associated with Quetzalcoatl, the elements of the story that bear upon the conquest relate to his disappearance from the central plains to a place in the east. It was repeated among his worshipers that Quetzalcoatl was expelled from Tula by Tezcatlipoca, the god of the night sky. Quetzalcoatl went east, to the coast of the Atlantic Ocean where he immolated himself on a pyre, emerging as the planet Venus. In another version, he fled to Cholula, where he remained 160 years before moving on to Cempoala, only to be persecuted by Tezcatlipoca until he fled to the desert and committed suicide. This movement of Quetzalcoatl may be a symbolic account of the steady advance of the Aztecs, who are identified with the war god of Huitzilopochtli, another enemy of the peace-loving Quetzalcoatl. Still another legend has him departing on a raft made of snakes and disappearing beyond the eastern horizon, promising his followers that he would return one day; since Quetzalcoatl's calendar name was Ce-Acatl (One Reed), it was taken as an indication that he would return from the east during the year of his calendrical sign. The year 1519 was equivalent to the Aztec year Ce-Acatl. Because one of the representations of Quetzalcoatl, in addition to his guise as a plumed serpent, was as a light-skinned man with a beard, it was a short step for the Aztecs to assume that the light-skinned bearded man coming from the east on a "raft" was Quetzalcoatl, or that the Spaniards were his emissaries coming to regain the throne by ousting the Aztec rulers.

Although Moctezuma first affirmed this possibility based on his interpretation of the legend of Quetzalcoatl and the other omens he experienced, he soon rejected that idea.[28] Jacques Lafaye believes that the "massacre of Cholula, the holy city of Quetzalcoatl, together with other indications, must have dispelled that terrible misunderstanding."[29]

The Spaniards did appear to share an element of immortality with the gods in their ability to withstand the ravages of a disease that was conquering the Amerindians in overwhelming numbers. While the Indians were dying of smallpox, the Spaniards were unimpeded. The Spaniards had developed immunity because of their exposure to these diseases in their homeland, but the Amerindians, for whatever reason, had never been exposed to smallpox, measles, or typhus and were immediately and mortally affected.[30] Within the mindset of the sixteenth century: "Such partiality could only be explained supernaturally, and there could be no doubt about which side of the struggle enjoyed divine favor. The religions, priesthoods, and way of life built around the old Indian gods could not survive such a demonstration of the superior power of the God the Spaniards worshiped. Little wonder, then, that the Indians accepted Christianity and submitted to Spanish control so meekly. God had shown Himself on their side, and each new outbreak of infectious disease imported from Europe (and soon from Africa as well) renewed the lesson."[31]

In *Plagues and Peoples* William McNeill attributes a large part of the success of the Spaniards in the conquest to disease epidemics; this theory motivated his own subsequent research into the effects of disease on human populations. He does not discount the other arguments offered for the Spanish victory: the skill of Cortés in finding allies among the Indian peoples of Mexico and rallying them against the Aztecs; Moctezuma's early belief that the Spaniards were representatives of the god Quetzalcoatl returning to reclaim their homeland; the magical effect of horses and gunpowder. The horses were soon shown to be mere animals, and gunpowder, too, had its limitations; some historians reject outright the supposition that the Aztecs ever thought the Spaniards were gods, and even if this assumption had been a consideration, it was soon dispelled by the mortality of the Spaniards. For example, on the Spaniards' Night of Sorrows, when the Aztecs drove Cortés and his men out of Mexico City, killing many of them, an epidemic of smallpox was also raging in Tenochtitlan. The military supremacy of the Aztecs did not lead to a decisive defeat of the Spaniards. As McNeill observes: "The paralyzing effect of a lethal epidemic goes far to explain why the Aztecs did not pursue the defeated and demoralized Spaniards, giving them time and opportunity to rest and regroup, gather Indian allies and set siege to the city, and so achieve their eventual victory" (p. 2).

It is not sufficient to consider only the political impact of the deaths of the Indian leaders during the time of their possible victorious assault against the Spaniards. McNeill emphasizes the psychological implications of the nature of the conditions of disease at that time. It was assumed by both Spaniards and Indians that "epidemic disease was a particularly dreadful and unambiguous form of divine punishment."[32] The Spaniards and their descendants in Mexico preferred to maintain the conquest mystique and did little to emphasize the devastation caused by the new infectious diseases. Few echoes of the epidemiologic and demographic factors appear in the literary texts, especially in those before the mid-twentieth century. Exemplary are the narratives of Ireneo Paz, whose express purpose was to review the history of the conquest for nineteenth-century Mexicans. Paz credited to the inherent attraction of European civilization and divine approval what should more equitably be attributed to the devastating effects of infectious disease epidemics.

Writing at the turn of the century, Justo Sierra noted that smallpox was called "the divine sickness" by the Amerindians because they believed it to be witchcraft in the way it spread with incredible swiftness among the Indian populace, killing Cuitlahuac himself, while leaving the Spaniards almost unscathed. Sierra observed that "the divine sickness . . . prepared Cortés' triumphal way."[33] In contrast, however, is Alfonso Teja Zabre's *Historia de México* (History of Mexico), first published in 1964 and directed to Mexican schoolchildren. Despite its subtitle, "A Modern Interpretation," the author employs a rhetoric that stresses the miraculous rather than the scientific. He makes no mention of the disease factor; among his primary explanations for the success of the Spaniards are the genius of Cortés and the protection of luck: "In the Conquest of Mexico, Cortés seems guided by a hand that saves him and leads him along the best paths,"[34] an attitude that echoes the nineteenth-century text of Eligio Ancona's *Los mártires del Anáhuac.* Ancona's treatment is paradoxical: his fictive narrator is the only one to refer directly to smallpox and its malign effects on the Aztecs, yet the rhetorical stress emphasizes luck.[35]

Recent investigators point out that the physical effects of the contagious diseases had reduced agricultural production and adversely influenced the will to bear children, to survive in a world devastated and inimical to the Amerindian cosmology.[36] Nevertheless, in literary sources on the conquest theme, the belief extracted from the cross-cultural encounter with illness was that the Spaniards were God's favored people. Even as staunch a Mexican patriot as Ancona has Geliztli, the Amerindian heroine of *Los mártires del Anáhuac,* warn her lover, the warrior Tizoc, that "the gods protect the foreigners."[37]

Awareness of the devastating tragedy brought by the new diseases to societies already under tremendous stress puts into perspective the roles of those who have become scapegoats in the nationalist interpretation of the conquest of Mexico. The success of the conquest cannot be attributed to the traitorous acts of La Malinche or the Tlaxcalans. The uncontrollable circulation of pathogens supported and exacerbated the military, political, and cultural imperialism of the conquest.

Military and religious customs, epidemiological factors, and the cult of Quetzalcoatl explain in part why the Spaniards were able to overcome the disadvantages of their situation. Their small numbers were obviated by the local allies they were able to make and by their superior technology with gunpowder, horses, and the wheel. But the Spaniards were also able to take advantage of the Aztecs because of their knowledge of the Amerindians. La Malinche functioned as translator and interpreter of Amerindian customs; in order to understand the unique position she enjoyed together with the price she and her descendants have paid for that special role, some aspects of family life and the attitude toward women in the Aztec world must be considered.

The emperor had one principal or legitimate wife, but because polygamy was accepted, he also had many others and numerous offspring.[38] The royal wives had a privileged position and were often highly accomplished and respected for their views and talents. Nevertheless, in *La mujer azteca* (The Aztec woman), María Rodríguez affirms that women were not encouraged to do anything more than cook, spin, and weave, and noble women in particular were not supposed to be engaged in any activity to earn a living.[39] Women, including those of the nobility, had limited political rights, and noble women were just as subject to the authority of father or husband as were commoners. Women were excluded from succession and were not permitted to exercise any official governmental role. At home, girls were instructed in their primary role, motherhood, and in performing daily household activities: "Girls worked in the household until they were sixteen to eighteen, when they married; boys took mates in their early twenties."[40] María Antonieta Rascón, writing in *Imagen y realidad de la mujer* (Image and reality of women), suggests that women in Aztec society were given respect for their roles as mother, agricultural producer, and home administrator.[41] Alfredo López Austin concludes that although women in urban populations were able to acquire a position of prestige, "society in general exalted what was masculine."[42]

Most marriages were monogamous, although relations outside marriage were not prohibited for men. In fact, sexual relations with slaves were not considered sinful, as the women were deemed bought objects.[43] Terrible punishments, however, were meted out to unfaithful wives. For women, virginity and fidelity were the highest womanly virtues, and marriage, like the reproductive process, was regarded as a sacred institution.[44] Aztec norms for female behavior persisted after the conquest, since they resembled patterns of behavior advocated by the Catholic religion.[45] La Malinche, first considered one of the primary indoctrinators of Catholic dogma among the Amerindian people, nevertheless is popularly identified as an example of a woman who deviated from expected female behavior. Her activities as translator, guide, and political go-between were extraordinary for both Aztec and Spanish societies. Her role as transferred slave, or, in European terminology, as mistress to Cortés the invader, ironically was one that Amerindian women were often forced to perform; yet the judgment against her as an infamous emblem of female transgression echoes a centuries-long opinion that is only now being revised.

CHAPTER THREE

The Creation of Doña Marina in the Colonial Period

ALTHOUGH CORTÉS was responsible for the significant part that La Malinche played in the conquest as Doña Marina, his own writings about her are remarkably reserved, as sparing of words as possible despite her numerous roles. He briefly refers to her in *Letter Two* as his translator: "my interpreter, who is an Indian woman from Putunchan (Tabasco)."[1] In *Letter Five*, after having described so many important events without bothering to refer to the Indian woman who had played such a significant—but obviously to him subservient—position, Cortés is only a bit more expansive in his narrative to the king: "If he [the Amerindian Canec] wished to learn the truth he had only to ask the interpreter with whom he was speaking, Marina, who traveled always in my company after she had been given me as a present with twenty other women. She then told him that what I had said was true and spoke to him of how I had conquered Mexico and of all the lands which I held subject and had placed beneath Your Majesty's command."[2] Cortés used Marina's role as translator to verify his own deeds and loyalty to the king; her indirect discourse served as a reflection of himself. Such self-serving practices would be incorporated into characterizations of him by subsequent writers, most notably Carlos Fuentes in *Todos los gatos son pardos*. Because Cortés himself provided so little information on the full ramifications of the activities of La Malinche, we must read the subtext as well as the surface signs in order to determine the context within which to understand her role and their relationship.

Both letters in which the references to La Malinche occur also contain Cortés's version of two especially controversial events of the conquest. In *Letter Two* Cortés mentions her in relation to the discovery of the conspiracy in Cholula and the events leading up to the massacre of the Cholulans, an exploit of great significance for the success of the conquest and for contributing to the so-called Black Legend of Spain's role in the New World.[3] It is also of great significance with regard to the "black legend" of La Malinche's role; according to the accounts of Cortés, Gómara, and Bernal Díaz del Castillo, she was the key source of information regarding the planned ambush of the Spaniards. Similarly, *Letter Five* refers to the 1524–25 voyage to Hibueras (today's Honduras), during which time Cortés ordered the torture and assassination of Cuauhtemoc; for La Malinche it was also the time of her marriage to Juan Jaramillo and the subsequent diminution of her role in the life of New Spain. The significance of these juxtapositions will be developed later in this chapter.

Cortés refers to the Indian woman as "Marina," without the title "Doña" usually used by Bernal Díaz. Cortés himself is referred to by a form of her name, "El Malinche," when he is addressed by the Indians. As Bernal Díaz tells us: "He was given this name because Doña Marina, our interpreter, was always in his company, especially when ambassadors arrived and during talks with chiefs, so they called Cortés 'the captain of Marina' in their language, or 'Malinche' for short."[4] This observation of La Malinche's accompaniment of Cortés at all the major meetings with chiefs and other important officials emphasizes the significance of her intervention in the negotiations despite the reticence of Cortés. Although he did not give official recognition to her presence in the *Letters*, the Indians who witnessed the transactions acknowledged her role by calling him "Malinche." Tzvetan Todorov's wry remark, that "for once, it is not the woman who takes the man's name,"[5] reminds us that the situation remains unusual to this day.

The *Historia verdadera de la conquista de Nueva España* (*The Conquest of New Spain*) of Bernal Díaz del Castillo has served as the source for biographical information about La Malinche. Although there is no way to prove his version right or wrong, it has been accepted in the historical tradition of Spain and Mexico. In the past his text was considered basically factual, while it has also been acknowledged that he "carefully selected portions of her life that enhance her stature as a participant in the Conquest. His elaboration of these episodes makes her into a true heroine."[6] The contemporary reader may well wonder which aspects of his narrative were invented and which actually occurred; but whatever the answer, we can evaluate the elements he chose to include.

In contrast to the paucity of textual information regarding the Indian woman on the part of his leader, Bernal Díaz provides a detailed and vivid portrait of this "most excellent" woman, the first descriptive phrase he applies to La Malinche.[7] In the words of Julie Greer Johnson, "Bernal Díaz is the only early colonial writer to make a woman a major figure in the historical events unfolding in Spain's American possessions."[8] Throughout his text, Bernal Díaz describes the intelligence, beauty, and amazing acts of heroism of La Malinche, as well as her unusual strength, spirit, courage, and resourcefulness. He also praises the abilities she displayed during the various military incursions she was forced to endure, commenting: "Doña Marina, although a native woman, possessed such manly valor that . . . she betrayed no weakness but a courage greater than that of a woman."[9] Bernal Díaz emphasizes the sufferings and tribulations of the Spaniards, which La Malinche shared without complaint (he considered this atypical for females). He compares her to models from the Bible and the Spanish literary tradition that were well known to his readers.

Bernal Díaz's second reference to La Malinche is also positive in the way he substantiates Cortés's comment that she was one of the twenty young women given to the Spaniards as a present by the Tabascan chief;[10] he singles her out: "One of the Indian ladies was christened Doña Marina. She was a truly great princess, the daughter of *Caciques* and the mistress of vassals, as was very evident in her appearance."[11] Because of her beauty and other excellent attributes, she was first given to a prominent conquistador, Alonso Hernández Puerto Carrero; when he left for Castile, she was transferred to Cortés, "to whom she bore a son named Don Martín Cortés."[12] This concise phrase referring to the birth of a child in 1522—after the major events of the military enterprise—may lead a reader to bypass its significance. By providing that information immediately after referring to her noble status and before elaborating on the other contributions of Doña Marina as translator and guide, Bernal Díaz reveals his own implicit attitude toward the significance of her role. He affirms her noble Indian lineage first, as proof of her appropriateness for her subsequent function in the formation of another family line, the mestizos, for all of whom Cortés and La Malinche serve as symbolic parents.

After providing the context within which to locate La Malinche, Bernal Díaz then adds background information on the birth and youth of La Malinche in the following chapter. The Spanish reader of Bernal Díaz's text would readily notice that events in the early life of this young Indian woman corresponded to events during the childhood and adolescence of Amadís de Gaula, the exemplary Christian knight of a fictional work of the same name. As Johnson points out: "Both Doña Marina and Amadís are of noble lineage and as children, they become victims of efforts to deny them their birthright. After the departure of their fathers—one dies and the other undertakes a

Anonymous, Lienzo de Tlaxcala Manuscript (courtesy Archer M. Huntington Art Gallery, The University of Texas at Austin, Archer M. Huntington Museum Fund, 1964)

journey—their mothers, with the aid of family servants or slaves, abandon them in secret. Amadís and Marina are then reared at some distance from their homes and by people whose culture is different from their own."[13] When Doña Marina and Amadís are each re-united with their families as adults, their Christian religious beliefs lead them to forgive the ills done to them. Johnson points out that in their reconciliation scenes, "both young people serve as defenders of the faith, Amadís by exemplifying good in his performance of noble deeds and Marina by symbolizing the conversion of an entire race of pagans. They accepted without question God's will in determining their destiny."[14]

In addition to the implicit presence of the Spanish subtext of Amadís, Bernal Díaz strengthens his case for the nobility and righteousness of Doña Marina by explicitly comparing her forgiving attitude toward her mother and half-brother with that of the biblical Joseph. Like Joseph confronting his brothers in Egypt, the Marina of Bernal Díaz's narrative has also grown in political power and wisdom because of the train of events begun as a malign act to rid the family of an unwanted sibling. La Malinche's discourse at the encounter with her family, as reported by Bernal Díaz using the form of indirect monologue, also stresses cultural values the Spaniards considered as their important gifts to the Indians:

> They were afraid of her, for they believed that she sent for them in order to kill them, and they cried. And when she saw them crying, she comforted them and told them not to be afraid, that God had been very gracious to her in freeing her from the worship of idols and making her a Christian, and allowing her to bear a son to her lord and master Cortés, and in marrying her to a gentleman such as Juan Jaramillo, who was now her husband; that she would rather serve her husband and Cortés than anyone else in the world, and would not exchange her lot to become leader of all the provinces of New Spain . . . and this seems to me to imitate what happened to Joseph and his brothers in Egypt, when they fell into his power in the episode with the wheat.[15]

As Prescott observes in his *History of the Conquest of Mexico*, Bernal Díaz ends this important account with an additional solemn comment regarding its veracity, "And all this I say, I heard most assuredly, and I swear it, amen," a variant of his usual claim that his version is the accurate one, not Gómara's.[16] As informed modern readers, however, we should make note of the textual location of the speech that he reproduces as an eyewitness: he inserts the reunion of Doña Marina with her family as part of his introduction of her to his audience, at the narrative moment that corresponds to her first encounter with the Spaniards. The irony of this textual juxtaposition should not go unnoticed. Doña Marina's encounter with the Spaniards in Tabasco was the result of her having been disinherited by her family. She is reunited with them only after she has fulfilled her functions for the conquerors, during the voyage to Honduras, after which she disappears from the historical record if not from literary texts. Other readers—most notably the Chicana writers discussed in chapter 8—wonder about how much suffering it must have caused her to have been sold into slavery after being a princess. For Bernal Díaz and Bernal Díaz's Marina, however, the end result is the important thing, that is, the assimilation by Marina of Spanish culture. Bernal Díaz presents her initiation into Spanish culture and its results all in one chapter as the appropriate context within which his readers may then place the subsequent deeds of Doña Marina as related in the following chapters. Bernal Díaz configures the sign "Doña Marina" as filled culturally with the attributes of a worthy *Spanish* mother.

After establishing Doña Marina's credentials in terms of lineage and nobility of deeds, Bernal Díaz then briefly asserts that it was her talent for languages that "was the great beginning of our conquests. . . . I have made a point of telling this story because without Doña Marina, we could not have understood the language of New Spain and Mexico."[17]

Just as Cortés and Bernal Díaz refer to Marina in her role as translator, Gómara also introduces her to his audience in relation to this skill. In his chapter 26 (entitled "Doña Marina" in the English edition), Gómara states that Marina was brought to the attention of Cortés after he expressed his annoyance that Father Aguilar could not understand the languages of the Aztec messengers. When he learned that one of the twenty women given to him by the Tabascan chief could speak to the Aztecs and to Aguilar, Cortés acted quickly: "Cortés took her aside with Aguilar and promised her more than her liberty if she would establish friendship between him and the men of her country, and he told her that he would like to have her for his interpreter and secretary."[18] (One should note that Gómara, while known for his irony, could not have surmised how much more than her liberty Cortés was to bequeath to Marina.)

Gómara does not disagree with Bernal Díaz about the reasons for Marina's presence, but he does not attribute to her the same background. According to Gómara, she was the daughter of wealthy parents from a village called Viluta (Oluta) near Jalisco (Coatzacoalcos), having been "stolen by certain merchants during a war and sold in the market place of Xicalanco . . . not very far from Tabasco, and that afterwards she had fallen into the hands of the Lord of Potonchan (Tabasco)."[19] Gómara's account presents her as a faithful slave girl who acted as interpreter and bore Cortés one of his several sons. He will refer to her in his text as "our Indian woman interpreter" or as Marina, but never with the same affection and esteem displayed by Bernal Díaz. His tone may well be a reflection of the attitude of Cortés, whose perspective he is said to have followed faithfully.[20] Clearly, if Gómara wished to enhance the achievements of Cortés and show the superiority of the Christian religion, a description of the intense love relationship between Cortés and an Amerindian woman, in the manner of such modern apologists as Gustavo Rodríguez and Jesús Figueroa Torres (discussed in chapter 5), would be counterproductive.

It does appear that with regard to Doña Marina, Gómara allows himself to express his disapproval of Cortés's actions, albeit by indirection; after he describes in particular detail certain aspects of the fateful trip to Honduras, Gómara makes a parenthetical comment in the first person: "It was here, I think, that Juan Jaramillo married Marina while drunk. Cortés was criticized for allowing it, because he had children by her."[21] The comment is instructive not only because of its critical nature but because it implies a lack of will on the part of Jaramillo for his own actions and the summary transfer of Marina from one Spaniard to another as if she had no individual determination (which may well have been true for most of her circumstances). One contemporary Mexican biographer of La Malinche, Mariano Somonte, disagrees radically with Gómara; he not only suggests that the marriage was planned before the trip to Honduras but also adds that the union was favorable for Jaramillo, since "it incorporated him into history";[22] for Somonte, Doña Marina's role is clearly more significant than that of Jaramillo.

Her lack of importance for Gómara is reemphasized in his penultimate chapter, as he recites the list of progeny of the conquistador: "Cortés had three daughters and a son by Doña Juana de Zúñiga [his second wife]. . . . Cortés left another son, Don Martín, whom he had by an Indian woman [here the name of Doña Marina is added by the translator in a note], and Don Luis by a Spanish woman, and three daughters, each by a different mother, all Indians."[23] The fact that Gómara leaves out the name of the mother of Don Martín is significant; the production of the child was the important fact, not who carried him nor her role in the conquest. Gómara never sees La Malinche as anything more than an objectified extension of the will of Cortés.

Translator, guide, mother—all key positions in the enterprise of the conquest; yet we are not sure where La Malinche was born—Oluta, Painala, or Jaltipán—nor the exact date of her birth. It is generally accepted that she was born either in 1502 or 1505 on the day called Malinal (or Malinalli), hence her Indian name *Malinalli*. Gutierre Tibón follows Don Joaquín García Icazbalceta, who believes that her original name comes from the Aztec calendar and that the Spanish *Marina* was chosen for its similarity to her Indian name. *Tenepal*, also part of her Indian name, shows the general custom of including an additional appellation.[24] There is also the suggestion that the Spanish *Marina* was the source of the Indian reference to her as *Malintzin*, *tzin* being a Nahuatl suffix showing respect and the *r* of the Spanish, not present in Nahuatl, being converted to *l*; *Malinche* would hence be the Spanish corruption of *Malintzin*. It is important to remember that the records can only suggest the naming process; we should not think we know with certainty her original name.

We may also assume without knowing for certain that she was the first-born daughter of a cacique and so a member of the privileged, educated class. The Mexican historian Manuel Orozco y Berra suggests that Doña Marina must have attended one of the schools for noble women, in order to explain her knowledge and cultured ways despite her having been a slave at the time of her transfer to the Spanish conquistadors. Most historians agree that after her father's death, which occurred when she was quite young, her mother remarried another cacique, with whom she had a male child. It is possible that Malinal's mother then sold her into slavery, conforming to the Joseph-Amadís paradigm, in order to safeguard the inheritance of the son and his right to rule, the version that Bernal Díaz offered. The group of Mayan traders to whom she was sold in turn sold her to the Tabascans. They subsequently chose her to be one of the twenty women given as a gift to the Spaniards. The practice of exchange of women was common among the Indians and acceptable, too, among the Spaniards; neither side saw the transfer of women as an unusual custom. It would be expected, then, that Marina would already have been conditioned by her socialization as a slave among the Amerindians to obey the commands of her new masters.

As has been noted above, one of the major episodes in which Marina acted on behalf of her new masters occurred at Cholula. Her actions in support of the Spanish cause have been interpreted as loyalty to the Spaniards, a loyalty that later would be interpreted as a betrayal of the Indian peoples. The incident reveals more about the subordination of slavery, however, and the state of intense rivalry among the various Amerindian peoples, and should be viewed from that perspective.

Gómara and Bernal Díaz are in general agreement regarding the main details. Gómara's account actually suggests that before any action on the part of Marina, the Spaniards were being warned by the Tlaxcalans about the perfidy of the Cholulans, their long-time enemies and allies of the Aztecs. According to Gómara: "Now, it happened that the women who had been given to the Spaniards upon their entrance into Tlaxcala heard of a plot to kill them in Cholula, with the connivance of one of the four [Tlaxcalan] captains; but his sister, who was in the service of Pedro de Alvarado, divulged it to her master."[25] His account refers to the help of the Indian women, who forewarned the Spaniards in Cholula to expect some sort of ambush. The Cholulans were planning to follow Moctezuma's orders to surprise the Spaniards as they left Cholula on the way to Tenochtitlan, a plot whose specific details Marina discovered and also divulged to her masters. Gómara describes Marina's participation in the events in a rather succinct manner, stressing the decisiveness of Cortés above all else.[26] Bernal Díaz focuses, with greater detail, on the role of Marina in the discovery of the plot. He also relates that their Indian allies were suspicious of the Cholulans and initially warned Cortés to be alert to danger. Doña Marina was sent to speak with the chiefs, "as she well knew how," a statement that shows her independence in communicating the spirit of the Spanish wishes while being permitted leeway as to the exact wording.[27]

It was Marina who discovered the actual plans of the ambush. She was informed by an old woman, the wife of a Cholulan cacique, says Bernal Díaz, who took a liking to Marina because she was young, good-looking, and rich. The old woman wanted to save Marina from certain death and promised to marry her to her son. Bernal Díaz presents as a dialogue Marina's various questions and responses to the plan of the old woman, dramatizing for his audience the crucial scene in which Marina shows her astuteness in handling both aspects of the Cholulan plans—that which pertained to the ambush of the Spaniards and that which involved her escape by marrying the son of the chief. Bernal Díaz represents her as appearing to agree to obey the woman's plan in order to bide time and then escape to divulge the scheme to Cortés: "I am indeed glad that this son of yours to whom you want to marry me is an important person—we have been talking a long while, and I do not want them to notice us; so wait here, mother, and I will begin to bring my possessions, because I cannot carry everything out at once. You and your son, my brother, must look after them, and then we shall be able to go."[28]

The details of the Cholulan episode would be repeated in future texts, either to praise Marina for her loyalty to the Spaniards or to suggest that she betrayed "her people." Examination of the chronicles shows, however, that Marina was not the only Amerindian nor the first to divulge the possibility of an ambush, since the Tlaxcalans as enemies of the Cholulans had warned the Spaniards of the duplicitous nature of their foe at the onset of their sojourn in Cholula. Moreover, other women slaves also reported suspicious activity. Marina's role is significant nevertheless, for her report finally compelled Cortés to act decisively; he rounded up all the chieftains and had them killed.[29] In the Lienzo de Tlaxcala, the paintings that depict the Tlaxcalan version of the events of the conquest, the scenes of the Cholula massacre portray La Malinche in her usual position, with arm outstretched, pointing as if she were helping direct the events.[30]

In regard to the Malinche paradigm, then, the actions ascribed to her in Cholula relate her to the theme of betrayal, but only if one considers the Indians to have been all one people. The Tlaxcalans clearly did not act according to that belief and considered the Cholulans enemies, as their role in the massacre and sacking of the city proves. The other element of importance for the paradigm is the supposed opportunity of an encounter between La Malinche and an Indian suitor. Although she appears to be accepting the possibility of an Indian mate, her actions in effect reject him. Her renunciation of the Amerindian male is perhaps the most serious of the charges that cling to her image; it becomes a metaphoric act signifying the repudiation of the native in favor of the foreign. Her role as mistress to Cortés and her marriage to Juan Jaramillo provide further substantiation of the paradigmatic behavior called *malinchismo* today.

Bernal Díaz often gives credit to Doña Marina as the translator of record during the many interviews that took place between Moctezuma and Cortés once the Spaniards successfully reached the Aztec capital on November 8, 1519. Although the Spaniards were treated well at first, their presence soon became intolerable to the Aztecs. After a series of encounters, including the assault by Pedro de Alvarado on the Aztec warriors followed by the death of Moctezuma, the Spaniards decided that their safety required them to evacuate the city under cover of darkness.[31] On that Sad Night, "la noche triste" to the Spaniards, June 30–July 1, 1520, their escape was detected and they were forced to fight a pitched nocturnal battle amid the various causeways that surrounded the city. The Spaniards were weighed down by the gold and other booty they were attempting to escape with; many lost footing in the treacherous terrain, falling into the water and drowning, while others were captured. Bernal Díaz depicts the calamitous events that nearly cost all of them their lives; significantly, after telling of their hardships, he makes mention of the fact that Doña Marina was with them during the rout and was rescued with just a few other women: "I have forgotten to write down how glad we were to see our Doña Marina, and Doña Luisa, Xicotenga's daughter, still alive. They had been rescued at the bridge by some Tlascalans [sic], as had also the only Spanish woman in Mexico, María de Estrada." [32] The order in which Bernal Díaz reports the names of the women shows that notwithstanding the presence of one Spanish woman from Castile, Donã Marina was first in his thoughts. Bernal Díaz also makes note of the positive reaction of their Tlaxcalan allies regarding the safety of the women. [33] The chronicler reaffirms the enmity of the Tlaxcalans toward the Aztecs and their willing support of the Spaniards' attempt to overthrow their enemies.

Bernal Díaz's account of the reactions of the Spaniards' Indian allies are verified in the Indians' own documents. They also mention Doña Marina frequently, both in their accounts written after the conquest and by means of images recorded in the codices. Todorov reports that in the Florentine Codex that illustrates the first encounter of Cortés and Moctezuma, "the two military leaders occupy the margins of the image, dominated by the central figure of La Malinche." [34]

Despite the drastic reversals suffered during the Sad Night, the Spaniards were very fortunate in being able to recover from their wounds and regain their strength among allies like the Tlaxcalans. Cuitlahuac, who had been appointed ruler after the death of Moctezuma, soon died from smallpox after the siege, so that the Aztecs were not able to take advantage of their military victory. Cuauhtemoc was then named ruler, and he attempted to move aggressively against the Spaniards. Nevertheless, as it is recorded in all the chronicles, the Aztecs never regained military control, and on August 21, 1521, Tenochtitlan fell to the Spanish forces.

Cortés did not kill Cuauhtemoc at the time of his defeat but used his presence to check any Indian rebellions and help in the reconstruction of the city. As noted earlier, Cuauhtemoc traveled with Cortés and La Malinche on the journey to Honduras; some say Cortés feared leaving the young emperor alone in the city as a rallying point of rebellion. According to Cortés's admission to the king, he was apprised of a plot to assassinate him on the road, a treasonous intrigue attributed to Cuauhtemoc and his loyal entourage. Based on that version of events—which Rodolfo Usigli will question in *Corona del fuego* (1960)—Cortés tortured and put to death Cuauhtemoc and his followers. This act of cruelty is considered one of the most inhumane, gratuitous deeds of the many associated with Cortés and the conquest. According to the chronicles, Doña Marina was not directly implicated in what transpired, yet the versions of these historical events that filtered down into popular culture indicate that, by juxtaposition, the acts of "El Malinche" were subsequently imposed on La Malinche as well.

The martyrdom of Cuauhtemoc overshadows the situation of La Malinche on this voyage. For she was transferred from one man to another once again, this time by means of a rite indicative of European culture—the marriage ceremony. As the legal wife of Juan Jaramillo, she increased her identification with a European lifestyle, as Ireneo Paz has her acknowledge in his novel *Doña Marina* (1883). Marriage to a conquistador indicates the respect she enjoyed among the Spaniards, later to be condemned as her capitulation to the foreign culture. Little is known about Doña Marina after her marriage. It is interesting that the death of Cuauhtemoc occurs in the same time frame as the disappearance of La Malinche, "both of whom outlived their usefulness on that useless and wearing journey to Hibueras and back," as the historian Fehrenback observes.[35] In *Fire and Blood* he reminds us that the fateful journey had been motivated by the key theme of the conquest, that of betrayal: "Cristóbal de Olid, in the country of Las Hibueras, now Honduras, had betrayed the trust of Cortés and attempted to establish his own kingdom. In 1524 Cortés went to quell the rebellion, taking along both Cuauhtemoc and Malintzin as if he feared leaving behind in Mexico native leaders who could start a rebellion against him."[36] It is another of the grand ironies of the conquest that in seeking to avenge treason, Cortés acted in a treacherous manner himself with regard to both Cuauhtemoc and the woman who had acted so faithfully on his behalf.

During the decisive phase of the Spanish campaign, from the departure from the Tabascan coast, where she was encountered, to the fall of Tenochtitlan, La Malinche served as trustworthy translator as well as mistress and confidante to Cortés. Despite her faithful subservience, it seems likely that Cortés viewed their relationship more in terms of strategic and military than of emotional import, as Todorov suggests.[37] In popular culture, however, the romantic love affair between the two has usually been stressed, since it favors Mexican cultural norms.

The events that involved both La Malinche and Cortés after the success of the Spanish enterprise have also been interpreted in many ways, especially their attitudes regarding the birth of their son, Martín Cortés, in 1522, the arrival of Doña Catalina Xuárez, the first wife of Cortés, and the marriage of Doña Marina to Juan Jaramillo. As was noted earlier, Bernal Díaz believed it important to tell us as part of his introduction of Doña Marina that she had a son by Cortés and that she expressed her joy to her mother regarding all that had happened to her, from her union with Cortés to her marriage to Jaramillo. Bernal Díaz's rendering of her attitude has been handed down as part of the mythology of the conquest. Even an investigator as well versed as Irene Nicholson, the translator of *Balún-Canán* by Rosario Castellanos and the author of *The X in Mexico*, accepts as accurate the attitude expressed by Doña Marina via the text of Bernal Díaz. In the postindependence period, the elements of the Spanish version would be rearranged to deride and detract from her accomplishments in order to stress the negative aspects of her participation in the conquest. Any interrogation of that paradigm, however, would not come about until recently, as a small number of Mexicans and Chicanas have begun to question the patriarchal ideology from within which Doña Marina was first construed.

The discovery and colonization of the New World, with its scope and grandeur as well as pathos, served as a source of literary inspiration to many European writers. Ironically, as José Sánchez observes, aside from the chroniclers Spain did not incorporate the American scene into its literature in any serious way, despite the fact that Spanish literature enjoyed a "golden age" (Siglo de Oro) following the discovery and exploration of America.[38] Sánchez focuses on the dramatic genre and judges the lack of significant works on the American conquest to be one of the anomalies of Spanish literature. This phenomenon is additionally perplexing if one considers the influence the American encounter had on Spanish life. For Sánchez, this lack of interest, especially in the sixteenth and seventeenth centuries, has not yet been satisfactorily explained; but he adds: "This whole question of the vacuum of the Americas in Spanish drama from the political and historical points of view lies in the hidden and deep psychological characteristics of the Spaniard; his sense of pride, his desire for recognition, and his expectation of wealth—factors which the American conquest did not offer him at the time with any certainty. . . . No first-class play has ever been written on Cortés, Pizarro, or Columbus by a Spaniard."[39] Because little attention was paid to the conquest in dramatic literature, the Spaniards left an open space in which others might create the standard interpretation, and the Black Legend persisted in the form given it by non-Hispanics.[40]

Just as the Spaniards preferred to ignore the conquest as a theme, the colonists in New Spain did not emphasize the topic in their work. In the sixteenth century, Francisco de Terrazas (?1525–1600?), a descendant of conquistadors, had authored an epic poem on Cortés, but it was never completed.[41]

One of the more famous writers of New Spain, Don Carlos Sigüenza y Góngora, is credited with the composition of "La piedad heroyca de Don Fernando Cortés" ("The Heroic Mercy of Don Fernando Cortés"), a glorification of Cortés in the tradition of the Spaniards. It is not the poem, however, that signals Don Carlos's key role in the spiritual revolution that helped to formulate a Mexican national consciousness.[42] According to Octavio Paz, Don Carlos should be acknowledged for his positive appraisal of the pre-Hispanic Amerindian tradition. Paz points to a nonverbal text as proof of Sigüenza y Góngora's innovative perspective. As part of the celebration for the arrival of the new viceroy, Don Tomás Antonio de la Cerda, two arches were constructed in the city of México, one designed by Don Carlos, the other by his famous friend, Sor Juana Inés de la Cruz. The Arch of Triumph by Don Carlos included as a new motif figures of the Aztec emperors, as the title and written description of the arch made explicit: "Teatro de virtudes políticas que constituyen a un príncipe, advertidas en los monarcas antiguos del Mexicano Imperio" ("Theater of political virtues that are contained in a prince and that are noticed in the ancient monarchs of the Mexican Empire"). Sigüenza y Góngora considered the Aztec emperors to be worthy models of governance for the new Spanish viceroy, an irony that Paz implies was not intended by the creole but that we can appreciate today. It is additionally ironic that Sigüenza y Góngora expressed such clear admiration for the Aztec empire at the same time he feared and misunderstood the Indians who surrounded him in New Spain. Paz helps us to understand why Sigüenza y Góngora would praise the Aztecs at the same time he so conveniently ignored the bloody war against the Aztecs undertaken by his own ancestors: the "need to sink roots in America and to dispute the Spanish titles to domination led the creoles to exalt the Indian past."[43]

I have included the discussion of Sigüenza y Góngora's ambivalent attitude toward the Indians because of its usefulness in explaining why the conquest and its figures were not incorporated into the Spanish or colonial Mexican literary corpus until after the transformations wrought by Mexican independence from Spain. Just as sixteenth-century New Spain had desired a total break with pre-Hispanic civilization, in the origin of modern Mexico there was a need to vanquish the colonial past. As Octavio Paz concludes, for "the majority of Mexicans, Independence was a restoration, that is, an event which closed the interregnum established by the Conquest."[44] The narratives analyzed in chapter 4 appeared after the independence of Mexico. Their depiction of the Malinche figure reflects the rejection of Spain and the glorification of the pre-Hispanic Amerindians.

CHAPTER FOUR

Eve and the Serpent: The Nationalists' View

DURING THE period of independence, the cultural problem at hand was to attempt to separate the new Spanish American countries from Spain in more than the political sphere. This problem of separation of identity was verbalized by the writer and political figure Esteban Echeverría (1801–51) of Argentina, a great proponent of independence from Spain: "The arms of Spain no longer oppress us, but her traditions continue to overwhelm us."[1] Echeverría here personifies Spain, giving the country arms with which to hold tightly onto the Spanish American colonists in a political embrace that was severed by the wars of independence in the early nineteenth century. His metaphor is extended in the political allusion used by writers and intellectuals of the day in which the imperialist nation is referred to as the "mother" country; the colonies are then "children" who suffer from all the problems and guilt complexes attendant upon separation anxieties.[2] A logical development of this vocabulary is the employment of the image of the family to discuss political relationships among nations. In the Latin countries in particular, with their strong Roman inheritance relating to *patria potestas* (the power of the father), such terminology naturally inflicts additional burdens on the protesting colonists, who are looked upon as children rebelling against their parents.[3] The Spanish expression for the imperialist nation combines signifiers for both the mother and the father: *la madre patria*, literally "the mother fatherland." The quandary, then, for the young Spanish American countries was how to assert cultural independence from the *madre patria* while not faulting themselves as children because of their desire for separation.

One method of accentuating national identity despite a shared language and literary history is to formulate divergent perspectives that stress "difference." In Mexico, the way of showing that difference in perspective was to begin with the conquest, since this crucial event was the point of origin of the problem. A reinterpretation of the conquest from the perspective of the colonies was essential so that the children could begin to formulate their own "story." Ironically, the children could not help but repeat the traditions inherited from the mother country, and so the conquest was viewed with images and motifs drawn from European traditions.

Just as in the sixteenth century there had been a desire in New Spain for a total break with pre-Hispanic Amerindian civilization, in the origin of modern Mexico there was a need to disclaim the society of colonial Mexico. Destigmatization of the pre-Hispanic Indians was the necessary first step toward integrating into Mexican nationhood the Amerindian and mestizo figures who were appearing on the political scene. In his study of Mexican poetry, José Joaquín Blanco regards the cultural glorification of the pre-Hispanic world as a reflection of the political ideology of the romantic liberals of the reform period.[4] They constructed a mythic continuity between the pre-Hispanic world and postindependence nineteenth-century Mexico. The nineteenth-century narratives analyzed in this chapter also reveal a need to incorporate the pre-Hispanic past into a concept of national identity and national cultural patterns.

In reading the romantic writers of the postindependence period today, modern readers must set aside some familiar categories for evaluating fiction—stylistic intricacy, psychological subtlety, epistemological complexity. Instead, these texts function as a political enterprise, halfway between sermon and social theory, that both codifies and attempts to mold the values of its time.[5] Important considerations regulate our reading of the nineteenth-century novels that introduce into fiction the subject of the conquest. Not only does each author express his views on the conquest and the extent of his knowledge of the topic. He also illuminates aspects of the ideological reality of nineteenth-century Mexico: how he, as a representative of the political and intellectual enterprise, attempts to formulate a national identity. A brief consideration of the sociopolitical situation at the time of the production of each text will be useful before we review the actual discourse of the texts.

In 1826, when the novel *Xicoténcatl* was published anonymously, Mexico had just undergone a war to achieve its independence from Spanish rule, only to revert to monarchy with the establishment of the Mexican empire in 1821. Agustín de Iturbide, a first-generation criollo, was named Emperor Agustín I, a position he achieved after coming to terms with another rival, Vicente Guerrero. The newly independent Mexico did not remain at peace for long. Iturbide had been a military hero in the War of Independence, but his chief supporters "were conservatives who rejected the ideas of 1789 and reasserted the values of a hierarchical order for an independent Mexico."[6] Iturbide soon proved that he did not respect the constitutionality of his new government by dissolving congress, which provoked a revolt. Santa Anna, a military man whom Iturbide had first elevated in rank and then offended, proclaimed a Mexican republic in December 1823. Fighting among the Mexican military soon forced the emperor to abdicate. A republican constitution was adopted in 1824, but it proved of little value in instilling a republican spirit in the country, and governments were continually assailed by the military for most of the first half of the nineteenth century. Moreover, the idea of re-instituting a monarchy was also kept alive, although the monar-chists would not succeed in bringing it back into existence until 1864, under Maximilian and Carlota, who lasted not much longer than Agustín I. Thus, those patriots who believed in the republican form of government and hoped for a united Mexico that would emu-late its sister republic, the United States, suffered many assaults to their physical being, no less than to their dreams and ideology. The republican, antimonarchical sentiments expressed by the narrator of *Xicoténcatl* clearly place the author in opposition to the political events in newly independent Mexico and perhaps explain his need to have his work published anonymously.[7]

For many Mexican historians of the mid-nineteenth century, the political turmoil of the postindependence period was attributable to the influence of malignant foreign interference, an approach called the scapegoat theory by Edmundo O'Gorman in his discussion of metahistorical aspects of Mexican historiography.[8] The pattern of identifying a scapegoat to blame for the sociopolitical problems of the country is clearly manifest in *Xicoténcatl*, along with the ob-vious republican ideology. Significantly, the scapegoat figure chosen to bear the burden of guilt is La Malinche, who in this cultural script functions as a synecdoche to symbolize the several reasons that could explain the defeat of the republican Amerindians.

Despite being the first historical novel as well as the first of the narratives on the theme of the conquest, *Xicoténcatl* has not re-ceived much critical attention in Latin American literature, in part because of the mysteries surrounding its publication. Although written in Spanish, its publication by an unknown author precludes any certainty that "he" was Mexican. Antonio Castro Leal includes the text in his anthology of Mexican novels that have colonial themes, regarding it as both the first Mexican historical novel and the first *"novela indigenista,"* or narrative that presents an indige-nous topic with interest and sympathy.[9] After a thorough study of its style, however, Luis Leal concludes in an essay that the author was not Mexican, although he acknowledges that the work offers the first known presentation of La Malinche in the postindependence period.[10]

Although authorship of the novel cannot be determined conclusively, it is possible to prove that the work was well known in Mexico and a source of inspiration for subsequent works on the conquest theme. Daniel Wogan notes that there was a drama contest held in Puebla that required "that the plot should be taken from a certain 'Historia de Xicoténcatl,' printed in Philadelphia in 1826."[11] Three plays are known to have been based on the novel: José María Moreno y Buenvecino's *Xicohtencatl* (Puebla, 1828); Ignacio Torres Arroyo's *Teutila* (Puebla, 1828), and José María Mangino's *Xicoténcatl* (Puebla, 1829).[12] The plays have not been anthologized, and copies can be obtained only from special libraries, unlike the novel, which can be read in its reprinted form in Castro Leal's anthology.[13] The dramatists follow the author of *Xicoténcatl* by introducing the Amerindian woman Teutila as the love interest of both Xicotencatl and Cortés, which arouses the jealousy of Marina.

By exclusively using her Spanish name, Marina, while giving the other woman an Amerindian name, the narrator of *Xicoténcatl* makes it clear that Marina represents for him the Europeanized Amerindian, whom he excoriates. The narrator also prefers to use "American" to refer to the native Amerindians, whom he places in opposition to the Europeans or Spaniards.[14]

Although the author's subject matter deals ostensibly with the time of the conquest, his eye is clearly on the events of his own period and the precarious position of the republic of Mexico as a united country. His text mirrors the historical situation not in a general way but in a narrative that is structured on synedoche, in the way Hayden White describes this trope in relation to historical discourse, that is, one episode is selected to represent the whole historical event.[15]

The narrative plot focuses on events that relate to one of the major tribes to ally itself with the Spaniards, the Tlaxcalans, and the explanations for that alliance. The narrator follows the chronicle of the *Historia de la conquista de México* (*The History of the Conquest of Mexico*) by Antonio de Solís, quoting whole paragraphs verbatim. For the specifics of his plot, however, he invents characters and episodes to conform to his underlying thematic purpose.

According to the narrative, at the time of the arrival of the Spaniards the Tlaxcalans had an uneasy alliance with the Aztecs, and one faction among them was eager to join with the foreigners in overthrowing the yoke of oppression represented by Moctezuma.[16] Xicotencatl the Younger, general of the republic of Tlaxcala, purportedly advocated the view of his father, Xicotencatl the Elder, that the Spaniards should not be allowed an alliance with the Tlaxcalans.[17] The chronicles generally agree that Tlaxcalan support of the Spaniards was decisive in the military conquest, since their armies were numerous, well-trained, and enjoyed the reputation of being brave and usually victorious.[18] The narrator chooses to reconstruct the incidents associated with the Tlaxcalan polemic to emphasize the rivalries among the states as a clash between monarchic (Aztec) and republican (Tlaxcalan) forms of government, between patriotism and what he calls *patricidio*—murder of the *patria* or nation. The Tlaxcalan role in the conquest becomes a symbol of the destructive consequences that can befall a nation when its peoples are divided and, in the search for a solution to their disharmony, accept authoritarian rule to solder together the differences of the various groups.

The narrator's rhetoric makes obvious his preferences and animosities. An analysis of his treatment of Doña Marina demonstrates both his ideology and his modus operandi. Doña Marina does not appear until the second chapter, for she is not the most important woman in the narrative. She functions, rather, as the negative foil for the true heroine of the text, Teutila. Although Teutila and Doña Marina are both "*americanas*," only Teutila, in name and deed, shows that she is a faithful patriot to the American cause. She steadfastly refuses all opportunities to become Europeanized. Doña Marina, in direct contrast, symbolizes all the evils and misfortunes that Americans suffer when they accept European ways. Within this context, the narrator unreservedly delivers devastating attacks on the morality, integrity, and dignity of both Doña Marina and Cortés.[19]

The negative image of Doña Marina is intensified by the positive portrayal of Teutila, begun with her first appearance in chapter 1. In a chance encounter she meets the man who will come to represent the good Spaniard, Diego de Ordaz. With complete disregard for the canons of plausibility, the narrator allows the Spaniard and the American to communicate freely in what one assumes must be Spanish. In fact, during the entire narrative, no problems regarding communication difficulties or translation needs are mentioned, thereby obviating one of the major functions of Doña Marina as "la lengua" in the enterprise of the conquest.

Ironically, the narrator, who is so concerned with the malign effects of Europeanization, ignores or perhaps is unconscious of his marked indifference to possible dissimilarities between Amerindian and Spanish cultural concepts regarding the treatment of women, *pundonor* (honor code), references to the role of the divinity, and symbol systems. He treats the Americans as if they had the same thought processes as the Spaniards. To his credit, he does present evil characters on both sides, except that there are many noble and virtuous Americans and only one admirable Spaniard: Diego de Ordaz, whose actions in the narrative conform to the demands of the theme rather than to any historical record.[20]

The first chapter also details the conflicts among the Tlaxcalans themselves regarding how to behave toward the strange foreigners called Spaniards. Xicotencatl the Elder and his son are opposed to offering any support, but another faction, led by Magiscatzin, hopes to sway the Tlaxcalans to accept the petition of Cortés to count on the Tlaxcalans as allies. The narrator is clearly not a sympathizer with the Spanish cause, and as in a Greek epic, he consistently assigns certain epithets to his characters; those who support the Spaniards are labeled "monsters and traitors," while those who oppose them are always "brave and virtuous patriots" working in support of independence and liberty. The narrator also presents, through his mouthpiece Diego de Ordaz, what he considers to be the underlying motives of the Spanish conquistadors: their greed for gold and silver.

Although Teutila is the daughter of the chief of the Zocotlan nation, she had become the slave of Xicotencatl when her people were defeated by the Tlaxcalans. The parallels with the story of La Malinche suggest a number of interesting observations. Women were frequently transferred from one group to another during war as well as in peacetime, in order to solidify alliances.[21] Like La Malinche, Teutila is a member of a chieftain's family who had become the property of a more powerful state, a natural consequence of military conquest. Unlike La Malinche, however, she refuses to transfer her allegiance again to the powerful Spanish invaders. Instead, she remains faithful to her Tlaxcalan lover. Teutila as a Zocotlana has suffered the violence of the Tlaxcalans but considers them preferable to the "unbearable and insufferable" evils of the Aztecs. She verbalizes the theme of rivalry and hatred as it existed among the Amerindians: "My nation has always preferred an alliance with the Tlaxcalans because we find most unbearable the demands and tributes that the government of Moctezuma exacts from us, and the violence and haughtiness of his agents are entirely insufferable."[22]

How different is the trajectory of action in this book compared to that of Ireneo Paz, who has a very different agenda. As we shall see, Paz has his female character in *Amor y suplicio* first reject the Tlaxcalans as the weaker nation in favor of the more powerful Aztecs, only to disdain all the Indians in favor of the Spaniards as the bravest and most powerful—clearly elements that explicitly recapitulate the Malinche paradigm. Teutila represents the opposite pattern of behavior, the native who prefers the indigenous over the foreign. For both Paz and the narrator of *Xicoténcatl*, however, the recounting of the rivalries and animosities among the Amerindian groups reflects what the chronicles and the Amerindian writers have reported. For this narrative, Teutila chooses to accept the best the Americans have, in the person of Xicotencatl, while Doña Marina disregards patriotism and becomes a traitor when she joins in company with Cortés.

The narrator establishes the contrasting behavior of Teutila for each characteristic that is part of the Malinche paradigm. He recounts Teutila's refusal to be baptized immediately before he introduces the most famous christianized American, Doña Marina. Implicitly, then, the narrator is criticizing Marina for accepting so easily the ways of the European, which he has just characterized as corrupt, filled with intrigue and guile. By examining the introduction of Doña Marina, we see by what the narrator omits and chooses to include that he prefers to place her at the negative pole with respect to Teutila:

This Doña Marina was an American born in Guazacoalco, who after a series of misfortunes came to be a slave of the cacique of Tabasco. He then gave her over to Cortés after his country was subdued. The good talents and graces of this slave drew the attention of her master, who, after having her baptized with the name of Marina, placed in her his love and confidence so that in a few days she went from slave to his concubine and confidante. In this latter capacity she acted to the great advantage of Hernán Cortés, since the natives did not suspect her use of European wiles, and so she could ply her wiles of corruption and intrigue.[23]

By referring to the unhappy circumstances of her life as mere "misfortunes" (literally "accidents of fortune"), the narrator shows that he does not accord to Marina the same sympathy he feels for Teutila. The narrator follows the romantic penchant for attributing to destiny or fortune the events that befall one, so that Doña Marina was affected by destiny to fall into the hands of Cortés, just as Teutila became the slave of Xicotencatl as part of the spoils of war. The enslavement—physical and cultural—of Doña Marina was complete, for she soon functioned as a Spaniard. It was the sad fate of the unhappy Teutila, says the narrator, to fall into the hands of the "astute and false" American woman.

Doña Marina is shown to act falsely both to the Americans and to Cortés himself. In a scene that is unrestrained by plausibility and could prove shocking to readers (especially readers of the Spanish chronicles), Marina contrives to meet with Diego de Ordaz in order to profess her interest in him, an interest that is clearly sexual, although the narrator uses typical romantic circumlocutions with regard to sexuality. Marina's surprising revelation is that in her view, Cortés is her oppressor and a tyrant, that she is only his slave and not his lover, that she hates his "proud domination" (p. 101; "soberbia dominación") and much prefers the merit of Ordaz. She discloses that if she were free, she would abandon her oppressor and follow her inclinations toward Ordaz. Her confession, of course, is soundly rejected by Ordaz, who has already fallen in love at the first sight of the beautiful Teutila. Ordaz is repelled by the lascivious Marina and prefers the purity and nobility of Teutila. The corruption and vice of Marina, clearly depicted in the narrative, motivate Ordaz to elevate Teutila to the position of a divinity.

The contrast between the two American women is made explicit in the following scenes, whose elements merit careful review. Ordaz runs from the proffered arms of Marina to the sanctity of Teutila. At the moment that he confesses that he will adore her for eternity, that he feels a "noble and pure" passion, Doña Marina conveniently appears at the door, disrupting the edenic scene,[24] and accuses him of treachery: " 'Bravo, Bravo, Mr. Virtuous,' said Doña Marina, interrupting him. 'It suits you well to act the modest one in one room and come to another to seduce a slave so disgracefully. Out of the room!' "[25] Whereas Marina's previous expression of love to Ordaz was recounted as narrative, her spurious accusation of his treachery is presented as her direct address to Ordaz, a more dramatic form that underscores her own active falseness. Marina assures Teutila that Ordaz also tried to seduce her with words of love, convincing the real object of Ordaz's affection that she is just another pawn in his lecherous game. As soon as she poisons Teutila's mind against the Spaniard, Marina returns to Ordaz and tries to persuade him that her disruption of his confession of love for Teutila was not based on jealousy but was intended to prevent him from making a political mistake in allying himself with an enemy of Cortés. Her supposed concern for both Teutila on the one hand and Ordaz on the other is shown to be pure perfidy toward both. The narrator uses a traditional image to highlight his opinion of Marina by calling her an "astute serpent." Recourse to the biblical image of the serpent gives Marina a dual negative role: she is the serpent in the way she insti- gates evil as well as the Eve whose acquiescence allows the evil to enter paradise.[26]

Although the theme of betrayal is clearly linked to Doña Marina in *Xicoténcatl*, she is only one of the many characters to be guilty of traitorous acts. More narrative time is spent elaborating the betrayal of Magiscatzin and the patriotic endeavors of the two Xicotencatls, since the narrator clearly wants to show the evil effects that a civil war brings to a republic (read "Mexico in the postindependence pe- riod"). The political conflict between the two families within the Tlaxcalan nation becomes the key synecdoche that represents the larger conflict in the entire Amerindian region. While the actions of Doña Marina here do not appear to constitute the major source of betrayal leading to Spanish victory, she nevertheless plays a role in showing that native American compliance with the Spaniards was the true cause of the success of the conquest.

To represent the theme of military submission, the author chooses another important dimension of the encounter, sexual conquest, which in turn resulted in the birth of mestizos, the Mexican people. It is in relation to that point that he amplifies further the love tri- angles involving Doña Marina. As noted above, the narrator devel- ops the triangle Doña Marina–Ordaz–Teutila to contrast what he considers to be bad behavior with appropriate conduct, the sexual aspect functioning as a symbol of political control. As further em- phasis of the sexual-political interrelationship, the triangle Cortés- Teutila-Xicotencatl is introduced. Both triangles repeat similar ac- tions and images as further proof of their correlation. Just as Doña Marina schemes to get Ordaz alone, as the "little bird" (*pajarillo*) caught in her trap (p. 106), so, too, does Cortés consider Teutila a "little bird" (p. 97). The two scenes of sexual entrapment occur si- multaneously, although in the narrative that of Doña Marina and Ordaz is presented first so that the subsequent resolute nobility of Teutila resounds more emphatically.

The intricate devices undertaken by Doña Marina in order to se- duce Ordaz are elaborately presented, showing her to be as deceitful as she is lascivious. Ordaz is excused by the narrator for his inability to resist such insistent advances on the basis of romantic fateful- ness: "There are cases in which all the prudence of an honorable man cannot prevent the powerful force of fate from driving him astray."[27] In a scene reminiscent of the *"capa y espada"* plays of ba- roque Spain, Doña Marina uses subterfuge to lock him inside a small, dark bedroom. The narrator describes the physical aspects of the room because his modest romantic persona prevents him from describing the sexual contact:

> The room was very small and dark; one had to speak in close contact in order not to be heard; Ordaz was young; Doña Marina was beautiful and amiable, and . . . A belated sense of disillusion shook the honorable Ordaz from his lethargy and covered him with shame. "Plotting, seductive woman!" he said to her. "You have finally abused the honor of Diego de Ordaz. Open the door, for I prefer to expose myself to a thousand dangers than continue in the shameful situation into which you have drawn me."[28]

The "shameful situation" may at first reading appear to be no more than his being locked in the room with Doña Marina, but the style of expression of the above citation leads one to surmise that a sexual liaison was consummated, a conclusion that is confirmed explicitly by the narrator at a subsequent key point. For the paragraph above that describes their intimate proximity contains a series of conjunctive phrases joined by means of semicolons; this syntactic configuration, which shows the coordination of major sentence elements, also reveals the underlying semantics of the text: that the two major figures of the scene copulate at the point in the narrative that starts with "and" and is followed by discreet ellipsis points. The actions that took place in the interim signified by this textual space are clarified when it is announced that Doña Marina is pregnant. At that point Ordaz wonders if he is the father of the child she carries, a sign of his "weakness" (p. 118), that is, his own sexual surrender to Doña Marina's wiles that fateful night. The narrator not only makes clear that Ordaz had sexual relations, but emphasizes the promiscuousness of Marina. That Cortés is the father, however, is also proven conclusively for Ordaz and the reader: "Happily for Ordaz all his concern was no more than apprehensions that were dispelled at the time of Doña Marina's delivery, for then he found out that on the night of his intimate adventure, the scheming woman had been already carrying in her womb the fruit of her affair with Hernán Cortés."[29]

Marina's promiscuity is not supported by the Spanish chronicles. The invention here of a sexual adventure between Marina and Ordaz functions to underscore several other related themes. It serves first as a synecdoche for the sexual interactions between Amerindian women and Europeans that engendered the Mexican mestizos. The

narrator shows support for the nurturing role when he permits Ordaz to be pleased that he had a part in giving life to a child (p. 118).
Nevertheless, true to the philosophy of the Enlightenment, which
he shares with the narrator, Ordaz worries about the educational opportunities awaiting the child of that union.[30] His concern for the
mestizo substantiates that Ordaz serves as a positive symbol of
Spanish behavior, in direct contrast to so many other actions of the
Spanish in the narrative that support the Black Legend.

Marina's sexuality and Ordaz's masculine surrender also serve as
counterpoint to Teutila's relationship with Cortés. As the symbol of
the rapacious Spaniard, Cortés sets as his goal the sexual conquest of
the American betrothed to Xicotencatl. In this love triangle, Teutila
is that part of the American world that remains faithful to its roots
and never capitulates to the foreigner, preferring death to surrender.
Cortés first tries to convince Teutila that her "barbarous" lover does
not deserve her beauty, but she forcefully rejects his advances, calling him the real "monster" and "barbarian" (p. 107). The expression
"sexual politics" helps us to understand the political allegory represented by this unusual love match, since the fierceness of Teutila's
rejection of Cortés as a lover in no way represents an available ave-
nue of action for an Amerindian woman captive. As noted above, exchanges of women were common among the Amerindian groups,
and Teutila herself was the prize for Xicotencatl's victory over her
people. Her resolute rejection of Cortés, therefore, is a symbol of resistance to the conquistadors in contrast to the more general compliance that Marina symbolizes.

When Ordaz finally manages to leave Marina's clutches, albeit too
late to prevent their sexual union, Marina races to Teutila's room and
thus by her presence interrupts Cortés's attempt to overwhelm Teutila by force. Through the juxtaposition of the behavior of the virtuous Teutila with the immoral Marina in parallel scenes, the narrator stresses the patriotism of the one and the perfidy of the other.

The narrator invents a third love triangle in which the character
of Doña Marina undergoes further condemnation. According to the
chronicles, Doña Marina is credited with acting on her own ideas
independently of Cortés in certain key events, especially following
her own instincts with regard to Spanish-Amerindian relations. An
example is her behavior in Cholula as documented by Bernal Díaz,
when she informed the Spaniards that the Cholulans planned to betray their trust and massacre them. In this text she is not at all involved in the Cholulan incident but instead becomes part of the
Xicotencatl-Teutila love relationship.

When Xicotencatl is unsuccessful in his attempt to free Teutila from Cortés's control, he turns his attention to Marina. Xicotencatl's actions also seem to comply with the needs of the narrator to condemn Marina, rather than to follow any canon of plausibility. After listening to Ordaz's confession of his love for Teutila, Xicotencatl admits to his father that he is not jealous but pleased that Ordaz could serve as her protector during her time of slavery. Easily relinquishing his right to Teutila, Xicotencatl then professes a love for Marina, whom he considers to be in the same position as Teutila, an unfortunate and unwilling slave in the possession of the Spaniards. Xicotencatl comes to this conclusion after an interview with Marina in which he confronts her directly with the Amerindian interpretation of her alliance with Cortés: " 'Are you still American?' he asked her. 'Does the flame of patriotic love still burn in your bosom? Or are you so corrupted and contaminated by the magic arts of those men, whose ways can distort all ideas of what is just and unjust, good and evil?'"[31] Xicotencatl is the first to suggest that Marina lacks "patriotic love of her nation" and that she acts like a corrupt Spaniard. His accusation is in itself unjust in view of the text's depiction of national rivalries, since she is not Tlaxcalan and thus shares no *patria* with him, except, as he perhaps suggests, in the general American sense.

The narrator prefers to blur the boundaries of group distinctions when he alludes to patriotic attitudes that relate to America. Following that perspective, he allows a faction among the Aztecs to express disdain for Moctezuma and a preference for an alliance with Xicotencatl and the side that opposes union with the Spaniards. In this thematic constellation, Moctezuma represents another version of betrayal of the Amerindian cause, for like Magiscatzin, he succumbs to the Spaniards because of his own weaknesses.

Xicotencatl's responsiveness to Marina is betrayed, however, just as Moctezuma and Magiscatzin are also deceived by their trust of the Spaniards. Marina leads Xicotencatl into thinking she is the involuntary slave of Cortés, awaiting patiently the moment when, in her words, she can "be useful to my people, and expiate with my subsequent conduct the criminal appearances of my present life."[32] As implausible as it may appear to the modern reader, her confession convinces Xicotencatl to believe her innocent pose as a woman without protection, forced to suffer the ill treatment of the Spaniards because of her solitary position "without support, without defenders, without friends, without relatives, alone and abandoned by the whole world."[33] Ironically, the description of Marina's position

conforms with that of the chronicles, yet in the text these characteristics are discounted in order to stress the one unforgivable element,
that "she is much loved by the strangers, which in truth is not the
best recommendation"[34] according to Xicotencatl the Elder.

Doña Marina is repeatedly censured for her intimacy with the
Spaniards. The narrator notes: "The brave Tlaxcalan fell little by
little into the trap of his astute and able compatriot. . . . Without
losing his love for Teutila, he also fell in love with the accomplishments with which she had embellished herself by her contact with
the Europeans."[35] The extent of her corruption by the Spaniards is
soon exposed when Xicotencatl's image of her as a praiseworthy and
patriotic woman is proven false. Xicotencatl the Elder begins to
doubt her virtue even as he offers the justification that she may be
simply a "virtuous woman who knows how to make the best of her
misfortune."[36] Xicotencatl the Younger shows his innocence by his
glowing description of a supposedly virtuous and gentle Marina,
making all the more terrible his discovery of her true, treacherous
nature. Her fall from grace in Xicotencatl's estimate is hastened by
the concrete evidence of her total submission to the Spaniards: her
pregnancy. "Is so much perfidy possible, so much deceit, and falseness, and artifice, and infamy? That unworthy American, spurious
daughter of these simple regions, a thousand times more detestable
than her corrupters, has shamefully abused the generosity of my
heart."[37] By repeating the adjective *tanta* (so much) before each pe-
jorative adjective, and by joining them together in a series, Xicotencatl reveals the profundity of his anger at the deception he has suffered. He accuses Doña Marina of leaving her adulterous bed and
approaching him knowing full well that in her "womb she carries
the fruit of her criminal love."[38] To rationalize his momentary aber-
ration, Xicotencatl calls Marina "unworthy prostitute" and "very
venomous serpent."[39] The imagery stresses that aspect of the Malinche legend which relates her to illicit sexuality; she is not the
Good Mother but a manifestation of Eve the Seductress, who leads
men into evil temptation.

Marina's pregnancy is considered distinct proof that she is deceitful, not only to the Amerindians but also to the Spanish. When Diego
de Ordaz hears of Xicotencatl's plan to marry Marina, he matches
the abuse Xicotencatl had applied to Marina, insult for insult, echo-
ing his very choice of words: "Perfidy joined with generosity, vice
with virtue, debasement with nobility."[40]

Although the good, sensitive Spaniard and the virtuous, patriotic
American call Marina "astute and perfidious," they both had been

attracted to her, the one accomplishing physically what the other only contemplated. Each condemns her, repelled by her pregnancy and its signification as submission to Cortés.

The narrator continues to add details to his depiction of her perfidy as he has the pregnant Marina attempt to entice Ordaz once more. When she is again rejected, she decides to act as a spy for Cortés, informing him of the actions of his enemies, the suitors of Teutila. As Marina describes herself to Cortés, she is "his faithful Marina suffering in bed with the pains caused by the fruit of his love, who watches over his interests even when he is perhaps searching for other new rivals with whom to share his caresses."[41] Despite her acknowledgment of his unfaithfulness, Marina pledges complete loyalty to Cortés; yet the narrator shows that even her loyalty to him will not be constant.

Although Marina is portrayed as that accomplice of "the arts of European corruption,"[42] she, too, comes to the realization that the Europeans are guilty of duplicity. Her rejection of the Spaniards is shown, ironically, to be related to the birth of the child who symbolizes the union of American and Spaniard. The scene of birth is a turning point in the narrator's treatment of Doña Marina and of her function in the text.

Doña Marina approaches the moment of delivery in great agony and fear of retribution for all the evils she has committed. The narrator specifically relates her growing physical agony to the increased spiritual anguish she feels when she thinks of her past conduct. She calls Father Olmedo to hear her confession, an occasion the narrator uses to repeat the highlights of her malicious and duplicitous conduct with regard to Ordaz and Teutila and her other political and amorous intrigues (p. 138).

Marina's act of self-realization highlights one of her key functions for the narrator, that is, to serve as a model of the evil effects of Europeanization. The narrative voice adds its own direct comment: "This American could have been an admirable woman without the corruption which she mastered since associating with the Spaniards."[43] Then, as if to prove redemption is possible, the narrator recounts the manner in which Marina herself brings about her recovery from perversion. Inspired by the maternal instinct, she declares that Nature has caused her to see the corruption of her tainted past, and as an indication of her newly found virtue, she calls for Teutila, her symbolic opposite. Teutila nurses her as she suffers from "milk fever," as the narrator labels her postpartum debilities. It is interesting that this reference to Marina's illness is one of the few times that maladies are mentioned in the text. No references to the real ravages of new diseases are introduced, but the idea that illness is a sign of moral debility and corruption pervades the text.[44]

In contrast to Marina's willingness to redeem her sinful ways, the depravity and corruption of Cortés are emphasized when he finally attends to her in her ailment. Instead of responding to the woman who has just given birth to his first child, Cortés reacts to the presence of the woman he has yet to conquer; he attempts to seduce Teutila. Just as Marina had once locked Ordaz in a room in order to overpower him sexually, Cortés now takes advantage of Teutila's offer to nurse Marina and locks her in the room, demanding that she submit to his will.

By juxtaposing various reactions to the birth of the first mestizo, the narrator illustrates the future actions of the Europeans with regard to the Amerindians. The (European) males will constantly be prepared to vanquish new women, moving on from conquest to conquest as the already impregnated women are left to care for the children. If we think of the women as the sign of American land, then the symbolism of the plot action takes on political and economic meaning as well. Ironically, in this narrative the non-Europeanized Teutila embodies the virtuous and saintly woman, the representative of the Virgin of Guadalupe, despite the fact that she refuses to be baptized.[45]

Doña Marina functions in a more complex manner, for she is the sign for both the lascivious woman and, as a natural consequence of her sexual behavior, becomes the mother figure. "Ordaz, I am a mother" (p. 139; "Ordaz, yo soy madre") are the first words she utters after giving birth. After her identification with motherhood, as if in recognition of the service performed, she is made to search for salvation and becomes identified with the virtuous virgin figure of Teutila. Thus, despite the combination of political attitudes formed by the Enlightenment and a romantic stylistic expression, *Xicoténcatl* presents a conception of the role of the male and female in Mexico that appears constant from the time of the conquest through the modern era. The accuracy and longevity of the pattern of behavior presented by the narrator is confirmed as a sociocultural paradigm in both the sociological studies of twentieth-century investigators such as Elu de Leñero (¿*Hacia dónde va la mujer mexicana?*) and literary analyses such as those of Rosario Castellanos and Luis Leal already mentioned in chapter 1.

With regard to the Malinche paradigm, the more vivid portrait in this narrative is not that of Marina the mother but of the perfidious, malicious, poisonous snake. At no point does the narrator show Marina acting in a positive, constructive manner. She is never described performing the various deeds attributed to her by such favorable chronicles as Bernal Díaz's *Historia*. In contrast, she is consistently shown as a sexual monster, which substantiates her identification as "La Chingada," the term used to signify the woman who opens herself to the other.

This portrait of La Malinche conforms with the anonymous author's general thesis, that the effect of the European invasion on Mexico was both pernicious and inimical to the political, cultural, and sexual life of America. *Xicoténcatl* does not offer a comprehensive account of the historical episodes associated with the conquest, for its rhetoric makes clear that the narrator's purpose is to teach his contemporaries a lesson by using an episode of the conquest as an illustration of his point. The beginning of chapter 4 clearly announces this contemporary political subtext: "Nations! If you love your liberty, join together your interests and your forces and learn for once that there is no power that will not break up in the face of your unity, just as there is no enemy so weak that will not conquer you and enslave you when you lack that unity. Tlaxcala is a living example of this truth."[46] Xicotencatl becomes the spokesman for the republican cause when he declares that "the government of one single individual does not seem to me to be tenable . . . [for its great inconvenience is] the natural propensity of man to abuse power and when the power of a single individual dominates, there is no law but his own will. Unfortunate is the people whose happiness depends on the virtues of one ruler!"[47]

It is Cortés, symbol of the "one ruler," the immoral monster, the corrupt, who has impregnated Marina-America, and his example is presented as the negative pattern that Mexicans should reject: both the authoritarian rule they inherited from Spain and the decadent moral behavior. The narrator offers for his readers, instead, the positive example of the Tlaxcalan republican government and the righteous love of Xicotencatl and Teutila. This couple represents pure and noble love and politically the native, republican form of government. The narrator shows what happens when the paradigm of Cortés-Marina is followed: the good couple die without producing an heir, and the good Spaniard, Ordaz, also departs American soil without union with Teutila. The rule of the despot prevails. Just as Marina finds salvation, however, so, too, can her heirs, by rejecting the model of behavior represented by Cortés-Spain.

The portrait of Doña Marina presented in *Xicoténcatl* offers definite support to the cult of La Malinche as the evil temptress, betrayer of *la patria*, the first *malinchista*, and La Chingada. None of her positive contributions are described, save for her ineluctable role as mother of the mestizo. Even in that role, it is the presence of the child that seems to effect her transformation to a Mexican—no longer European—consciousness. The portrait constitutes a literary transformation of the metamorphoses taking place in Mexican society. The work should be viewed as part of the project of a generation eager to free the Mexican and American *patria* from ideological and political dependence on Spain. This portrayal forged by postindependence politics will reappear in the modern period not only in an essay by Octavio Paz, "Los hijos de la Malinche," but in artifacts of popular culture and books destined for foreign consumption, such as Irene Nicholson's *The X in Mexico*. She elucidates for the non-Mexican, English-speaking public the importance of the theme of betrayal in Mexican culture: "Treachery is elevated to the rank of original sin, worshiped, and attributed both to the Spanish greed for conquest and to the Amerindian refusal to give battle."[48] And who is the symbol of that treachery? "Malinche betrayed the Indians . . ." Nicholson uses Paz's essay to substantiate her view that modern Mexicans consider themselves the sons of Malinche and are therefore "traitors in their own minds."[49] Perhaps a change in attitude regarding La Malinche and her role in Mexican history can be accomplished once the roots of this rhetoric are exposed.

Although I do not presume to be able to refer to all the texts in which La Malinche appears, I think it is instructive for comparison to bring to the reader's attention that among the nineteenth-century writers attracted to the theme of the Mexican conquest was the Cuban Gertrudis Gómez de Avellaneda (1832–1894). First published in 1846 in *El Heraldo de Madrid* in serialized form, *Guatimozín, último emperador de México* (Guatimozín, the last emperor of Mexico) appeared in Mexico in 1853 and was a success, according to Hugh Harter.[50] Avellaneda's fourth full-length novel appears to be the culmination of her early fascination with the theme, for in her youth she had written a play, now lost, on the topic. Although she appears to follow the romantic nationalist tendencies to sympathize with the "noble" Aztecs and consider Cortés to be cold and calculating, Harter suggests that her characterization of Marina serves as a persona for the author herself.[51] Like the author of *Xicoténcatl*, she uses the historical theme to convey a message related to her own historical circumstances, but in a more personal vein. Avellaneda had been in love with Gabriel García Tassara and had had a child with him who died nine months later, during the time she was writing *Guatimozín*. Thus, when Marina expresses a love for Cortés that defies all conventions with tragic results, her situation resembles Avellaneda's own. Although Marina's role does not receive great elaboration, her confession of overwhelming love for Cortés appears in the penultimate paragraph of the narrative: "I am nothing more than that: a woman who is crazy with love for you."[52] Avellaneda's use of Marina, then, is interesting from a biographical perspective, but its general outline follows a romantic rendition of La Malinche not unlike the portrait found in Eligio Ancona's *Los mártires del Anáhuac* (The martyrs of Anahuac). Ancona's novel appeared in 1870, not long after Mexico had successfully overcome a second European invasion.

Throughout the nineteenth century, Mexico had suffered a series of internal political struggles that often led to civil wars. President Benito Juárez and the liberal faction in Mexico had just succeeded in winning the War of Reform (1858–1861), as the latest in the series of military and political conflicts between the liberals and conservatives was called. In the face of mounting deficits, Juárez suspended payment of the foreign debt, an action that quickly brought Spanish, English, and French troops to Mexican soil in late 1861 in an attempt to collect revenues by force. Under the leadership of the Spanish General Juan Prim, the Spanish and English armies soon agreed to depart.[53] Napoleon III instructed his armies to remain, however, and used the incident to begin a war of occupation that led to the French-imposed monarchy of Maximilian and Carlota, established in 1864. Although many Mexican conservatives supported the foreign rulers, Juárez and the liberals fought back. By 1867 most of the French troops that upheld Mexico's second empire had withdrawn, leaving Maximilian without the necessary military support to overcome Juárez and his republican army. The republican victory stimulated new interest in national themes within the literary world, as Ralph Warner notes: "If one adds up these factors: the termination of a foreign intervention through the success of Mexican arms and the reaffirmation of national spirit as a result of the necessary cooperation that took place to oust the troops of Napoleon, then it would not be a surprise to observe the appearance of novelists that focus on Mexican topics."[54] According to Warner, Eligio Ancona (1835–1893) and Ireneo Paz (1836–1924) are among the Mexican authors whose texts responded to renewed interest in themes relating to Mexican historical realities. He calls *Los mártires del Anáhuac* by Ancona the first novel to deal with the theme of the conquest, discounting *Xicoténcatl* as a Mexican novel despite the significance and influence of its Mexican theme.[55]

Ancona's novel appeared in 1870, the product of a young journalist from Mérida, Yucatán, who was a republican in sentiment. His opposition to the monarchy of Maximilian and Carlota had caused his exile and imprisonment in 1866, and in 1867 he actively fought against the monarchy as a member of the Liberal troops. Perhaps the strong republican and nationalist beliefs expressed by his fictitious character Tizoc against the tyranny and tortures of Cortés reflect the author's own patriotic feelings for a Mexico free from foreign imperialist domination, a viewpoint he shares with the anonymous author of *Xicoténcatl*. Ancona verbalizes for his nationalist readers the long-preserved historical memory of violence, torture, and cruelty associated with the conquest. He formulates his version of the events and characters of the conquest within a paradigm that has become the standard Mexican nationalist tradition, conferring negative values on the Spanish and Amerindian figures associated with the Spanish imposition of power.

Just as he labels the rule of Cortés a system of terror, he also calls Moctezuma "that contemptible monarch," censuring the emperor for his weaknesses in dealing with the foreigners and his despotism.[56] He shows his interest in forging a positive link between the pre-Hispanic inhabitants of Mexico and their contemporary Amerindian and mestizo heirs, however, by idealizing those Amerindians whose republican political sentiments he considers appropriate for his Mexico.

Neither the author of *Xicoténcatl* nor Ancona spend as much narrative time on La Malinche as will Ireneo Paz, since she is not the focus of their stories but is ancillary to the main message. Unlike the earlier work, however, Ancona's version is paradoxical; he does not begin his narrative with a completely derogatory portrayal. While he stresses the popular motifs of betrayal and sexual collusion associated with her image, he introduces her to his readers with the story of her birth, which provides a justification for her role as traitor to her people. Her perfidious actions are determined by the script given to her by destiny.

As in all his characterizations and portrayals of actions, Ancona manipulates the role of Malintzin/Marina, the two names used to refer to her, so that he may stress his underlying theme. The conquest may have been inevitable, but the injustices and cruelties were unnecessary and should have been avoided. The conquest becomes an event determined by fortune, the Amerindian gods, the god of the Christians; all the forces of predestination willed it to occur. Each character and episode is cast in this deterministic mode, which reflects romantic ideology. No matter how brave and righteous the Aztecs or the Tlaxcalans may be, Cortés is never abandoned by the good fortune that determines his success.

Moreover, unlike those of other writers, Ancona's characters on both sides refer to the divine presence as a guide to their actions. The Aztecs as well as the Christians believe that they are being tested by the gods. By showing the sufferings of the people, he stresses that the excesses of both religious groups are equally harmful to the peace and tranquility of the nation.

Castro Leal suggests that Ancona followed the chronicle of Bernal Díaz, adding only the original love story between Tizoc and Geliztli and a few additional characters that nevertheless fit the historical frame.[57] Ancona adds more than the love story, however, for he also provides commentary that conflicts with Bernal Díaz's perspective on the figures of the conquest. Ancona's observations have contributed more forcefully to the palimpsest of each sign. He fuses his republican sentiments with a romantic belief in destiny and the power of love to influence the actions of his characters. Whether Tizoc or Malintzin, Amerindian male or female, his characters are motivated by love to risk their lives and suffer eternal malediction if necessary to be with their beloved. Through his superimposition of this romantic outlook on the characters of the Amerindians, Ancona contributes details not found in the chronicles that reflect the needs of his own time period.

In general, each author's attitude toward La Malinche can be grasped by examining the author's treatment of her life before her encounter with the Spaniards. Whereas according to Bernal Díaz, La Malinche's mother and stepfather sold her into slavery to rid themselves of an unwanted heir, the author of *Xicoténcatl* succinctly describes her as merely an American who after "a series of misfortunes came to be a slave of the cacique of Tabasco."[58] The terse phrase "a series of misfortunes," as noted earlier in this chapter, reveals the unsympathetic way the narrator treats Marina; she is the evil temptress and traitor to the American cause. In contrast, Ancona transforms the story of the Amerindian Malintzin's birth and early childhood into a romantic melodrama of predestination that adds to the tragedy surrounding her life.

Ancona relates with abundant and dramatic detail a minidrama replete with dialogic exchanges among the principals that creates great sympathy for the Amerindian woman. After his initial sympathy, however, he then treats her in the same disparaging manner as *Xicoténcatl*. Thus, the newly baptized Marina is allowed to explain with great pain and sorrow the early scenes of her life. She recounts to Padre Aguilar that her birthplace was Painala (as Bernal Díaz recorded), a Nahuatl-speaking area. Ancona adds a new note when the narrative attributed to her also relates that she was born under an evil sign. Marina confesses that her parents were informed of the prophecy by the priests and soothsayers of their religion. The malediction, which will be repeated in the text many times, predicts her relationship with foreign invaders who will bring tragedy to her people: "When that child reaches adolescence she will love the greatest enemy of our race. This love will provoke her to deny the gods, sell out her brothers and hand over her nation to the foreigner."[59] The prediction of the priests is a capsule version of the negative interpretation of La Malinche's role in the conquest and, typically, does not take into account the historical circumstances of her position as a slave woman in the complex social associations of Amerindian society.

Ancona's reference to the evil sign under which she was born does not originate with Bernal Díaz but appears to have been drawn from Amerindian legends regarding the goddess Malinal Xochitl. This sister of Huitzilopochtli shares a related name similarly derived from the Amerindian calendar, and her ill-starred biography was also conferred upon Malintzin.[60] Moreover, Ancona's narrative requires an evil female character as a foil for his positive heroine Geliztli. Like Teutila, Geliztli represents American resistance to the European invasion: in contradistinction to Marina, she resists Cortés's amorous advances and favors an Amerindian lover, Tizoc. Only Marina favors the Spaniards, since she is predestined to fall in love with the foreign chief and to shape her actions to his every wish and need.

Ancona transforms each aspect of Malintzin's early life to conform to the evil prophecy so that her fated role can be fulfilled. In his version, her father dies during the ceremonies in honor of her birth. When her mother eventually remarries, the stepfather is an evil, severe figure who wants to have her sacrificed to the gods in order to rid Painala of the evil decreed at her birth. He also wants to assure that his own son will inherit the kingdom, since it would normally go to Malintzin as the first-born child. (María Rodríguez insists, however, that according to Aztec customs, a woman could not inherit the throne;[61] see chapter 2.) Her mother is soft-hearted and hides her beloved daughter to protect her from becoming an offering to the gods. Ancona thus transforms the evil mother of other versions into a sympathetic figure, as does Ireneo Paz in *Doña Marina*. The only evil woman, the only one associated with betrayal, is Marina, "she who sells her brothers." Notice how the motif of the biblical Joseph, introduced by Bernal Díaz, has been inverted here. Instead of a Doña Marina who was sold into slavery yet declined to seek vengeance, here she is the one to sell her brothers, an active figure instead of the passive recipient of evil actions presented by Bernal Díaz.

As the two parents discuss what is to be her destiny, each repeats again and again the evil deeds predicted for Malintzin, so that the malediction functions in the way epic epithets do, reminding the reader of a person's key characteristics. Malintzin "is destined to love an enemy of our people and because of this love, sell out her brothers and her nation,"[62] a description that defines and circumscribes her actions in the rest of the novel. When Cortés hears the story about Marina and the prophecy, he believes it to be another sign that he has divine guidance in all his actions in Mexico. On the one hand, he tells her that Spain, as her adopted *patria*, will be forever grateful for her support; the narrator, however, adds another dimension to the prophetic words that is revelatory for future events: "At the same time, the young Aztec woman thought she heard another voice that arose from the deep recesses of her consciousness and that said to her: 'And Anahuac will curse you eternally for the betrayal with which you have just been stained.'"[63]

Marina's facility in learning Spanish, her astuteness and shrewdness in ferreting out spies and enemies against the Spaniards—all these attributes and actions are suggested as being divinely inspired. For example, when Marina is asked by Cortés how she was able to learn Spanish so effortlessly, she replies that her teacher was "the god of the Christians" (p. 474: "el Dios de los cristianos"). Nevertheless, in true romantic fashion, Ancona also attributes her actions to her great love for Cortés: "And in effect, a miracle had taken place in Marina, not by the god of the Christians, whose eyes probably did not observe with much favor that crusade of terror and destruction, but by that child-god of Greek mythology depicted with blindfolded eyes who is called Eros."[64] Ancona's comment is illuminating: in this passage he disassociates the Christian god with the destructive aspects of the conquest at the same time that he seems to accept the possibility of other divinities that work on the human psyche.

Nevertheless, elsewhere he will reiterate that the Aztecs as well as the Spaniards believed in divine motivation behind the events of the conquest. For example, the Amerindian heroine Geliztli tells Tizoc that she has heard reports that the Spaniards are protected by the gods. Such accounts cite the supernatural experience of a sister of Moctezuma who had died and returned to life after her burial. The Aztec princess was brought back to life through an encounter with a divine presence who prophesied to her: "The warriors who sail in those large vessels are the ones who are to subdue Anahuac by means of arms and destroy the cult of the gods. . . . When the priests of those men preach about the holy water, you will be the first to receive it, and you will encourage after you all the rest of the Aztecs."[65] It is ironic that despite Geliztli's loyalty to the Amerindians, she repeats as a prophecy their eventual submission to the Spaniards. At the same time that the importance of Christianity as a force in the conquest is presented, Ancona also shows that the Aztecs' own religious beliefs in prophecy and acceptance of the supernatural worked against them in their dealings with the Spaniards, a conclusion Todorov reiterates using a twentieth-century semiotic perspective (see chapter 2).

Just as the prophecy regarding Malintzin seems to temper her free will as an agent of destruction, so, too, are there reasons given for the way Moctezuma acted in relation to the Spaniards. As an excuse for the docility of the Aztec ruler, Tizoc suggests that the Spaniards have used magic to bewitch the emperor. Geliztli's response relates their power to divine sources: "If the power that the white men from the East exercise over us were not supernatural, then how could they have imprisoned, in the midst of his people, a ruler of such vast domains?"[66]

The fatalism expressed by Geliztli is repeated in a key scene of great dramatic irony that also shows the inventiveness of Ancona and his perhaps unconscious deconstruction of Bernal Díaz's text. Whereas Bernal Díaz uses biblical allusions to strengthen his portrayal of Doña Marina's acceptance of Christianity, Ancona ironizes the biblical images as they apply to the Amerindian Geliztli. In both cases, however, the authors show the inevitability of Cortés's victory.

Ancona invents an intrigue in which Tayatzin, the head priest of the Aztecs, originates a scheme to get rid of Cortés; his plan has elements that parallel the story of the biblical Judith. Although Ancona does not commit the solecism of having the Amerindian priest verbalize the allusion, his narrator brings the subtext to the surface by labeling the chapter "La Judith del Anáhuac (The Judith of Anahuac). Ancona includes various contradictory motifs in the narration of this scene that reveal his own ambivalence toward the characters as the implied author. The priest Tayatzin is called "a fanatic" (p. 534) by the narrator, yet his project to eliminate Cortés is one that Ancona the implied author would applaud. Tayatzin instructs Geliztli to arrange a private banquet with Cortés, at which time she is to give him a narcotic that will put him to sleep. He will then be entrapped by the Aztecs, who will prepare him for sacrifice to their gods.

Although Geliztli willingly attempts to carry out the duplicitous act, somehow she drinks the wine and Cortés escapes unharmed. Her comment when she realizes what has happened is again revelatory of the theme: "The stranger was the favored child of the gods and they without doubt had made the narcotic relocate from his glass to that of the unhappy Aztec woman."[67] This explanation does not issue directly from the mouth of Geliztli but is presented as an indirect interior monologue, giving the impression that it comes from the narrator as well as from Geliztli. It is the narrator who provides the irony by calling her Judith, for unlike the biblical character, she is not destined to be successful in ridding her nation of its oppressor.

Although Ancona calls Moctezuma a despot and his empire a tyranny, he does not condemn the Tlaxcalans; he treats them as republicans worthy of great esteem, as they were portrayed in *Xicoténcatl.* The Tlaxcalans led by Xicotencatl the Younger are republican heroes who oppose any union with the Spaniards, but the members of the senate favor such an alliance. Tizoc predicts in a statement of dramatic irony that the Aztecs are doomed if the Tlaxcalans decide to befriend the foreign invaders: "'Unfortunate Anahuac,' interrupted Tizoc with a prophetic tone, 'if the brave republic of Tlaxcala opens its arms to the common enemy of our race.'"[68] The rhetorical effect of such comments on contemporary readers of the narrative, who knew the story well, was related not to the nature of the prophecy but to the authorial suggestion that the Aztecs and the Tlaxcalans share a common race and a common enemy. As in *Xicoténcatl,* ancient and real rivalries among the various nations were meant to be forgotten in the face of the new and more threatening force from across the seas.

The imagined character Tizoc is the personification of this intended Amerindian union; Ancona uses Tizoc's actions as a synecdoche to express his own attitude concerning the unity of the Amerindian cause against the foreign invaders. Tizoc is the son of Mazatl, a prince from an enemy nation of the Aztecs who was captured and had relations with an Aztec woman as part of the rituals surrounding his impending death as a victim to be sacrificed to the gods. Although the child of this intersocietal affair, Tizoc is brought up as a priest. He longs for the life of a warrior, a more prestigious role in Aztec society. His complete identification with Anahuac is exemplified in his love for the Aztec princess Geliztli, a daughter of Moctezuma.

The good love and patriotic behavior of the pair Tizoc-Geliztli constitute the positive side of the coin whose negative is the Cortés-Marina relationship. As symbol of American patriotism, Gelitzli is the spokesperson for the censure of Marina. For example, although the narrator does not refer at all to Marina's role in the massacre at Cholula at the time he narrates the terrors of the event, he has Geliztli chastise Marina for all her iniquities, including her role in

Cholula: "In spite of the color of your appearance, you seem to be a compatriot of the white men of the East more than of the coppery Aztecs. You help the foreigners in their iniquities . . . and there are some who are sure you are responsible for the Aztec blood that was spilled in Cholula. You have adopted a nation that is not yours and you have renounced Anahuac, that saw your birth." [69]

Geliztli's comments are devastating, coming from the noble, virtuous Amerindian who prefers Tizoc to Cortés, coppery Americans to white Europeans. Against her will, however, Geliztli becomes one of the members of a love triangle, with Marina and Cortés, when Moctezuma offers her in marriage to Cortés as a sign of their political union. Geliztli, however, having already expressed her love for Tizoc, considers herself a sacrificial victim. The characterization of Geliztli works in contraposition to that of Malintzin, who gives in to her passion for Cortés and the white men. It should be noted that the theme of racial difference, mentioned by Geliztli almost in passing in her critique of Marina, is a motif that will be reelaborated by Ireneo Paz in his narratives as he attempts to incorporate the Amerindian into the Europocentric paradigm of national consciousness.

In most literary treatments of Marina—in *Xicoténcatl*, for example—her role as mother of the first mestizo is considered sgnificant, often the one redeeming factor in the face of all her negative acts. Ancona, however, treats the topic of the birth of the mestizo child in a unique way. It is not Marina who is highlighted as the first mother in his narrative but Geliztli. The circumstances of conception, her reactions, and the fate of the child can be read as both an allegory of Spanish treatment of the Amerindians and a condemnation of Marina and her behavior as lover and mother. Marina's role is recalled only by indirection in its contrasts with Geliztli's presentation, since many of the elements in the Geliztli pattern contradict the established Malinche paradigm.

Contrary to Marina, who seeks out Cortés, Geliztli acquiesces to a meeting with her intended spouse only when she is convinced by Tayatzin to follow the plan to poison the Spanish leader. When Geliztli mistakenly takes the narcotic and falls into a swoon, it is Cortés who exploits her temporary defenseless state by having sexual relations with her. The unconscious state of the woman is emblematic of all the Amerindians upon whom Spanish rule has been imposed without their consent.

The first mestizo in this text is the son of Geliztli and Cortés. He becomes not a source of consolation for his mother, as he is considered for Marina in other narratives, but the symbol of her degradation and defeat. Cortés's sexual conquest here functions as a synecdoche for the entire enterprise of the conquest, a motif that will be more fully elaborated in Paz's texts.

The fate of the mestizo child also becomes a synecdoche for the destiny of mestizo Mexico, for the mestizo who is a product of two cultures and shunned by both. Geliztli considers the child the symbol of her degradation. She willingly gives him to the priest Tayatzin after he convinces her that he also raised Tizoc, another product of intersocietal rivalries. Tizoc had been taken into the priesthood of Aztec society, but Tayatzin has more nefarious plans for the interracial child: since the child resembles his father, the conqueror, Tayatzin aims to sacrifice him to the Aztec gods in a symbolic attempt to blot out the intruders. Geliztli learns too late of Tayatzin's intention to sacrifice the child in the traditional ritual in which the victim's heart is torn out.

The treatment of the child is not seen as an acceptable rite but is censured by both the mother and the narrator: the mother, through her terrified reactions, and the narraor, by his use of accusatory descriptions. He depicts the horrible details of the event, calling the sacrificial stone an "impure stone" ("inmunda piedra"); the priests who enact such a ritual are shown with their "sardonic smile" ("sonrisa sardónica"), while the crowd watching with pleasure is labeled "fanatic" ("fanática") (pp. 604–605). Ancona thus condemns human sacrifice as a ritual among the Aztecs; but just as he censures the actions of the Amerindians, he also shows that the Spaniards were guilty of human sacrifice in the way they exercised their war practices in order to conquer and subdue the Indians. Although Ancona's narrator seems to accept the power of Christian divine guidance in the success of Spaniards against the Amerindians, he laments the excessive use of destructive force and violence, as we observed earlier in his comment about "the god of the Christians, whose eyes probably did not observe with much favor that crusade of terror and destruction." In general, Ancona separates the acts of the conquistadors from a sincere and devout Christian faith. As narrator he points out that these Spaniards who presume to pray with reverence also commit atrocious acts: "Those men who were absolved by their Christian priest, just a few months ago had sacked the treasures of Moctezuma, violated the virgins of Anahuac and stained their hands with the blood of defenseless victims of Cholula."[70] His procedure is thus more nuanced than that of the author of *Xicoténcatl* in the way he exposes the abuses of both groups.

Of all the writers of the nineteenth century, only Ancona has his narrator refer directly to smallpox and its effect on the Aztecs. In describing the death of Cuitlahuatzin, he attributes it to a new disease among the inhabitants of Anahuac that was brought to the New World by one of the slaves of Narvaez and notes that it was responsible for an extraordinary number of victims. It is interesting that he does not elaborate further on the dread disease that killed so many Amerindians, perhaps because the disease factor did not represent a direct attack by the Spaniards, who remain the true object of all his denunciations.

For Ancona, "the martyrs of Anahuac" probably refers to the pair Tizoc-Geliztli, who were doomed by history from the onset of their love relationship. Nevertheless, the pair of interracial lovers, Cortés and Marina, who function in opposition to the Amerindian couple, are also shown as suffering an agonizing destiny. Marina's fate is to be remembered only for her perfidy, while Cortés is mistreated first by the monarchy for whom he labored and then by his mestizo progeny. No statue in his honor has been erected in Mexico. Ancona shows that no special advantages came to Cortés for his part in the conquest, just as no good came to Marina.

Ancona's political aims were to praise republicanism and identify certain Amerindians with the republican form of government. In contrast, Ireneo Paz seems to have been more intent on incorporating the mestizo into the definition of Mexican nationality. For that reason, as we shall see in the next chapter, his portrayal of La Malinche and other Amerindian women is conditioned by his interest in the progeny they engendered with the Spanish males.

CHAPTER FIVE

Doña Marina Recast:
From the Postintervention Period
to 1950

BEGINNING IN THE postintervention period, after the second presidency of the Zapotec Benito Juárez (1858–1870), there appeared to be a need for nationalist writers not only to incorporate the Indian heritage into the definition of "Mexican" but also to valorize positively that previously ignored and disdained element.[1] The narratives of Ireneo Paz can be read as part of the nationalists' enterprise of consolidating the Spanish and Indian elements.

Of the many novels produced by Paz on historical themes, he wrote two that focus on the conquest due to his specific interest in instructing his contemporaries about the nature of their past: *Amor y suplicio* (1873; Love and torment) and its continuation, *Doña Marina* (1883).[2] Both texts reveal in style and content his adherence to the romantic ideology and rhetoric of his period; at the same time, they show his personal reading of the conquest as a series of sexual encounters. His use of sexual relations to represent the military, political, and cultural dimensions of the conquest indicates that his texts, like *Xicoténcatl*, mirror the historical situation in a narrative structured on synecdoche.

The modern reader should remember that the target audience of Paz's novels belonged to the bourgeoisie and upper classes. These people possessed certain conceptual categories that included traditional European patriarchal attitudes toward the family and social institutions, coupled with a set of religious beliefs based on Roman Catholicism that defined social as well as sexual hierarchies. In addition, while it appears obvious today that Mexico is composed largely of an admixture of Amerindian and white Europeans, the positive Amerindian contribution to the formation of the Mexican nation was generally neglected and undervalued by the government and the scholars of his time.[3] Even in the text *Xicoténcatl*, which elevates the American to a high moral position, the Indian contributions to Mexico are not yet shown to serve as a viable part of its heritage, as symbolized by the fact that only the immoral and corrupt Marina gives birth. During the Porfiriato, from 1876 to 1910, Europeans and non-Mexicans in general were considered more valuable than and superior to the "primitive" Amerindians, especially with regard to economic and cultural contributions. Nevertheless, the ideological agenda of such nationalist writers as Ireneo Paz can be read as an attempt to incorporate the Amerindian into Mexican identity so as not to ignore that aspect of Mexican nationality.

Paz's attitude toward Spain is likewise different from that of his predecessors, who still felt the yoke of European authority. Unlike the narrator of *Xicoténcatl*, whose agenda was the criticism of anything related to the Spaniards, Paz wrote at a time when Spain was attempting reconciliation with her former colony. His text makes transparent that his objective is not to "resuscitate rancors that have already begun to be extinguished ever since the illustrious General Prim came to tell Mexico that Spain is not her stepmother, but her worthy mother" (Paz describes political relations in the same familial terms used by other Spanish Americans).[4]

Whereas the political goal of the narrator of *Xicoténcatl* was to warn against the evil authoritarian, antirepublican forces holding sway in newly independent Mexico, Paz has other nationalistic goals. He fulfills the need to valorize the "Indian" (he does not use "American" as did the earlier author); at the same time, he elevates the Spanish contribution by tempering the cruelty and atrocities attributed to them. It is worth reviewing Paz's open, direct address to his readers, for he clearly relates his narration of the conquest to the conditions of his own time: "And if we have a word of pardon and oversight for the Spaniards of over three centuries ago who came to martyrize our grandfathers, how can we not express a feeling of fraternity for the [Spanish] Republicans of today who are instructing us with their deeds, who electrify us with their words, and who place themselves at the head of European civilization?"[5] Paz says that the Spanish of his day have something good to offer and represent the best of European civilization, the polar opposite viewpoint to that of his predecessor, who could only equate the Europeans with corruption.

In *Xicoténcatl* and *Los mártires*, sexual alliances with the Spaniards were the emblem of doom for the Indian peoples; for Paz, however, that union produces the greatest good—the Mexican people. Both the mother—the Indian female—and the father—the Spanish male—are shown by Paz in the best possible light.

Also indicative of Paz's romanticism is his rendering of the historical event by means of a love conflict, in which love is thwarted and duels are fought, men accomplish either heroic actions or das-

tardly deeds inspired by the love of a particular woman. Nevertheless, his rewriting of the conquest in terms of individual sexual encounters conforms to the patriarchal social and cultural view of
women as objects of exchange and shows their necessary submission to the superior male figures.

The human events of the conquest are organized, clarified, and
made meaningful within this sexual frame of reference. The actions
of the individual Indian women are emblematic of the interrelations
between the Indians and the Spaniards; that is, the rejection by each
Indian woman of her Indian lover in favor of a Spaniard is meant to
convey the triumph of the Spanish conquistadors over the Indian
peoples. Perhaps this romantic attitude has been carried over as an
influence in the formation of one of the versions of the conquest
in popular culture that bases the Spanish victory on La Malinche's
overwhelming love for Cortés. Her emotions led her to betray her
Indian people and embrace the Spaniard and all he stood for—his European culture, religion, and system of values. Focus on the love
story offers in romantic rhetoric the historical reality of the transfer
of control over the Amerindian female by the Indian male to the European male.

The preference for the Spanish male not only serves as a synecdoche of the military and political battles of the conquest but also,
according to Jacques Lafaye, describes a phenomenon observed in
colonial society: "If we may believe foreign witnesses, the creole
women (revealing a trait of malinchismo of considerable interest for
the historian of attitudes), preferred to marry a gachupín [a penin-
sular Spaniard], rather than a creole, provoking the jealous hatred of
the latter."[6] That Lafaye classifies the behavior pattern under the
rubric of *malinchismo* provides further proof that the Malinche
paradigm is a key subtext for female-male relations in Mexico.

In the Paz scenario, even though a woman might inspire a man to
action, she is nevertheless a sexual object whose exchange among
tribal groups is a reflection not of her free will but of submission to
patriarchy and male power by an inferior nation. This exchange of
the female is a symbolic expression of the real power exchanges that
took place because of the military and political events associated
with the conquest.

In *Amor y suplicio* Paz configures the obscure story of Otila and
her various lovers according to the same paradigm as that of the legendary Malinche and Cortés.[7] That Otila's conduct anticipates the
behavior I have labeled as the Malinche paradigm suggests that Paz
considers it the major behavior pattern of the conquest. He repeats
the paradigm in the actions not only of the eponymous Doña Marina

but also of Princess Tecuichpuic, daughter of Moctezuma and betrothed to Cuauhtemoc, known by her baptismal name of Doña Isabel in the second novel, *Doña Marina*. The love interest each woman chooses represents a rejection of her own group and a preference for the Spaniard.

Paz indicates the characters' inclination for Spanish customs in the same way as the narrator of *Xicoténcatl*, by selecting Spanish names for them. Thus, the daughter of Maxixcatzin is called Princess Otila, just as her spurned rival bears the now familiar signifier Xicotencatl, although he functions as a very different signified in *Amor y suplicio*. Maxixcatzin, too, is not the enemy he was in the first novel, as indicated perhaps by the more Indian-looking spelling of his name. La Malinche is always referred to as Doña Marina and is treated in a relatively complex manner compared with the rather straightforward functions given to the other female figures.

The first part of *Amor y suplicio* relates through the same plot actions the political and amorous situations of the various indigenous peoples before the arrival of the Spaniards. The historical conflict between the Aztecs and the Tlaxcalans is symbolized by a complex love triangle composed of the beautiful Otila, princess of the Tlaxcalans, the brave Tlaxcalan general, Xicotencatl, and Guatimozin (also known historically as Cuauhtemoc), nephew of the emperor Moctezuma II, ruler of the Aztecs and other Mexican peoples. In this text, Xicotencatl and Guatimozin are rivals for the love of Otila, just as they are enemies from two different nations. The beautiful Teutila, who had been the faithful beloved of Xicotencatl, does not appear in any form; her function as representative of the American rejection of the Spaniard has no place in this text.

When Xicotencatl is rejected by Otila in favor of the Aztec, he cruelly attacks her for the love she expresses for his rival, suggesting that she is a traitor on both the personal and political levels: "How much evil you do to protect an enemy. You hate those who were born at your side, those who have breathed the same air as you. . . . You hate your brothers and you love a stranger!"[8] With this speech Xicotencatl, the spurned male figure, initiates the theme of betrayal that is so significant to the Malinche paradigm. Furthermore, when he is unsuccessful in his fight against each of Otila's lovers, he blames his military failures on her disdain of him, calling her "this atrocious serpent" (p. 163: "esta atroz serpiente"). It should be noted that the presence of this image, as in the narrative of *Xicoténcatl*, reflects the implied author's perspective; it could not be part of the Indian worldview, in which the serpent is not a negative image as it is among the Christians.

Otila does not act remorseful nor does she feign ignorance as to the enormity of her willingness to sacrifice her homeland and her gods for the love of a stranger, a man outside the tribe. She herself expresses her willing sacrifice to Guatimozin: "For you I would abandon father, relatives, homeland, duties, and whatever else that is holy on this earth!"[9] The narrator, it should be noted, pardons Otila's traitorous actions on the grounds of her enamored state: "How could Otila hesitate between a compatriot and a lover? Let us not judge her severely, she was in love, with all the strength of her eighteen years."[10]

In spite of the great love between Otila and Guatimozin, they both know that there exists a long-standing and deep-seated hatred between their peoples, a political situation that becomes an obstacle to their union. When Guatimozin first acknowledges his adoration for Otila, he considers himself to be extremely unfortunate because of the irreconcilable differences between the Tlaxcalans and the Aztecs, or Mexicans as Paz calls them in the text: "To be in love with Otila was tantamount to wanting the impossible. The hatred which existed between the two peoples was irreconcilable, and Maxixcatzin would first kill his daughter before he would hand her over to a Mexican warrior."[11]

By having the two lovers as well as other characters relate the crimes of the Aztecs against the Tlaxcalans, Paz acknowledges the importance of state rivalries and their real impact on the events of the conquest. In a dramatic way, therefore, he portrays another of the factors that historians emphasize to explain the success of the Spaniards despite the overwhelming numbers of Amerindians. The presence of this animosity, it should be noted, also diminishes the singular impact of La Malinche's cooperation with the Spaniards.

The basis for the hatred between nations is referred to by the elder statesman Xicotencatl in a speech to his son, which provides dramatic irony for the reader as he exhorts his son to prevent not only a despot from seizing control of power but "foreign domination" as well: "Thus it it, my dear son, that while you live you should never permit a single individual to usurp the power of your people, let alone allow foreign domination."[12] Despite his warnings, however, foreign invaders do seize control of his nation, just as the strangers take possession of the women. The relationships between the women and the men, moreover, serve as early indicators of the political takeover.

Although Paz has Otila express her choices of lovers as if they were independent actions on her part, contradictory evidence regarding her ability as a woman to act independently is also manifest. When Guatimozin worries that it will not be easy for Maxixcatzin to "hand over" ("entregar") his daughter to a stranger, his choice of a verb is significant. The idea of handing Otila over as an object reveals an association between women and objects that merits further analysis. For involved in the personal relationships of Guatimozin, Otila, and her father are issues regarding state power, survival strategies, and conflicts between powerful emotions—the need for vengeance versus the love of peace. Although it may seem that the narrator suggests that Otila as a young woman is in charge of her actions and may choose her lover, the attitude expressed by her father as chief of the Tlaxcalan nation indicates that she is, nonetheless, a sexual object whose exchange from one group to another involves a transfer of political power. In contemplating the duel to be fought by the two Indian suitors, Maxixcatzin acknowledges that an alliance between her and the enemy prince would assure peace between the two nations.[13] The two men discuss their possible political relationship and refer to Otila as the prize that seals their pact; Guatimozin explicitly refers to her as "the price of our alliance."[14]

Despite the love for Otila that father and lover share, she is still in their eyes an object, her body the prize exchanged between one group and the other. It is also significant that Don Juan de Velázquez de León, the Spaniard with whom Otila subsequently falls in love and whom she favors over both Indian lovers, also views women as objects. When Maxixcatzin describes Otila in glowing terms, Velázquez's response shows that he thinks of her as an object to be possessed: "You are the owner of a rich jewel."[15] Velázquez considers himself to be the most fortunate of the conquistadors because his beloved is so beautiful: "I believe that there can be no other conquistador with better fortune."[16] We should note that he uses the word "fortuna," which has a dual signification in Spanish as both "fate" and "wealth." Otila, the jewel who would have become the possession of the Aztecs through her alliance with Guatimozin, rejects the Mexican in favor of the Spaniard to become the Spanish "fortune." In a parallel series of actions recorded in the chronicles, the Tlaxcalans became allies of the Spaniards in their battle with the Aztecs. Here again, political fortunes can be followed in the symbolism of sexual relations.

Otila and the other Indian women are again seen as objects for barter when Cortés meets with the Indian ruler and asks for women as part of the tribute owed to him by the conquered Tlaxcalans. Cortés puts it bluntly: "In order to guarantee our alliance, I would like you to provide us with some women. You surely know that conquered peoples have an obligation to place their women at the disposition of the conqueror."[17]

Cortés's comment is also an indication of Amerindian attitudes about the function of women as objects, for as Pescatello reminds us, it "was a social courtesy among several Mexican tribes for families to present their daughters to guests or allies as a token of friendship" and "presentation of women as gifts or tokens of friendship was considered an important procedural part of Indian foreign relations."[18] The attitude expressed by Cortés and accepted by the others in this text highlights all the more the atypical behavior of Teutila in *Xicoténcatl*. Her irregular conduct, however, conforms to her textual function, since her morality and steadfast American patriotism contrast with the deviant behavior of Marina. Ironically, Marina's compliance was the norm during the conquest; as Pescatello indicates, "the gift of women created lasting kin relationships and also aided the Spanish in their conquests since Indian kinfolk paid homage to the Spanish male as an idol and also served him as a relative" (p. 134).

The treatment of the Spaniard as idol or god is a constant in Paz's text. The first time Otila sees Velázquez she compares him to a god: "More than a man, he seems to me to be a god. Isn't it true that he is handsome?"[19] Her reference to him as a god recalls the myth that caused the Indians to believe at first that the Spaniards were indeed emissaries from Quetzalcoatl.[20] Although Otila and her people do not literally take the Spaniards to be gods, they do accept the religion of the Spaniards and thus worship the Spaniards' god while rejecting their own religious beliefs.

The Indians' acceptance of Spanish religious beliefs is symbolized in the interactions between Otila and Velázquez and noted in their dialogues. The arduous process of christianization, which involved many friars, soldiers, tears, and travail, becomes transformed into an amorous and lyrical exchange. Just as the friars demanded that the Indian women be baptized before the Spaniards had sexual relations with them, Velázquez, representative of the conquistadors, proposes to Otila that she should convert to Christianity. "Let us depart to Castile / Where Christians we will be," he sings to her. Otila exclaims that she listens to his song in "religious ecstasy," and that he speaks to her "in the language of the gods."[21]

The references to religious conversion are just one aspect of the narrator's detailed justification of the transfer of Otila's affections from the Aztec prince to the Spanish conquistador. The narrator also refers to the importance of her poetic imagination in forming the concept of an ideal mate; Otila's dream lover, so to speak, does not correspond to the reality presented by her own tribesmen, with their "copper skin" and "feathered clothing," but was reflected more accurately in the foreigners, first by the Aztec prince, who was "more beautiful and more noble because he was a descendant of kings."[22] The full realization of her dream lover was achieved with the arrival of the Spaniard, whose white skin does not go unnoticed and who entrances her as the "white man who . . . has caused me to go sleepless." Then "Velázquez appeared before her eyes and she became dazzled. Soon her dreams came to be realized with complete perfection."[23]

Otila's comments bring in two important ideas that are the subtexts for her perspective. The inclusion of references to the skin color of her lovers introduces, albeit with a delicate brush, the prevailing nineteenth-century idea of racial hierarchies, expressed among others by Count Joseph-Arthur de Gobineau, according to which the white race was considered superior to the darker-skinned races.[24] The second observation relates to the politics of the conquest. In condoning Otila's change of affection, the narrator refers to what would be called a change of heart as a change in "organization"; he deliberately uses a lexical item from the political, not the amatory, vocabulary. Thereby Paz signals to the reader the presence of the synecdochic relationship between Otila's love interests and the conquest of the Indians by the Spaniards.[25] Poor Otila feels fighting within her the competing images of Guatimozin and Velázquez de León, a battle within the framework of sexuality that mirrors the actual historical military conquest of the land. As if to strengthen further the allegory, the narrator records how she begins to justify her positive feelings for the Spaniard by referring to the hatred between her people and the Mexicans as a justification for ending their relationship: "'Guatimozin will never return to see me,' she said, 'there is between the two of us an abyss that neither he nor I can bridge. His nation and mine hate each other. In Mexico there are beautiful princesses and he will be happier marrying a Mexican. . . . The love between us is madness. But should I love this stranger? Does he love me? I will ask the soothsayers. . . . The gods will be the ones to resolve the future of the daughter of Maxixcatzin.'"[26]

Destiny, that favored romantic motif, ordains that Otila should give herself to Velázquez, just as her people, the Tlaxcalans, should ally themselves with the Spaniards. She also convinces her father that, in the same manner in which she may retract her pledge to Guatimozin and affiliate herself with Velázquez, he, too, may nullify his pact with the Aztecs by aligning himself with the Spaniards (p. 207).

We should note that before the arrival of the Spaniards, Otila had acknowledged to Guatimozin, in graphic and detailed terms, the facts of war between their two nations; these facts, however, emerged as a detriment to her love interest only after the appearance of Veláz-quez.[27] Her initial willingness to forget Aztec cruelty against her people was echoed by her father, who was willing to forgo vengeance in favor of peace, although not before he offered his admonitions to the Aztecs in the form of fatherly advice to his prospective son-in-law. Maxixcatzin's advice to Guatimozin echoes the political view-point expressed by Xicotencatl in the earlier novel: "Perhaps at some time your kingdom will be great and flourishing; but for this to happen you need to do away with the tyrannical oppression with which you dominate all the states that love you and not the ones that fear you. Govern with kindness and you will maintain a powerful em-pire."[28] This political philosophy repeats concerns of the anony-mous narrator of *Xicoténcatl*, yet the ideas are attributed to a very different speaker, showing that the concepts belong to the later pe-riod and are not necessarily a reflection of the time of the conquest.

Just as Otila was enraptured by the handsome, godlike Spaniard whose image erased all her memories, all her past (p. 195), the Amer-indian nations behave in a similar manner. The narrator of Paz's novel also addresses the reader directly to consider how to rectify the violence of his own period in light of the conquest. It is almost as if he re-creates the period of the conquest as a lesson that conflicts can occur but that they can be as successfully reconciled as the love affairs of the Amerindian women and Spanish males in his novel.

Although Marina appears only briefly as a character in *Amor y suplicio*, the root paradigm I have labeled with the name La Malin-che is clearly evident and developed as a positive pattern. Paz's pre-sentation of the conquest through the synecdoche of a love relation-ship is reemphasized in *Doña Marina*. By introducing the Malinche paradigm in the first novel without the use of the conventional fig-ures, he showed that the actions of La Malinche and Cortés were predestined. At the same time as he strengthens the paradigm, he also mitigates the blame placed only upon Doña Marina as the sym-bol of Indian capitulation to the Spaniard. His presentation of a number of Indian women who voluntarily choose Spanish over In-dian males emphasizes the attractiveness of European civilization and the validity of Doña Marina's choice. Insofar as Doña Marina's actions are not unique, she is not a traitor but the exemplary female figure in the opus of national unity. *Doña Marina* further validates her intentions by praising the result, the birth of the mestizo child.

First Paz must prove that Doña Marina is a worthy mother, which he accomplishes by describing her as being so beautiful that she is considered a goddess: "She seems a goddess! Hers is not a natural beauty but a supernatural enchantment!"[29] By calling her a goddess he follows a custom based in the legends of both cultures, since her Amerindian name refers to the goddess Malinalli, while her physical beauty is also compared with that of a goddess in the European tradition.[30] Paz supports the comparison by describing her effusively page after page in order to concretize her many characteristics, attributing to Doña Marina a sacredness as the mother of the Mexican people that, ironically, she will later be denied by Octavio Paz in *El laberinto de la soledad*. Here Ireneo Paz stresses the nobility and virtue of the Indian woman whose coupling with the noble and brave Spaniard produces the mestizo, who is also endowed with these positive virtues.

The description of Doña Marina is typically romantic in the Latin American way, laden with syncretic elements: her eyes are black as the *azabache*, a native American stone, while her teeth are—typically European—"a nest of pearls." Paz finally epitomizes her exquisite physical characteristics as superior because she was sculpted by the divine hand: "the artist who formed her was the author of all nature."[31] Thus he indicates that he views Indians as human beings on the same level as the Spaniards, siding with Fray Bartolomé de Las Casas in a debate that raged in the colonial period.[32] Nevertheless, he also makes clear that Marina's physical attributes are exemplary for any group; for the Christians she would be like an angel, while pagans would deem her a goddess of paradise.

More important than her outstanding physical attributes are her moral qualities; Paz elaborates upon the comments of Bernal Díaz, who had noted her "manly valor." The narrator notes that "when Marina decided to fight, she fought until the end without fear of anything or anybody, until she conquered or was conquered, but she never left undone her womanly or at times manly activities."[33] It is ironic that in regard to her beauty she is judged according to a typical female standard, while her strength and fortitude are described in glowing, masculine terms as worthy characteristics of a brave soldier. It is interesting that Paz mentions her "manly valor," an element ignored by other writers to the point that modern readers have forgotten this aspect of her characterization that relates her to the subtext of the Amazon women.[34]

Paz emphasizes her good heart and compassion, encoding the positive virtues associated with the Virgin Mary onto the icon of Doña Marina in order to encourage the reader to identify her with that positive image.[35] In addition to description, he shows her goodness and compassion in action when she attempts to save from severe punishment the Spaniards Pedro Gallego and José de Jaramillo, the two men who will become the love objects of Doña Isabel, the daughter of Moctezuma, and herself. Her goodness is such that even the hard-hearted Cortés melts under her remonstrations.[36] However, as will be shown below, her role as a savior applies only to the Spaniards.

In marked contrast with previous texts, Paz continues to elaborate on each aspect of Bernal Díaz's characterization of Doña Marina so that she appears to be a clearly superior human being. Paz relates her intelligence and perspicacity to her success as an interpreter. Her ability to function as a translator, neglected in other narratives, is described as no mere transfer of words from one language to another, but as an ability to read the hearts and actions of men: "This talent was very useful to Marina in her role as interpreter, on a multitude of occasions, even in regard to languages she didn't know. It was enough that she saw some facial lines, the movements of the mouth, the expression of the eyes, so that right away she was in possession of the whole situation. Her gaze always recorded in a second all the details of whatever scenes she witnessed."[37] Such descriptions convey to the reader that Doña Marina is almost superhuman in her capabilities, a paragon of interpreters. These aspects of her character will be shown when she successfully uncovers plots to assassinate Cortés that will be foiled by her astuteness. In one incident, she single-handedly strips the would-be assassin of his dagger and saves Cortés from death.[38]

Her loyalty to Cortés, "the man who lifted her from slavery and elevated her almost to his level,"[39] is also described in superlative terms. She is compared favorably with Moses, for even he was not loyal to Pharoah, whereas Doña Marina is forever faithful to Cortés, even when he does not return that faithfulness himself. For Marina, being his slave (*sierva*) is the most gratifying position imaginable: "I am happier being the servant of Don Hernando than if I were the Queen of Spain."[40] Paz seems to be describing what he considers to be the attributes of the mother of the Mexican people—the dedicated, unselfish love, the intelligence and fortitude, the bravery and beauty—all in one almost perfect female.

Unlike the lascivious Marina of *Xicoténcatl*, Paz's heroine exhibits modesty and sexual restraint, a portrait that deviates from the Malinche of popular tradition. Cortés, however, is portrayed as sexually active. One of the scenes that vividly re-creates this contrast of characterization occurs early in the text to verify her modesty and humility, important characteristics for the mother of the Mexican people. Doña Marina is in her room undressing when Cortés, anx-

ious to see her, surprises her in a state of seminudity: "'Ah,' she ex-
claimed, giving a slight cry as she tried to cover herself when the
conquistador entered the room. Cortés was well able to see the
nudity of his beloved even though she hurriedly tried to cover herself, so that without being able to contain his impetuosity, he rushed
to her and covered her neck and arms with kisses."[41] Marina appears
timid in the face of Cortés's passion, but when he suggests that she
could eject him from the room, her remonstrations reiterate her
status as slave to his desires:

> "Do you wish perhaps to throw me out of the room?"
> "But you are my master, sire, and you can do whatever you
> please . . ."
> "Thank you. . . . If it does not offend your modesty, you may
> continue getting dressed in front of me . . . while we speak of
> business matters."
> "But we shall be able to speak of business only when you stop
> kissing me."
> "It's been so long since we've seen each other that I hunger for
> your caressess."
> "All right, sit there; but you must be prudent. . . . Do you
> promise me?"
> "I promise you."[42]

In this dialogue, Marina appears to be a prim Hispanic version of a
Victorian miss and Cortés the initiator of sexual advances. Although
he will be shown as tiring of her later on, her love and attraction for
Cortés never wane. Rosario Castellanos will dramatize the essence
of this scene in *El eterno femenino* (1975), emphasizing as does Paz
that Marina has to caution Cortés that they cannot conduct their
political agenda if he continues to kiss her (see chapter 7); Castellanos, however, will use the scene satirically to deconstruct the
ingrained popular image of a lascivious Malinche.

In the same scene, Cortés asks his beloved why she doesn't ask for
help with her dressing routine. Marina answers in a way that reaffirms what the chronicles mention about her participation in the
battles of the conquest: "Don't you remember that I am a woman
used to the battlefield?"[43] Cortés's reply follows the material found in
Bernal Díaz's text that describes the soldierly qualities of Doña Marina: "I can never forget that before and after combat, when we have
had to walk all night or take flight through the mountains, you always appear presentable in your dress, with your resplendent aspect . . .
your teeth as brilliant as ivory, and this has filled everyone with

great admiration."[44] While Cortés in this text gallantly compliments his mistress, in his own *Letters,* we remember, he barely mentions her presence. This portrait of the soldierly Marina always ready for combat should be compared with the image of the *soldaderas* of the Mexican Revolution; perhaps La Adelita of the famous ballad also had her origin in this aspect of the Malinche paradigm.[45]

Paz also indicates an attempt on the part of Cortés to distinguish his Indian Marina from the tribe of the enemy Aztecs, for the Aztecs, or Mexicas, were considered the least commendable by European standards. In praising her cleanliness and other fine attributes, he says, "You belong to a very different race from that of the Mexican one."[46] Although it is probably true that La Malinche was not an Aztec, she nevertheless shows Amerindian solidarity in her defense of the women of other nations. It is Cortés who repeats that she is different by virtue of her discourse and discretion. Marina's reply is a model of romantic wisdom: "I am discreet and wise with you because I love you; you find me gracious and filled with enchantments, because you love me. . . . What miracles does love not perform?"[47] The theme of overriding love between these two figures of different cultures will be repeated by a number of subsequent historians, most notably by Gustavo A. Rodríguez in his monograph of 1935; he believes firmly in the love between Cortés and Doña Marina, which in his opinion continued well beyond her marriage to Jaramillo.[48]

Despite Marina's expression of loyalty to Cortés, however, her behavior appears to be motivated by her considerations for the child fathered by Cortés. It is for the love of that child that Marina sacrifices her own feelings, especially when it comes to other men who also propose to her. While the choices she makes because of the child are unique in Paz's text, the paradigm of the sacrificing mother functions here as it does in *Xicoténcatl* and later in Gorostiza's *Malinche.*

Just as Otila's rejection of Amerindian men reflected in a synecdochic manner the power structure of the conquest, Doña Marina is also made to enact the reality of the power system in her attitude toward Amerindian lovers. Paz creates a character, Cuauhtlizin, identified as the son of Moctezuma, who announces his desire to marry Marina, much as the author of *Xicoténcatl* contrived for Xicotencatl to propose to Marina. While Cuauhtlizin as the brother of Doña Isabel, formerly Princess Tecuichpuic, does not appear in the chronicles, Tecuichpuic is a historically verifiable character. Paz involves her in a love relationship with Lieutenant Pedro Gallego, although some chroniclers believe her first Spanish lover was Cortés and that she had a child by him.[49] For Paz it is important to show

Marina's attitude toward coupling with native Americans; thus he invents an episode in which Cuauhtlizin visits Tecuichpuic in her palace and falls deeply in love with Marina—enacting the romantic possibility of love at first sight.

When Cuauhtlizin insists on pressing his love for Marina, as he, too, calls her, she continually replies that she is not free, that she cannot love him. At this juncture, as if to remind Paz's readers, Cuauhtlizin repeats the history of Marina's background, much as it appears in Bernal Díaz's chronicle—that she was one of twenty slaves given to Cortés by the chief of one of the eastern nations and that she serves the Spaniard as interpreter and advisor. The Indian prince adds that he knows Cortés loves her and that she reciprocates his love. Despite this acknowledged love between the two people of different races, Cuauhtlizin invites her to run away with him to the mountains, where they could live together happily and in peace. He describes an idyllic place where they will live in harmony and isolation: "We will build a little cabin and there we will form our kingdom."[50] But to his query, "Do you accept, Marina?" she finally admits that she cannot go with him to start a new kingdom because she already carries within her the start of another race: "I carry a child of Malinche within me."[51] It is not only the news itself that is significant here, but also to whom the important revelation of an expected child is addressed.

It is essential to note that Paz appears on the surface of his rhetoric to be narrating an amorous encounter between a suitor and his lady love; yet the use of the word "kingdom" brings the discourse into the realm of politics and reveals the symbolic nature of the encounter, especially when we consider the reason for Marina's refusal to accept his invitation: she is carrying the child of Cortés (to whom she refers as "el Malinche," a name that connects him closely to her role in the conquest). The child is more than the actual embodiment of their spiritual union. I would suggest that one may translate the episode for its synecdochic representations so as to read the conversation as a political exchange.

As Cuauhtlizin's repetition of the story here reminds us, the transfer of females through which Malintzin became Doña Marina symbolizes the military exchange of power from the Indian states to the Spanish foreigners. Cuauhtlizin, as representative of the Aztecs, describes in romantic vocabulary his recognition of the political exchange of power: he knows that Cortés-Spain is attracted to the Indian female-land and that she reciprocates. Therefore, he offers Marina the possibility of aborting that union with the Spaniards and reuniting with the Aztecs to form a joint Indian kingdom. His invitation arrives too late, however, for the various nations that chafed under Aztec domination envisioned a better situation under Spanish rule. Moreover, the Indian-Spanish union produced an immediate heir, the child of the Marina-Cortés affair, a tangible result that could not be denied, a natural "by-product." This allegorical reading, it should be noted, is followed in part in Gorostiza's play when Cuauhtemoc tells Doña Marina that he had hoped to start a new empire under a more just system, but she tells him that his plan is too late to be useful (see chapter 6).

The announcement to Cuauhtlizin of the impending birth is also politically symbolic, for at least within the narrative this is the first indication that Marina is pregnant; El Malinche—Cortés—has as yet no knowledge of this news. Marina, the symbol of both American land and Amerindian resistance to the Aztecs, reveals to the Aztecs first that she is so deeply involved with the Spaniards in the creation of the mestizo population that the prince's proposal to begin anew an Indian kingdom is doomed. Perhaps more than her love for Cortés, her maternal role functions here to separate her from the Indians, while it symbolizes, too, the reality of the new "kingdom" that is forming, to be inhabited by the mestizo.

Cuauhtlizin pays with his life for his pursuit of Marina, another synecdochic configuration of history by Paz. Here he presents sexual politics couched in an elaborate romantic style. Paz's Cuauhtlizin is driven by his love for Marina to seek her out in the courtyard of her Coyoacan home, palace of Cortés as well. His act is dangerous; he is a trespasser both physically (on the land now in Cortés's possession) and emotionally, for his mission is to try to convince Marina to reject Cortés and unite with him. He is taken prisoner, however, in the garden of the palace of Coyoacan. Marina had escaped from the soldiers, but Cuauhtlizin was too overcome with love to resist. According to the narrator, Cuauhtlizin is not perturbed by his impending death because, like a good romantic hero, he would rather die than be without the woman of his choice, who preferred another. On the other hand, Cuauhtlizin's rhetoric also presents the idea that his death is inevitable because he is the rival of Cortés not only romantically but militarily as well: "Even if he were not the lover of Marina, he had thought a million times that he would use his most faithful weapon to stab deep into the heart of his hated rival."[52] When Cuauhtlizin dies with Marina's name on his lips, his rejection already foreshadowed by the abandonment of the Tlaxcalan and the Aztec in *Amor y suplicio*, Paz announces for his readers the symbolic import of his passing: "finishing with this sad fortune, with the last male of that race, the noble line of the Mexican emperors."[53]

While the noble line of the Aztecs may have died on the male side, the child sired by Cortés with Marina proclaims symbolically the new political structure uniting Indian female and Spanish male. The Indian does have a role in this new structure, but it is a subservient one.

In relation to the discovery of Cuauhtlizin on Cortés's property, the narrator introduces motifs that reveal a belief in Marina's malign sexual powers. One woman says, "What the devil does that Marina have, that she is such a dangerous woman?" while her friend responds, "I don't know, but she sure is attractive to all men."[54] These comments about the Malinche figure will be echoed in the text of Garro's *Los recuerdos del porvenir*, as the townspeople apply the same paradigm of behavior to Julia (see chapter 9). Here Paz relates his Marina to the sexually fatal characteristics that are part of the negative image of La Malinche; yet he does not stress this adverse aspect of her characterization, since he is disposed favorably toward her.

Despite examples in the text that record Doña Marina's past intercessions to save the lives of Spaniards, Marina leaves Cuauhtlizin to face alone the wrath of the Spanish guards. I consider her actions emblematic of her historical behavior in Cholula with regard to the Aztecs and their allies—leaving them to fend for themselves while she sides with the Spaniards.[55] Although the Cholula massacre is not referred to in Paz's narrative, its thematic significance regarding Marina could be considered the subtext for this invented episode. Marina admits that Cortés will hang the Indian because of jealousy: "It is clear than that D. Hernando is jealous of a disturbed and ignorant prince."[56] Her final decision not to plead for clemency for Cuauhtlizin is motivated by feelings that would be labeled "malinchista" today; that is, on the personal level she favors the foreigner over the native. On the one hand, Marina declares that she would not want anyone to harm Cuauhtlizin.[57] She concludes, however, that to speak out in his favor (as she had done already for the Spaniard José de Jaramillo) would protect his life but indicate a relationship between them, and not even his life would be worth that risk to her reputation.

Her reference to Jaramillo, as she struggles with her conscience to decide whether or not to speak out in favor of Cuauhtlizin, is a narrative device that makes us compare the actions of Marina with regard to her suitors. She verbalizes the hierarchy of her affections: "Oh, no, never, not even out of compassion, would I love Cuauhtlizin more than Jaramillo, nor Jaramillo more than Cortés. For that man is my god!"[58] The political structure is clear: at the bottom is the Indian, then the common man, and over them the leader, in this case Cortés, who is likened to a god. I would suggest that Marina's hierarchy of love interests reflects the Mexican power structure, not only at the time of the conquest but during the Porfirista period in which Paz was writing and in our own period as well.

Despite her rejection of Cuauhtlizin as a consort and her inability to save his life, Doña Marina says that she always has great sympathy for the Indians and their difficult existence under the Spaniards' rule. It is ironic that she makes such a statement, unproven in the text, to Cuauhtlizin's sister, Doña Isabel. Her expression of sympathy comes at a time when Isabel has been humiliated by Cortés's refusal to save her lover, Pedro Gallego, friend of Jaramillo and one of the conspirators in a plot against Cortés. Marina tells Isabel, "Although I never have asked for favors for Spaniards but always for those of my race, today, since it's for you, I am going to speak to Don Hernando."[59] With this statement, La Malinche presents herself in the role of intercessor on behalf of the Indians, who will try to help a Spaniard since he is the lover of the daughter of Moctezuma. Her relation to Cuauhtlizin, however, did not work in the Indian male's favor. Since even the daughter of Moctezuma is willing to risk her life for the love of a Spaniard, who is no more than a lieutenant in rank, the pattern whereby Indian women choose Spaniards over Indian men in the formation of the new Mexican people becomes clear. The importance of this theme is evident, for Paz spends a great deal of narrative space on the development of the relationship and the amorous exchanges between Isabel and Pedro, reiterating rather than adding new elements to his basic theme that the sexual preferences of the Indian women reflect the larger picture of military and political exchanges of power.

Whether an Otila, Isabel, or Marina, each Indian woman demonstrates that when given a choice, she prefers the foreign male for a consort instead of the Indian. Paz presents Marina as making choices between her suitors because historically she was known to have been given in marriage by Cortés to one of his soldiers, Juan de Jaramillo. Paz suggests an explanation for this historical event when he has Doña Marina offer a rationale for their relationship; she notes early in the text that "in contrast to the other Spanish soldiers, [Jaramillo] always treated her with consideration and with distinction."[60] Perhaps for this reason the Marina who would not attempt to protect the Indian Cuauhtlizin for fear of Cortés's jealousy intercedes on behalf of Jaramillo. The text calls her ability to save Jaramillo from the wrath of Cortés a "true miracle," another affirmation of Marina's relation to the paradigm of the Good Mother.[61]

Although modern readers may find puzzling the marriage of Marina to Juan Jaramillo after she already had a child by Cortés, the chroniclers all agree that the exchange took place, while they offer various explanations of what was apparently an extraordinary event. For example, Gómara suggests that Jaramillo was drunk when he married Doña Marina, an unwilling suitor.[62] In contrast to such a flimsy rationale, it is instructive to read the justifications offered by a modern apologist of both Cortés and Marina. Mariano G. Somonte explains the event as an expression of the cultural conditions of polygamy that existed in Mexico as well as the institution known as *la barrangania*, or official concubinage, that existed in Spain.[63] Paz, however, transforms Marina's situation into another synecdoche of La Malinche's role as woman in the enterprise of the conquest. That is, she acts in the same manner as Otila in her relations with Indian and Spanish males, rejecting her own race in preference for the European.

In Paz's text, Jaramillo asks Marina to promise to choose him in the event that she is abandoned by Cortés. The reason he can suggest this exchange rests not only on his love for her but on the fact that Cortés has a wife, which Marina had guessed but had never before been told. The shock of hearing that Cortés's wife is about to come to Coyoacan is as unsettling to Paz's Marina as it will be in Celestino Gorostiza's play, although here Marina does not act out of character. The dialogue between Marina and Jaramillo emphasizes her fear that she will be replaced in Cortés's affections.[64]

Despite Jaramillo's attentions to her, and despite the presence of Cortés's legitimate wife, Paz's Marina always expresses her loyalty to Cortés. She repeats in many different ways the one idea that "I cannot belong to another, nor can I belong to anyone other than Hernán Cortés. He is my life, the other half of my soul, my adoration."[65] Though these thoughts appear sincere and emotionally valid based on her actions in the text, the reader knows that she will be abandoned by Cortés, and Paz as novelist must somehow deal with the historical marriage of Doña Marina to Jaramillo.

Paz handles this relocation of Marina in a typically romantic way. Perhaps unconsciously, he signals to the reader the inventiveness of his treatment by calling his Jaramillo by the name José instead of the historically verified Juan that appears in all the chronicles. Paz is the first writer to offer an account that allows for Marina's willingness to marry Jaramillo. She explains that she is motivated by more than her jealousy of Cortés's wife or her love for Jaramillo. Rather, her reason is significantly related to her motherly concern for her child. In the love triangle Jaramillo-Marina-Cortés, Paz makes Cortés the passive figure, while the absent factor, the child, ironically compels Marina to leave Cortés. Paz has her verbalize the plan, which is for-

·mulated after Doña Catalina dies mysteriously soon after her arrival in Mexico.[66] Marina decides that her child needs a father who is above suspicion: "I need to arrange as soon as possible my marriage with that young man who has a clean name with which to cover that of the son of Hernán Cortés. It is better that he be his father and not an assassin . . ."[67] This negative comment regarding Cortés is noteworthy, since Paz appears to have Marina revert here to a typical Mexican prejudice against Cortés despite his Europhilia as narrator and his protagonist's usual expressions of devotion. Marina's role as self-sacrificing mother, giving up her beloved to marry a more suitable father for her child, leads her to marry Jaramillo. Their union, however, does not take place until they are all on the journey to Hibueras, which is the chronology given by Bernal Díaz. Not only does the marriage to Jaramillo occur then, but it is also the occasion of her reunion with her mother and half-brother. It is also on that fateful journey that another significant, albeit probably unrelated, event occurs: Cortés decides to accept as true the accusations of betrayal against Cuauhtemoc and tortures and assassinates the young ruler, taking advantage of the location remote from Tenochtitlan. Although these events are well known in the mythology of the conquest, Paz includes only those that refer to the life of Marina; Rodolfo Usigli will take the events relating to Cuauhtemoc as the subject of his play *Corona de fuego,* which will be discussed in chapter 6.

A modern reader may wonder whether Marina's earlier description of Cortés as an assassin is an unconscious reference by Paz to Cortés's subsequent treatment of Cuauhtemoc. The journey to Hibueras, nevertheless, is divested of the negative events relating to Cuauhtemoc and is transformed instead into a positive spiritual and cultural affirmation of Marina's acceptance of Spanish values. It is important that her nobility is enhanced regarding her lineage so that she stands out as the worthy Indian forebear of the modern mestizo to whom Paz directs his cultural message. His transformation of the traditional rendition of Marina's childhood shows the importance he places on identifying positive, aristocratic Indian women as the appropriate role models for mestizo Mexico.

Paz once again is inventive in his treatment of history and does not re-create the information exactly as given by other narratives but recasts the facts to suit his own thematic purposes. As we have observed, tradition has it that it was Marina's mother who sold her to traders to get rid of the daughter from her first marriage in order to ensure the inheritance of the son of her second marriage.[68] Paz's Marina, however, offers a singular explanation to Jaramillo that accentuates even more the positive role of her mother and the negative behavior of her stepfather. In a scene that takes place before the actual reunion with her mother, Marina recalls that her stepfather had been the one to develop the plan to get rid of her: "My mother must have resisted a great deal before committing such a villainous act, because almost every morning I saw her appear teary-eyed."[69]

It is interesting to compare this scene with that of Ancona's text. Just as Ancona labels the stepfather as the originator of the plan to sell Malintzin to slave traders, Paz also prefers to repeat this basic plot structure, but the changes he includes that differentiate his version from that of Ancona's show his sympathy for the Malinche figure. Whereas Ancona stressed that Malintzin was born under an evil omen, for Paz her birth was a sign of joy transformed by the tragic circumstances dictated by destiny when her father died and her mother remarried. The perfidious act of selling a child is here attributed to the Indian male, while the mother figure again appears free from sin, as befits the narrator's need to establish an aristocratic maternal line. In addition, other points that the narrator stresses here in the reconfiguration of Marina's life story relate to the cultural agenda of the narrative as a whole. Her preferential attitude to the Spaniard in contrast to the Indian male and her own absence of sin are again reestablished.

For example, in regard to her own attitude toward sexual encounters, she makes it clear to Jaramillo that she will enjoy his embrace only after the priest joins them in matrimony,[70] a circumspect behavior radically different from the traditional portrait of La Chingada, who is never given the opportunity to consent to a sexual encounter. Jaramillo gives credence to Marina's own view when his comment after hearing her story exculpates her from any sinful activity. For him, she is "an honest woman who has sinned only because of fate."[71] So much for the version of La Malinche as "wily serpent." Romantic fatality, not willful degeneracy, led her to accept Cortés as a lover.

Once Paz has attributed these positive qualities to the Indian progenitor of the mestizo, his next objective must be to justify her selection of the white man. In recounting to Jaramillo her first view of the Spaniards, she describes the men as "white warriors" who are handsome in appearance and speak beautifully just as their eyes also show their goodness. Her praise of the Spaniards here repeats her earlier assessment, which was in effect a comparison of racial qualities. In a long indirect monologue attributed to Marina, Paz openly justifies the Indian women's preference for the Spaniards on the basis of two different ways of life symbolized by each man:

And then when she began to make comparisons between the two men who had declared their passion to her, between Cuauhtlizin and José de Jaramillo, she always found the latter to be more handsome, more noble, more intelligent, more manly, and above all, more civilized. Cuauhtlizin could not offer her anything but a savage love; in order to love him, she needed to divest herself of the polish that she had achieved through education and return once again to the simpleness of savagery; she would need to flee from the Spaniards who were a part of her life and whose customs were now her own; she would need to abandon the religion of the true god that was firmly entrenched in her heart; and finally, she would have to return to the mountains like the wild beasts and exile herself forever from everything that now formed her likes and needs. José Jaramillo was more fitting to her aspirations. To be able to present herself as an equal before the Spaniards, to leave her condition as a savage in order to be the mistress of her house as a free woman, to be in a position to know the European coasts traveling there at the side of her husband . . . all this developed as an ideal for her in her hours of respite.[72]

These ideas expressed by Marina summarize what the rejection of the Indian heritage meant to the Mexican, from the colonial to the revolutionary periods—a dissociation of the "primitive," the "savage," in favor of the "civilized," synonym of "European." Marina's rejection of the Indian represents a repudiation of primitivism, of an old religion and an impoverished way of life; embracing the Spaniards physically also brought spiritual benefits—a new religion and a new way of life ("the European coasts")—as well as economic power: "to be a mistress of one's own house like a free woman."

A reading of these concepts within the context of Paz's historical period reveals that the inequality of races implied by Paz in his text reflects the doctrines much in vogue at the end of the nineteenth century regarding racial superiority. Paz appears cognizant of the European attitudes on race, for he also has Cortés compare Marina favorably with regard to the other Indian women, especially to the Aztecs or Mexicas; his comments praise Marina in a way that answers any negative criticism directed to the Indian nature of the mother of the Mexican people: "You belong to a very different race from that of the Mexican." Paz's attitudes toward the Indians and the white race regarding racial superiority appear to be an adaptation of some of the theories popularized by Count Gobineau and filtered through the prism of Mexican nationalism.[73]

While it is true that Paz's novel reflects the ideological and socio-logical subtexts of his historical period, he does not require his reader to recall an exterior body of historical information in order to understand the actions of the novel. Assuming the role of historian, he includes what he deems appropriate instead of relying on the reader's knowledge of history. Of course, reliance on Paz's notes and historical commentary necessarily confines the reader to Paz's per-spective; it is interesting that he admits that in forming his nar-rative presentation, he has adjusted the various versions offered by the chronicles so that they conform to "the style of a work of this nature."[74] Thus, his vision of the conquest is personal, yet it none-theless expresses a national impetus to find an identity with which the Mexicans can live—to create a sense of continuity from the cat-aclysmic conflict of the conquest to the chaotic mestizo present of the Porfirista years.[75]

Paz's historical novels on the conquest differ from the earlier ones in the way he retells the nation's central historical reality in terms of emblematic sexual relations. His rewriting of the conquest in terms of sexual encounters follows the patriarchal social and cultural view of women as objects of exchange and shows their necessary submis-sion to the superior male figures. Paz also fulfills his nationalist goals by showing that it was inevitably decreed by destiny/the gods that the beautiful Indian woman should reject her Indian lover in favor of the superior Spanish male. Paz offers a positive interpreta-tion of Mexican *mestizaje* and thus provides his readers with a posi-tive conception of themselves and their history, a way of defining social reality that dramatizes its conflicts while recommending a so-lution that fits the social and political ideologies of his time. Instead of La Malinche as scapegoat, his Marina's acceptance of the lan-guage, religion, values, and customs of the foreigner are not deni-grated. In an inverse procedure to that found in *Xicoténcatl* and *Los mártires*, her actions are considered an abandonment of provin-cialism and acceptance of civilization. We should note that this kind of selection made by the women of Ireneo Paz's novels—the choice of a European/Spanish consort in rejection of an Indian mate—may have fit the needs of the nineteenth-century type of nationalism, but by the 1960s a very different attitude will be in place. As we shall see in Elena Garro's "La culpa es de los tlaxcaltecas," the protagonist Laura does not choose the man who represents the Hispanic tradi-tion but instead prefers to go back to the Indian spouse and the In-dian way of life.

Although the approach toward Marina varies in each of the three nineteenth-century narratives discussed, the authors all use the Indian woman as a metaphor for American land, so that the events surrounding her sexual possession function as an allegory of the military and political conquests. The use of woman as a metaphor for land also appears in other nineteenth-century Latin American narratives and reveals a patriarchal attitude toward woman as an object to be conquered.[76] Moreover, the Mexican authors express, within the framework of the conquest, verbal patterns based on the land-as-woman metaphor that parallel patterns analyzed by Annette Kolodny in *The Lay of the Land* (1975). In that critical study she discusses the sexually charged process that prompted pioneer men to express their enterprise as the conquest of virgin land, which they rapidly "deflowered." Masculine social power is expressed in sexual imagery that conflates the two areas of activity and reinforces once again the patriarchal structures of society. Conflict, whether the sexual theme masks or exposes social, military, or economic oppositions, is resolved when the inferior group, represented by the feminine, submits to the dominant force, depicted in the masculine image. From its nineteenth-century narrative form into the twentieth century, the Malinche-Cortés paradigm, while transformed in details, remains the most powerful configuration of sociosexual relations in Mexico.

During the period after the publication of Ireneo Paz's narratives up to the publication in 1950 of Octavio Paz's essay on La Malinche, many biographical histories that focused on Doña Marina were produced.[77] Although these texts were considered nonfiction by their authors, much of their writing reads as a romantic gloss on the narratives by Ireneo Paz. The following discussion does not presume to present a comprehensive survey of all the relevant texts but offers rather a representative sampling of the predominant perspective on La Malinche in the aftermath of the revolutionary period.

The fated love affair that overwhelmed the two figures from different backgrounds is treated as fact by such cultural historians as J. Jesús Figueroa Torres, *Doña Marina: Una india ejemplar* (Doña Marina: An exemplary Indian woman), Gustavo A. Rodríguez, *Doña Marina*, and Federico Gómez de Orozco, *Doña Marina, la dama de la conquista* (Doña Marina, lady of the conquest). Their studies give no credence to the negative portrait of Doña Marina as presented in *Xicoténcatl* or *Los mártires*. Rather, they express a strong belief in the love between Cortés and Doña Marina, as they prefer to call La Malinche.[78]

According to Rodríguez, Marina was a fourteen-year-old Amerindian in the prime of her beauty when Fate introduced her to the thirty-four-year-old valiant and daring Spaniard; both fell in love irrevocably and for eternity.[79] He firmly rejects the view of historians who say that Cortés pretended to be in love with La Malinche in order to assure himself of her loyalty: "No! He loved her all his life, as we will demonstrate later, and he was loved in return by her with a tremendous and sincere passion."[80] For Rodríguez, Doña Marina's love for Cortés endured well beyond her marriage to Jaramillo.[81] To illustrate his perspective, he refers to the voyage made by Cortés to meet with Pánfilo Narváez, Governor Velázquez's emissary sent to subdue Cortés. This mission was obviously an important one for Cortés, for failure to overcome these opposing Spanish forces would mean the end of his command. Rodríguez comments that Marina accompanied Cortés on his journey to battle with Pánfilo de Narváez because not only did he need her as interpreter but, more importantly, "because of the love that the two then avowed."[82]

In referring to the Night of Sorrows, Rodríguez writes that the actions of Cortés also proved the great love he had for Marina: he arranged for a large number of soldiers to watch over her and also placed her in the center of the army, which was his own location as well. It is interesting to compare this biased approach to the partisan perspective of Bernal Díaz, who wrote that all of the soldiers were pleased to see that Doña Marina had been saved. Rodríguez writes of the same situation that "Cortés was filled with contentment as were the soldiers."[83] His desire to affirm the love of Cortés for his Marina leads him to attribute the pleasure to Cortés by name and refer only in general to the other soldiers, who appear as the subjects in Bernal Díaz's description.

It is also significant that Rodríguez never makes mention of the possibility of epidemics affecting the outcome of battles, but he does consider it important that the Indian allies of Cortés were attracted to the "white man" and were pleased to come to his aid.[84] Rodríguez's perspective in the 1930s does not differ much from that of Ireneo Paz in the 1880s. Through all the events of the conquest, Rodríguez praises both Cortés and Marina and claims that whatever actions either took, their love—"splendid and enduring" ("espléndido y duradero")—was their primary motivation and their son Martín was the "fruit of this passion" ("fruto de esta pasión"). Again, the encoded aim of Rodríguez follows that of Ireneo Paz—to glorify the "fruit" of their passion, the mestizo.

In 1949, a collection of essays under the title *Cortés ante la juventud* (Cortés in the presence of youth) was published, the effort of a group of historians in training. Although many of the essays include some reference to Cortés's companion, the study by Guadalupe Fernández de Velasco, "The Importance of Doña Marina in the Conquest of Mexico," focuses on her role. Fernández de Velasco notes that although the history texts all dedicate some space to the "companion" of Cortés, considering her an essential factor in the conquest, very little is known about Doña Marina even in 1949: "To speak in a worthy manner about Doña Marina and all that she means to us, is a difficult and risky undertaking. . . . It seems impossible that dealing with a person of such importance in the Conquest of Mexico, almost nothing is known of Doña Marina."[85] While the author does not elaborate on the reasons that make it such a difficult and risky enterprise to "speak in a worthy manner" about her, Marina is clearly for him an important, difficult, and resounding character, both real and legendary.[86]

In contrast to the positive motifs included in the biographical texts mentioned above, the negative images associated with La Malinche/Doña Marina in the nineteenth century evidently have prevailed, not only in literary texts but in both popular cultural forms and the plastic arts, forms of discourse that are not the focus of this study.[87] The view of La Malinche that pervaded Mexican culture by the mid-twentieth century can be ascertained in the way she is treated by Octavio Paz in *El laberinto de la soledad*. Before reviewing his work, however, we should first briefly consider the images of La Malinche formulated in the historical art of Diego Rivera and José Clemente Orozco to which Paz refers. Their murals provide a pictorial reconstruction of the conquest that also reflects the social revolutionary passion and nationalist fervor that flourished in the postrevolutionary period. Each painter depicted La Malinche according to his ideological frame of reference. Rivera's murals in the Palacio Nacional, painted between 1929 and 1951, conform to his Marxist, *indigenista* outlook; he focuses on the positive virtues of the material foundations of ancient Indian life and portrays the conquest as an evil scene that reversed the beneficial values of Indian life. Just as his image of Cortés looks to Benjamin Keen like "a poor deformed devil," his portrayal of La Malinche's back suggests his own disrespect for her role.[88]

Orozco, in contrast, provides the iconography that corresponds to a more eurocentrist perspective. His mural *Cortés and Malinche*, found over the staircase in the National Preparatory School, portrays La Malinche as the Mexican Eve. Orozco, however, uses the allusion to Eve in the positive sense; that is, she does not represent the negative icon of the woman responsible for original sin and the fall from paradise projected by the anonymous narrator of *Xicoténcatl*, by Ancona in *Los mártires*, or by Octavio Paz. Rather, she is the submissive Indian woman representing the American land's fecundity.

José Clemente Orozco, *Cortés and Malinche* (courtesy Instituto de Investigaciones Estéticas, UNAM, Mexico)

As Keen notes, "The conqueror, a superb figure of a man, extends a protective hand toward a thoroughly Indian Malinche, and their union clearly represents the union of Spanish and Indian elements in a new Mexican synthesis."[89] The positive portrait of Cortés shows how Orozco countered the indigenist approach of Rivera by valorizing the Hispanic contribution to mestizo Mexico. His Malinche, then, is projected as a stolid, fertile Eve, protected and dominated by the Spanish male. Whether of the indigenist or Hispanist camp, both artists reveal nonetheless the patriarchal attitude toward women as object, a perspective that also informs Octavio Paz's discussion.

In the chapter "Los hijos de la Malinche," translated by Lysander Kemp as "The Sons of Malinche," Paz offers the definitive view of La Malinche for the mid-twentieth century.[90] He does not critique the myth but presents its development and shows La Malinche's relationship to the biblical Eve as well as to other Mexican figures, such as La Chingada and La Llorona. Instead of the positive portrayal of Doña Marina associated with Ireneo Paz, the negative version of her behavior is continued in his essay.

Paz sees La Malinche as representing "the cruel incarnation of the feminine condition," for he posits an innate feminine vulnerability that transforms all women into "chingadas." In *El laberinto* he describes women as Other for men. He writes as a Mexican male whose concept of woman has been formed by the polarities of the Virgin and the Malinche figure, from within a tradition that is a combination of Arabic, Hispanic, and Amerindian attitudes. As a Mexican, moreover, Paz tries to understand the patriotic cry of the male, "Viva México, hijos de La chingada" ("Long live Mexico, sons of 'La chingada'"). He considers the phrase, with its inclusion of "La chingada" as "mother," to imply a dual reference: to the violent origin of the mestizo nation as a cruel encounter between two cultures, with the Indian woman placed in the role of the violated one, the *chingada*, and to the personal origin of each individual Mexican. La Chingada as defined by Paz is a mythic mother, the woman who has suffered the most corrosive of actions against her person—a violation that is both physical and psychological.

Once he establishes the idea of the mother as La Chingada, the meanings of the verb *chingar* are discussed. His development of this point in the essay leads to a return to what he sees as the basic polarity of life—a difference between the masculine and feminine economies, to use a contemporary term. For Paz, *chingar* is a masculine verb, while the passive form connotes feminine characteristics. The idea that the masculine principle violates while the feminine suffers the act of aggression becomes a perspective of life for the Mexican of Paz's description: "To the Mexican there are only two possibilities in life: either he inflicts the actions implied by *chingar* on others, or else he suffers them himself at the hands of others."[91] It has become a value of Mexican society to prize the masculine role of the active *chingón* and denigrate the feminine *chingada*. The *chingón* or "macho" is the figure of respect, but it is a macho who is the Stranger, the one who comes from outside the community: "It is impossible not to notice the resemblance between the figure of the *macho* and that of the Spanish conquistador. This is the model—more mythical than real—that determines the images the Mexican people form of men in power: caciques, feudal lords, hacienda owners, politicians, generals, captains of industry. They are all *machos, chingones*."[92] Just as the macho who has provided the paradigm of behavior for powerful figures is related to the conquistador, the woman who is La Chingada, or the mother violated by force, is related to the conquest by reference to La Malinche.

Paz considers La Malinche as another signifier for La Chingada, in fact the historical transcription of the meaning of *La chingada*, because she is the symbol of both the submission and the violation of the conquest. He places the Virgin of Guadalupe in counterpoint to the figure of La Chingada, the violated Mother. If Guadalupe is "pure receptivity,"[93] La Chingada is an even more passive figure; she offers no resistance to violence, and her open passivity is translated sexually into her role as an object of submission, leading to her loss of identity as anything more than "*La chingada.*"

Paz brings to the surface the root paradigm for Mexico when he equates La Chingada with the historical figure of La Malinche. The paradigm he presents describes the basic relation of the Indian female violated by the Spanish male as reflecting the enterprise of the conquest. At a later point in the chapter he concretizes the point I have taken as the major paradigm for my study: "The strange permanence of Cortés and La Malinche in the Mexican's imagination and sensibilities reveals that they are something more than historical figures: they are symbols of a secret conflict that we have still not resolved."[94]

The importance of that observation merits further comment, but first it is worth noting another aspect of Paz's perspective. One would agree with him that La Chingada can be equated with La Malinche, who has become the symbol of submission in Mexico, of betrayal: "The symbol of this violation is Doña Malinche, the mistress of Cortés. . . . Doña Marina becomes a figure representing the Indian women who were fascinated, violated or seduced by the Span-

iards."[95] Yet as powerful as the observation is, his masculine perspective with respect to La Malinche victimizes her by suggesting
that her actions with regard to her situation were voluntary: "It is
true that she gave herself voluntarily to the conquistador," comments Paz.[96] This statement disregards the narrowly circumscribed
position of women in both Amerindian and European society at that
time and seems perhaps to be a holdover from the romantic vision of
Doña Marina presented by Ireneo Paz and the historians mentioned
above.[97] Significantly, Paz does note that once Cortés no longer
needs the services of a translator and guide to the Indian culture, he
forgets his faithful companion. Just as Cortés's treatment of her after
the conquest reveals the reification of Woman that marks patriarchal society, it would also suggest that her own will had little to do
with the actions she performed.

Notwithstanding this one modification, Paz offers in synthesis the
important aspects of the popular version of the Malinche paradigm.
She is the manifestation of La Chingada in relation to the macho
conquistador. She is also at the opposite pole with respect to the
other vision of the Mother, the Virgin of Guadalupe, whose image is
that of the good, all-suffering, pure mother.

La Malinche not only endures as the negative female image, but
with regard to Mexican patriotism she appears at the opposite pole
to that of Cuauhtemoc, the last emperor of the Aztecs. Paz points
out the positive role that Cuauhtemoc plays for Mexicans as the
true father of Mexico, the hero of the conquest in spite of having
been dethroned, tortured, and assassinated by Cortés. Cuauhtemoc
is a closed figure, a positive icon in Mexico, while La Malinche is the
symbol of negative openness, the traitor to his martyr's role. While a
statue has been raised in his honor, her actions have become reified
in the term *malinchista,* which Paz explains when he compares the
two symbols: "Cuauhtemoc and Donã Marina are thus two antago-
nistic and complementary figures. There is nothing surprising about
our cult of the young emperor . . . and there is also nothing surprising about the curse that weighs against La Malinche. This explains
the success of the contemptuous adjective *malinchista* recently put
into circulation by the newspapers to denounce all those who have
been corrupted by foreign influences. The *malinchistas* are those
who want Mexico to open itself to the outside world: the true sons
of La Malinche, who is the Chingada in person."[98]

By relating La Malinche to key symbols in Mexican culture—the
Virgin of Guadalupe and Cuauhtemoc as well as Cortés and the macho—Paz provides proof that the historical figure has also entered
the Mexican myth system. When he asserts that the pattern of be-

havior associated with Cortés and La Malinche has persisted in the imagination and sensibility of contemporary Mexicans, he is stating both the observation and the consequence of that observation. For he makes it clear that this pattern of behavior is an uncomfortable paradigm for the Mexican, who would reject both the Indian element symbolized by the submissive Malinche and the Spanish element represented by the violent and aggressive Cortés. The effect of such a rejection of La Malinche, says Paz, is a denial of the reality of the past and the origin of the Mexican nation: "When he repudiates La Malinche—the Mexican Eve, as she was represented by José Clemente Orozco in his mural in the National Preparatory School—the Mexican breaks his ties with the past, renounces his origins, and lives in isolation and solitude."[99]

Paz places the blame for the Mexican sense of isolation and loneliness on that rejection of Mother Malinche. Here, then, is the dual message from Paz and the significance of his observations for this study of the Malinche paradigm. First, he posits the existence of the Cortés-Malinche paradigm, which research as recent as that of Elu de Leñero, in *¿Hacia dónde va la mujer mexicana?*, has validated from a sociological perspective. My consideration of representative texts of the contemporary period in chapter 9 will also show that the paradigm functions as a subtext for works not ostensibly focusing on the conquest theme. Moreover, Paz seems to imply that until La Malinche is somehow integrated within the totality of the Mexican psyche and is no longer a figure to repudiate, the Mexican will not develop to his fullest potential, but will remain an orphan, a wandering soul in the labyrinth of solitude.

After the appearance of Paz's essay and his call for integration, a number of Mexican writers began to address the political, ideological, and cultural "drama" of national origin—the conquest—and evaluate the role of the founding couple of Mexican *mestizaje*.[100] It is primarily in the dramatic genre that the theme of the encounter of cultures in the conquest emerges, just as in the nineteenth century the predominant genre dedicated to describing the task of nation building was the narrative.

CHAPTER SIX

La Malinche on Stage

OCTAVIO PAZ's seminal essay provoked many negative reactions among Mexicans, but one cannot deny that he hit upon the root paradigm for male-female relations in the Cortés-Malinche model. The plays chosen for analysis in this chapter can be seen in one sense as responses to that essay. Their direct presentation of the conquest and the figures of Cortés, Malinche, and Cuauhtemoc offers a way to reestablish the broken bonds between the Mexicans of today and their past, a repudiation/rupture that Paz considered the major obstacle to the development of an integrated Mexican national identity. As Carlos Fuentes notes in his essay "Remember the Future," one must have a relationship with the past in order to have a future. Fuentes was preceded by Celestino Gorostiza, Rodolfo Usigli, and Salvador Novo in remembering/reconstructing the conquest period as a way to respond to the difficulties that Paz observed for Mexicans who rejected their origin. Each author reconfigures the events of the conquest as a way of offering to his audience a positive view of the *patria*. At the same time, the presentation of La Malinche in these texts reproduces the patriarchal perspective described in Paz's essay, in which La Malinche is the image of the passive object manipulated by males in expression of patriarchal ideology.

In selecting plays, my intent is not to refer to every play that deals with the Malinche figure but only to those that are known to have contributed to the paradigm. The plays studied in this chapter—*Corona de fuego* (1960; Crown of fire) by Rodolfo Usigli; *Cuauhtémoc* by Salvador Novo (1962); *La Malinche o La leña está verde* (1958; La Malinche or The firewood is green) by Celestino Gorostiza; and *Todos los gatos son pardos* (1970; All cats are gray) by Carlos Fuentes—are anecdotal or personal transmutations of the historical sources. The following chapter will focus on plays that transcend the historical world to offer new contexts, as well as satirical commentary, for the relevant historical characters.

It is ironic that among the first known dramas in contemporary Mexico to bring the figures of the conquest on stage are works by Celestino Gorostiza and Salvador Novo, who with fellow members of their experimental theater group Orientación were "so many times vilified for their supposed anti-nationalism," as Frank Dauster observes.[1] Their plays of the late fifties and sixties, however, introduce the theme of Mexican national identity through a rereading of the conquest. Although Rodolfo Usigli is not considered a full participant in the Orientación experiment, he is a contemporary of the group and contributed a play on the same historic event as his version of the origin of Mexican nationhood.[2] I begin with his study of the Malinche figure because *Corona de fuego* is the first of the plays to continue the traditional portrayal outlined by Octavio Paz.

Usigli is one of Mexico's best-known playwrights and one of its most prolific. His reputation rests mainly on his historical dramas, especially the *Corona* trilogy and *El gesticulador* (The imposter). He used the term "antihistorical play" to designate the relationship of his text to the historical event, a highly controversial idea when he first presented it. As Dauster has noted, "for Usigli the most important thing was not the truth of the historical detail but its importance in the development of the concept of nationality, the true subject matter of the trilogy."[3] Yet Usigli's views on the relationship between literature and history would not have been questioned or attacked had they been read within the context of Hayden White's *Metahistory.* Usigli implies what White makes explicit, that in discussing the discursive practices of history or fiction, "it is not a matter of choosing between objectivity and distortion, but rather between different strategies for constituting 'reality' in thought so as to deal with it in different ways, each of which has its own ethical implications."[4] Usigli's ideas concerning the use of historical details in his plays have been studied at some length.[5] In *Corona de fuego* he is not "the slave but the interpreter of the historical event."[6]

What differentiates this *Corona* from the other two is not so much its underlying thematic statements or its attitude toward history but Usigli's formal decision to make *Corona de fuego* his first attempt to write tragedy in the canonical Greek form, complete with choruses and in verse—an "ambitious experiment," as he himself said.[7] Since literary conventions bear their own historical specificity, one may well ask why he chose the form of tragedy for a play on an archetypal Mexican theme. I would agree with Francisco Lomelí, who suggests that Usigli's use of the tragic form is appropriate for representing a national view of a people and its long history of suffering.[8] Usigli follows the Greek dramatic unities of time and space, situating the actions chronologically from February 27 to 28, 1525. The circumstances leading to Cortés's decision to kill Cuauhtemoc and his justifications for his behavior motivate the action. At the same time that the dramatist constructs his Aristotelian tragic form, however, he shows that Cuauhtemoc's martyrdom has nothing to do with the Greek Fates, or the romantic idea of irrevocable fate seen so clearly in Ancona's narrative; he weaves a plot based on a contemporary Mexican reading of the Aztec defeat, attributing it to betrayal, greed, and egotism.

The minor part of La Malinche conforms to her documented activities at this moment in the history of the conquest. She was considered to have played a major role only until the fall of Tenochtitlan in 1519; after that time, it appeared that her usefulness to the conquistadors was not as vital, and her voice and presence gradually diminished, a pattern Usigli follows.

It is interesting that he does not configure the clash of two opposing cultures in terms of a sexual battle, as in the historical narratives of the nineteenth century and, with a lighter brush, in Gorostiza's and Fuentes's plays. Instead, in his reading of the conquest Usigli is intent on furnishing for Mexico its founding father figure, whom he identifies as Cuauhtemoc.

Although the major agon of the play is the conflict between Cuauhtemoc and Cortés, I am intrigued by Usigli's treatment of La Malinche and his contribution to the reconfiguration of her image as an archetype for Mexico. The motifs traditionally associated with her role in the conquest are identified and developed. Rather than centering on one figure, however, the topoi of betrayal and its converse, loyalty—rejection of one's tribe or race and acceptance of the enemy—are generalized to become characteristics associated with the male Indian figures who stand in opposition to Cuauhtemoc, the tragic hero of the play. In showing the betrayal of Cuauhtemoc as a plot engendered by the other state leaders who had been subjugated by the Aztecs, Usigli emphasizes what has been called the second decisive factor in the success of Cortés's campaign against the Indians: "This is Cortés's exploitation of the internal dissensions among the various populations occupying Mexican territory."[9] At the same time he shows the discord among the Amerindians, he treats their disputes as factional divisions within a homogeneous group, since, in the words of Doña Marina, "the same blood joins us and sets us afire."[10] By having her acknowledge their unity of blood, the unity of nationhood is assumed, providing the context for the theme of betrayal. In contemporary parlance, the national leaders who betray Cuauhtemoc by selling out to Cortés would be called *malinchistas*.

While she may not be presented as an active member of the plot against Cuauhtemoc, in the imagery she is blamed for being the primary source of betrayal. One of the Aztec princes calls her "impure voice, traitorous voice . . . stain of oil on your race that enlarges day by day."[11] The image of her as an oil stain covering more territory each day is a graphic allusion to the increasing number of traitors to the Aztec cause that the play depicts.

While Cortés represents Spain and Cuauhtemoc all loyal Mexicans, La Malinche plays a multiple role, as can be seen in the way she is named in the text. The naming system here follows the "three functions of proper names: identifying, classifying, signifying,"[12] with the result that the choice of onomastic signifier discriminates among various social signifieds while referring to the same physical referent. Usigli's playscript and stage directions refer to her as Doña Marina, in the Spanish manner, while Cuauhtemoc calls her Malitzin;[13] the use of the indigenous form is an oral reminder that the woman is also Indian, just as her transfer of allegiance is indicated by her designation as Doña Marina. In turn, Cuauhtemoc calls Cortés Malinche, an Indian custom that acknowledges his close association with the figure of La Malinche in her role as his "lengua" or translator. Identifying Cortés as Malinche evokes the Indian woman behind him—and, of course, her betrayal of the Indian cause. The onomastic system of the play thus focuses linguistically as well as factually on the infamous couple that worked together against the Aztecs.

The alternation between Malintzin and Doña Marina on the onomastic level is reflected in the imagery, which also focuses on the two basic historical roles of La Malinche, as translator and as first mother; these two functions that she fulfilled for Cortés are also viewed as part of her betrayal of the Indians, the perspective Usigli promotes. The figurative language chosen to describe La Malinche as translator and mother conforms to the type of synecdoche called anatomical particularizing by J. David Sapir in his study "The Anatomy of Metaphor": "When a part replaces a whole, it serves at least two specifying functions. First, it characterizes the whole as distinct from other objects. Sail substitutes for ship, not simply by force of cliché, but because the sail fully characterizes the boat as something distinct from other objects. For any whole, however, there are usually quite a number of parts that conserve its specificity. . . . This leads to the second specifying function: the distinctive part chosen will foreground those aspects of the whole that are not only distinctive but are also taken as essential or directly relevant to the topic."[14] Sapir reminds us that the synecdochic process is based on hierarchical replacements, so that the selection of characterizing elements tells more than just the details of the total configuration; the details selected can also refer to the place of the object described in a social hierarchy. In the imagery relating to Doña Marina she has been divided into two parts—a voice and a womb. Since Woman is allowed to be womb, that aspect of her role is converted into a positive force; but the references to her voice are always negative.[15]

Usigli's technique is masterful in the way he joins concrete historical details of La Malinche's life with metaphors that relate her to universal female images. He accomplishes this feat of synthesis with a pun on the Spanish form of her name, introduced in a section chanted by the Mexican chorus:

> Marine voice deceitful and sibilant
> who changed the sound of the language
> of your people in order to alter their thought.[16]

By using the signifier *marine*—*marina* in Spanish—as an adjective, the chorus relates Indian Malintzin to her Spanish role as Marina. The rich imagery of the passage attributes to her a deceitful and sibilant marine voice that recalls the subtext of the siren, a water creature that lures men to destruction. In his *Dictionary of Symbols* Juan Cirlot suggests that the siren motif summons up the image of the temptress of men or, allegorically, invokes the torment of desire leading to self-destruction.[17] The effect of the passage is to highlight the characteristics of the translator as betrayer, as temptress whose voice is used to deceive. The second part of the chorus's description alludes to the second aspect of her anatomical particularization, the womb, in its evocation of her progeny, the product of her deceit:

> Well, your children and those who believe
> are echoes of that voice, and at the same time, splinters
> of the native wood that the lightning threatens
> and that the Spanish ax splits to make crosses.[18]

This "marine voice," then, which was described elsewhere in the text as "impure" and "traitorous," can be inverted as "Marina the Voice," which produces many "echoes," *ecos* being a metaphor that extratextually clearly refers to the Mexican people. The image, moreover, is also echoed in the text in the way several characters repeat references to her voice and link that voice to her other functions based on the womb: mistress and mother. Doña Marina herself associates her sexual role with activities of her voice: "I know what it is to fuse two worlds in my sex / And knowing that is sufficient and excuses me and saves me. / My translation is faithful and I spoke the truth."[19] In relation to that sexual role, La Malinche describes herself as "a woman in whom conquest and war fertilized a womb both persevering and long-lived."[20] Her identification as a "womb" serves as a synecdoche for the role of Indian women in engendering the Mexican nation.

As a voice she had the power of the word, of discourse, and engaged in a nontraditional female role that led to hostilities, atrocities, iniquity—the conquest of her race, her people. The message is that the woman who deviates from the norm—"marine voice, deceitful and sibilant"—brings evil. Redemption, however, is not denied her, as Usigli joins a tradition textualized in the nineteenth century in the novel *Xicoténcatl* and revitalized by Gorostiza in his play *La Malinche*. Usigli also posits her salvation through the role of motherhood, the most acceptable form of female expression being through the womb and not the voice.

In order to accomplish the feat of rescuing Marina from a solely negative role, Usigli realizes through imagery what was not possible physically and did not occur historically: at the same time as he safeguards the role of Marina as mother, he replaces Cortés with Cuauhtemoc as father of the Mexican people. Through a series of metaphoric substitutions, Cuauhtemoc's discourse inserts him into the place of Cortés so that the Indian assumes paternity for the reproductive labor of Malintzin. First, Usigli establishes that Cuauhtemoc is the origin of the Mexican nation that is to come, the "incredible, illustrious new world," "the world that has not yet arrived."[21] It will come because of his martyrdom, as Cuauhtemoc suggests:

And I, who have lost all the battles,
know that there will arise in the future
the Mexican nation for whom I die.[22]

He then redefines Malintzin as the instrument of conquest over the Spaniards: "I hope that in the fruit of your progeny / the Mexican conquers the Spanish / and the meaning of Mexico continues."[23] The body of La Malinche serves as a synecdoche for the land that will produce offspring/fruit fashioned in the image of Mexico/Cuauhtemoc.

In his desire to revitalize Cuauhtemoc, Usigli pays little attention to the Malinche figure and, like the nineteenth-century writers, keeps her within the constrained pattern of the traditional reading that reflects a patriarchal attitude to social configurations. To the end Cuauhtemoc and Cortés remain firmly at opposite poles, as warring nations whose battlefield once again is the womb/land that Malintzin/Marina represents.

Salvador Novo's *Cuauhtémoc* goes further than Usigli's play in praising his eponymous hero and devaluing Mother Malinche and Cortés. Novo almost appears to suggest that, through parthenogenesis, Cuauhtemoc is the sole creator of the modern Mexican nation. Novo's *Cuauhtémoc* also is more explicit in relating the events of the conquest to the contemporary period, for it begins with a framing device situated in the current period. His play pays the least attention to the role of La Malinche, since it has a very specific agenda to accomplish with regard to "Indianness."[24] His vision also continues Usigli's elaboration of the importance of Cuauhtemoc as symbol of Mexican nationhood.

For Novo's purposes, La Malinche, as she is called in his text, is portrayed primarily in the role of "la lengua," for she repeats the ideas that the Spanish give her to say. In her single interchange with Cuauhtemoc she serves as mouthpiece for the Spanish viewpoint. As a sign of her role as the extension of Spanish culture, it is Cortés who introduces her to Cuauhtemoc and then leaves the stage to the two opposing Indians. In her address to Cuauhtemoc, she shows herself also to symbolize the religious conversion that is part of the acculturation process:

> Malinche: The Captain has asked me to speak with you. He is not going harm you. His god is good, you know. I have already been baptized—and I go to Mass and to confession every day. . . . Why do you turn your back to me, sir?
> Cuauhtemoc: I don't understand your language, Malinche.
> Malinche: Do I speak badly the language of Anáhuac?
> Cuauhtemoc: You speak a language—that I will never know.[25]

The response of Cuauhtemoc on one level may allude to the belief that La Malinche was not a native speaker of Nahuatl but grew up in a Maya-speaking area.[26] His reference to an inability to understand her language is also a symbolic way of affirming his rejection not only of Christianity but of the European culture that La Malinche here represents. The exchange also recalls her popular role as the first to accept acculturation and become a *malinchista*.

Novo's text also represents the dual role of La Malinche in the way she is named by the characters. The script designates her interventions under the rubric Malinche, while Cortés and the other Spaniards refer to her by the Hispanicized Doña Marina. Malinche is also the name by which Cuauhtemoc addresses Cortés, thereby joining the two figures with the same sign and showing that for Cuauhtemoc/Novo, both characters possess the same signifying functions.

In addition to linguistic manipulation to join Cortés-Malinche and to distinguish Cuauhtemoc, Novo makes good use of a semiotic device to signal to the audience whom they should accept as the authentic Mexican. The Indian narrator tells the audience in the initial frame sequence that all the actors will wear masks of the different characters except the actor who represents Cuauhtemoc. The use of masks in the play can be related to Novo's recognition of what Usigli in *El gesticulador* labeled the role playing of the Mexican people. The young actors, defined in the frame as members of the narrator's village, will wear masks to signify the roles they play in order to represent the life of Cuauhtemoc. Only the narrator will perform without benefit of a mask, signifying that he is the only authentic figure on stage. While the others play roles that have been imposed, he alone is true to his nature and to the nature of "Mexicanness," equated here with the Aztec heritage as defined by Cuauhtemoc—in this representation. For again it must be emphasized that the narrator's group represents what they would like to think was the meaning and reality of the life of Cuauhtemoc, what they at their moment in time need to envision for themselves. That is why Novo's play terminates the historical action before the scenes of torture and death of the hero, scenes that signify his physical defeat by the Spaniards.

The final scene returns to the present moment and shows the unmasking of the players. As each actor removes the mask, each reveals that beneath the signifier of Spaniard or Indian betrayer of Cuauhtemoc there remains an Indian signified. The semiosis of the scene witnessed by the audience is clarified in the secondary code: "All the actors in turn deposit their masks on the floor as if they were burying them and raising themselves again, free of them and transformed."[27] The result of the gesture of unmasking signals victory for Cuauhtemoc and defeat for the couple Malinche-Cortés. It is not the fruit of their progeny that has been reproduced on stage or in the world represented by the stage. The final scene denies La Malinche the role as mother of the Mexican people, a function attributed to Novo's Cuauhtemoc in the final speech of the Indian narrator: "And Cuauhtemoc has not died. I know that he is in me; that he will live forever, in me and in my children—and in all who follow—who will be born in the land of Mexico—formed with the bones of our dead—nourished like the sun with the blood of our hearts."[28] Novo transforms the Aztec rite of sacrifice, which provided the blood of its victim to feed the sun god, Huitzilopochtli, into a positive image of procreation of Mexican nationhood.[29] In that way he ignores the contribution of La Malinche as mother of the Mexican people and denies any positive legacy for her while he maintains her identification with submission and betrayal.

In contrast to the plays of Usigli and Novo, which continue the negative treatment of La Malinche that Octavio Paz synthesized and popularized, *La Malinche o La leña está verde* by Celestino Gorostiza follows a less common tradition that has existed as a minor strand in the tapestry of conquest images. Although the play predates those of Usigli and Novo and did not serve as a model for their Malinches, it nevertheless shares with them a patriarchal perspective, which is superimposed on a more sympathetic view of La Malinche. As favorable as he thought his attitude to be, by working within the patriarchal structure Gorostiza's presentation of La Malinche as a woman is configured within that restrictive paradigm.

The title by which the play is known, *La Malinche*, clearly shows that its focus is different from that of the later plays, especially Novo's, for the Malinche role is clearly the subject of exploration. As Antonio Magaña Esquivel explains, the play was first presented as *La leña está verde* (The firewood is green) to avoid confusion with another work with the title *La Malinche*, although today it is Gorostiza's play that is known by the name of its female protagonist. Magaña Esquivel relates the title to "the fire that still burns in relation to the question of 'malinchismo' and the phenomenon of the conquest where Cuauhtemoc on one side, Cortés on the other, and Malinche between the two, continue serving as ideological flags for some obstinate few."[30] What would become a crown of fire for Usigli's Cuauhtemoc is here just building into an incendiary event. Moreover, the "green wood" of the title is repeated in the cradle song sung by La Malinche and represents an object that is burned ahead of its time to create heavy smoke; metaphorically it stands for obstacles that obfuscate. While Cuauhtemoc is the figure generally associated with fire metaphors because of his subjection to torture by fire,[31] this image may well refer to La Malinche in the context of the play. In the way her legend focuses on her as a traitor, a smoke-screen has been set up that prevents full comprehension of the events of the conquest and, by extension, of male-female relations, which are based on this root paradigm.

Despite the verbal imagery developed by Gorostiza's title, he relies more on visual images to create his desired effect: a revision of the major figures of the conquest. He anticipates, however, the concern of Usigli and Novo to relate the events of the conquest to the contemporary period. *La Malinche* ends like *Corona de fuego*, with a prophetic look to the future. Giving La Malinche the final words, Gorostiza not only, like Usigli, has her predict the animosity and hostility with which she and Cortés will be invoked; here she also appeals for comprehension that will lead to acceptance. By coupling the known reality of their infamous reputation with the idea that a change may take place, the playwright tries to accomplish with discourse what had been created by discourse.

In motivation *La Malinche* is similar to Usigli's *Corona de sombra;* it attempts to provide justification for changing contemporary negative attitudes toward La Malinche and Cortés, just as Usigli tries to change Mexican attitudes toward Maximilian and Carlota, another hated couple representing foreign interests in Mexico.[32] Unlike Usigli and Novo, however, Gorostiza considers La Malinche the important founding figure of the Mexican people. To show her vital role, he centers the play on the highlights of what is known about her life, with each of the three acts dedicated to an important episode in which she participated. Act 1 begins with her first encounter with Cortés in Veracruz, March 1519; the decisive events of October 1519, when she saves the Spaniards from being ambushed by the Cholulans, are presented in act 2; while the final act takes place in 1521 and signals her "dethronement" (Gorostiza's term) when Cortés's legal consort, Doña Catalina, arrives in Coyoacan.

The play is a romantic vision in the popular sense, for both La Malinche and Cortés act like lovers straight out of a *folletín* or romance made in Hollywood, as Kirsten Nigro observes in passing.[33] One need not refer to imported Hollywood patterns, however, since Ireneo Paz provided one of the early romantic/romanticized treatments of the pair as impassioned lovers in his texts, and subsequent Mexican historians have also sporadically supported this view, although it is not the popular perspective. One work Gorostiza's presentation closely resembles is Jesús Figueroa Torres's *Doña Marina: Una india exemplar:* "Doña Marina was the first citizen, the first Christian and the first Mexican who spoke Spanish, the first to mix her blood with the conquistador to give birth to a child, elements that forged a nation and a new race."[34]

The redemptive enterprise of Figueroa Torres, like that of other historians mentioned in chapter 5 who contributed to the romantic view of La Malinche, was overshadowed by the image reconstructed in Octavio Paz's essay. Gorostiza's play, however, supports the revisionist attempt to revalue the woman considered the mother of the Mexican people. By including the Cholula massacre he also shows his willingness to face squarely the negative incidents that Ireneo

Paz ignored; Gorostiza's treatment will be an attempt to justify her behavior on the basis of his theme: that the end—the Mestizo nation—was the greater good that justified all the actions of the conquest.

Unlike the essays that refer to her in the Spanish mode as Doña Marina, his script labels her La Malinche in recognition of her role in the process of *mestizaje*, although in the course of the action her name varies. Ironically, Cortés calls her both Malinche and Doña Marina, while Cuauhtemoc, ever the symbol of Indian Mexico, calls her Malintzin. As for "Malinche" being applied to Cortés as well, as in Usigli's play, here only Cuauhtemoc addresses Cortés in this manner. Significantly, the reference occurs after Cortés, in contrast with Usigli's text, protests the plan proposed by his soldiers to torment the Aztec leader. The use of "Malinche" in that context does not appear to encourage the negative association that Usigli elaborates.

Gorostiza introduces the audience to his positive vision of La Malinche in the first description of her made by Puertocarrero, who calls her "chief and daughter of chiefs and in truth, a great lady, the Indians call her Malintzin or Malinche as a sign of respect. We have baptized her with the name of Doña Marina."[35] By presenting all her names at once, Gorostiza reveals his project of reconciling the many roles of the figure, from Indian princess to Spanish lady, covering up the negative with images of respect. To do this, he inverts the chronological order of the naming process, however, for when La Malinche was given to the Spaniards she was not a "great lady" but a young girl who had not yet performed the deeds that would earn her the name of respect. He follows the achronological technique of Bernal Díaz, who also introduced his reader to Doña Marina by giving her full history (see chapter 3).

In order to transform the negative conception of La Malinche prevalent in Mexican culture and to justify the enterprise of the conquest itself, Gorostiza's presentation has to answer the question, often asked, as to why this Indian woman chose to support the Spanish conquistadors. He bases his answer on both personal and theological considerations, but in the development of these two themes he places his Malinche clearly within the paradigm of the patriarchy. As Nigro has observed: "Gorostiza makes Malinche the repository of two feminine qualities held sacred in Mexican society—devout Catholicism and motherhood."[36] Gorostiza's development of these elements, however, combines the themes of theology and love in such a way that the personal love story of La Malinche and Cortés and the result of their union, the mestizo child, take on a divine signification. Through the process of synecdoche, their love is transformed into a religious allegory that justifies the historical events. The sufferings and injustices attendant to the conquest become meaningful hardships that lead to the greater glory of God's will—the formation of the Mexican mestizo nation.

To support this thematic idea, human love and divine love become mixed in the imagery. It is significant that when La Malinche addresses Cortés she calls him "my god! my white god!" and that Cortés describes La Malinche as "the Guardian Angel that God has given me in this undertaking."[37] Although Cortés first speaks to La Malinche as a man in love, sexually aroused by the beauty of the Indian woman, she soon makes clear the divine subtext that motivates their actions:

> Cortés: Your compact brown skin that makes my white skin tremble with the same desire and the same fear with which it trembles before the mystery of this land, where I do not know whether joy or death awaits me . . . but toward which I go fascinated, without the power to do anything to prevent it.
> Malinche: Neither you nor I can prevent it. Thus have the gods willed it.
> Cortés: The gods?
> Malinche: Yes. . . . My gods, too. This moment . . . they announced it from the beginning of time. . . . We are playthings in their hands.[38]

In this dialogue and throughout the play we note the intersection of the themes of the conquest of woman and the conquest of land as part of the divine imperative that motivates the Spaniards' actions; we recall, too, the woman-made-land motif that appeared throughout the nineteenth century.[39] Thus, the gods demand that Cortés push forward into the Aztec territory, just as he is sexually stimulated to conquer the body of the Indian woman.

In another key speech, Cortés again unites God, land, and female imagery in a way that clarifies the relationships at the foundation of Gorostiza's subtext: " 'God is with us. He has shown us the road we have to follow in this land so prodigal and generous that she herself opens her bosom to us and bestows upon us the means to conquer her!' "[40] Cortés's reaction leads us to marvel, too, at how fortunate the Spaniards are! The land of America willingly opens its "seno"—its bosom (*seno* can also mean "womb")—to them under divine auspices, offering itself as willingly as the females identified with the land. La Malinche's rhetorical question justifying her union with Cortés—"Is there something wrong when a woman follows a man?"[41]—is thus answered firmly in the negative, as long as the man is also a representative of the "white god."

La Malinche again functions as the archetype of the pattern of acquiescence of the Indian female to the white male, which Ireneo Paz had so graphically delineated. In this play, not only is submission of the Indian female to the white male divinely sanctioned, but Cuauhtemoc is also brought into the motif to validate its effect. Here he is not, however, the symbolic father of Mexico, as he was for Usigli and Novo, although he still functions as spokesman for the indigenous cause. The Indian leader asks Cortés to order the return of the Indian women who had been stolen by the conquistadors. Cortés eagerly agrees to the restitution of this "property" but adds the caveat "if they are disposed to return."[42] Cortés has returned to these women, these objects of exchange, their free will—when it suits his needs. The women, however, are said to decide not to return to their Indian fathers and husbands but to remain with the Spaniards. Again, it is Cuauhtemoc who announces what in allegorical terms is the defeat of his own racial group: "Only three wanted to return. (With humor) That's the way women are. What one does, right away the others want to do, too. Now they all want to have a white child."[43] Cuauhtemoc's speech tells us that the Indian women prefer to follow the white man just as La Malinche had done first. At the same time that he announces what in essence is the symbolic rejection of the Indian in favor of the European, the stage directions indicate that he projects this verdict with humor, attributing their behavior to feminine capriciousness. Cuauhtemoc speaks for the male above and beyond the restriction of class or race, making gender the key operative of difference. The actions of woman as a category are identified as the origin of evil—here, cohabitation with the enemy. His comment puts him on the same side as all the other men in this great divide based on gender, just as he locates "woman" on the opposing side. The tropic process that takes place here is taxonomic particularizing,[44] in which the Indian women substitute for all the Indians who prefer European civilization, for which the white man serves as the particular replacement. At the same time Cuauhtemoc's humor trivializes the momentousness of the process alluded to through synecdoche, his critique also trivializes the behavior of women by basing it on their supposed eternal nature. Unconsciously, the rhetoric victimizes "woman" despite Gorostiza's attempts to vindicate the first woman-as-victim in Mexican culture.

In relation to the process of vindication, Gorostiza attempts to exonerate La Malinche from the charge of treason. He includes specific information from the chronicles and creates a context of credibility for her actions to condition the audience in favor of absolution. He links the concept of treason to the related themes of nationhood and oppression in order to justify her behavior. For example, La Malinche recounts Bernal Díaz's version of her past as the daughter of a chieftain sold into slavery by her mother after her father's death, a fate that destroyed her loyalty to Mexico: "I was banished to Tabasco as a slave and as a slave the Tabascans delivered me to the Spaniards. What else can I do but serve as a slave?"[45] In her lengthy debate with a youth who calls himself "a soldier in the service of Moctezuma"[46] and who turns out to be Cuauhtemoc, she converts her own life history of oppression into a synecdoche of the subjugation of the other nations by the Aztecs. In her confrontation with him, La Malinche voices the idea that the Aztecs are cruel oppressors of these groups and thus not worthy of loyalty. Finally, the youth attempts to attack her racial pride:

> Youth (ironically): And in order to liberate the members of your own race, are you going to permit strangers to enslave them?
> Malinche: Ah, so it depends on me? I didn't know that. And the others? The Cempoalans who come to ask Cortés to support them against Moctezuma and to offer themselves as intermediaries for an alliance with the Tlaxcalans? From the very chief of the Cempoalans, I know that even the closest relatives of Moctezuma fight among themselves, insult each other, and try to obtain advantages by threatening to ally themselves with the Spaniards. (Amused) And now it turns out that whether the Spaniards enslave the Mexicans will depend on me![47]

The strength of emotions revealed in the long and involved outburst that interrupts the discourse of the youth serves as a critique of those who call her a traitor and blame her for the Spanish victory. She herself, in this text, has attributed their success to the will of the gods, denying her own free will in the events of the enterprise. Furthermore, Gorostiza's Malinche expresses solidarity with the Indians for their hardships caused by the war with the Spaniards; ironically, however, Gorostiza also has her admit to having been stricken with remorse upon witnessing the massacre in Cholula: "It hurts me to see the people of my race dying and to think that all this is happening because of me."[48]

Despite her reference to guilt, an examination of the rhetorical devices used in the above emblematic interchange between La Malinche and Cuauhtemoc uncovers Gorostiza's techniques of audience manipulation that aim to convince the spectators to change their long-held unfavorable attitudes toward La Malinche. The unidentified spokesman for the Aztecs to whom La Malinche speaks becomes identified as the leader Cuauhtemoc only when Cortés appears on stage.[49] The youth/Cuauhtemoc, then, is simultaneously a symbol of Mexican youth of the past and of the future. As the very symbol of change, he articulates the vision Gorostiza would impart to his audience, that a united Mexico can be brought about through mutual esteem and respect: "We young people are working to change things, to enable Mexicans to value and respect each other. When we achieve this, which is not so difficult, we will establish unity among us all, and we will be a great nation, strong and happy."[50] This message appears to be the underlying goal of Gorostiza's didactic enterprise—the identification of a road toward a Mexican nation that is "strong and happy." Functioning as an agent of cultural formation, Gorostiza fuses the trends in Mexican mythology that tend to polarize the players in the conquest as good Indians versus bad Spaniards, in the manner of *Xicoténcatl*, or bad native customs versus good European civilization à la Ireneo Paz. By absolving both La Malinche and Cortés, the Europeanizers, and by identifying, from among the Aztecs, Moctezuma as the oppressor and the younger generation symbolized by Cuauhtemoc as seekers of peace and justice, then surely a united Mexico can be formed.

Gorostiza expresses his goal for a united Mexico not only through the voice of Cuauhtemoc but also by means of the mestizo child as an icon of unity. La Malinche, Cuauhtemoc, and the child constitute a unit that symbolizes the united future of Mexico. Significantly, their interrelationship is formed after the massacre of Cholula is recounted in act 2. First, Gorostiza establishes that La Malinche had expected Cortés to bring peace to the Indians and liberate them from Aztec oppression, an idea that the events at Cholula disprove. She herself is shown as a victim of her trust in Cortés's peaceful intentions. More significantly, her own body shows her victimization as a result of the Spanish incursion into American land: she carries the child of the conquistador. The blood that flows during the Cholula massacre anticipates the flow of her own blood during childbirth and links her through the image of blood to the fate of the Indians. These ideas are developed in a dialogue between Cuauhtemoc and La Malinche as each represents the voice of the different Indian factions in the conquest.

When Cuauhtemoc accuses her of being indifferent to the massacre of her "own blood," La Malinche counters by replacing the blood of one group with that of a newer and needier group: "Within my body a being has started to form that has neither your blood nor mine. Nor the blood of Cortés. It is a new being who wants to live and whose presence gives new meaning to my life. As for him, I cannot betray him! For him I shall live and fight against everything and against everybody, in spite of all the threats, all the punishments, all the sufferings, even martyrdom . . . even death!"[51] By means of this speech, she informs both the audience and the characters in the play of the impending birth of the child that will unite the two races. The child is the end that justifies the means, that is, the mother's actions that led to his conception.

As always in the Malinche story, the details surrounding the pregnancy—both the announcement and the arrival of the child—are used for the thematic purposes of the author and follow no historical chronology. Just as the presence of the child was the force of redemption of the woman in *Xicoténcatl*, so, too, for Gorostiza the child serves as the means of bringing salvation to La Malinche. It is significant that, once again, it is not to Cortés/Spain that she announces the news but to the representative of Indian Mexico. By configuring La Malinche's announcement of pregnancy within the context of Cholula and Cuauhtemoc, Gorostiza opposes the theme of betrayal to that of procreation. The concepts of *pater* and *patria* commingle when, as a mother-to-be, La Malinche replaces loyalty to her lover with that of devotion to her child, a paradigm held in the greatest respect by the sociocultural milieu that Gorostiza addresses. By converting La Malinche into the self-sacrificing, all-suffering mother, Gorostiza superimposes upon the image of evil Eve the more favorable one of Mother Mary. It is with the formation of this visual icon that he begins and ends the third and final act of the play, using technique to tell the theme.

The curtain opens on act 3 to reveal La Malinche holding her child and singing to him in Spanish. The final scene of the play repeats this initial icon except for one significant change. Instead of using Spanish she sings in Nahuatl, erasing for the audience the idea of her role as "*malinchista*." The visual and oral codes clearly contradict the signifieds associated with the signifier *malinchista*, for she no longer repudiates the native or embraces the foreign. Literally, she embraces the mestizo child, who functions as a synecdoche for the modern Mexican nation. It is for the sake of that child, "a new man and with whom we begin a new race in a new world,"[52] that she and Cortés will be exonerated for all their deeds and misdeeds. La Malinche continues with the author's message: "The parents are the ones who engender children, but the children are the ones who, according to their own stature, honor and exalt their parents. Some day they will make us great."[53] Gorostiza, as one of the children of that union, has fulfilled the prophecy of Mother Malinche by honoring her with his play while at the same time paying homage to her Mexican descendants.

Gorostiza's didactic aims are to vindicate La Malinche and free her from her role as victim or scapegoat and from the persecution she suffers as the first *malinchista*, traitor to the Mexican *patria*, by showing that the contemporary concept of nation did not function in the same manner in her time. He handles that project easily enough by having at various times La Malinche, Cortés, and Cuauhtemoc refer to the sociopolitical situation of rivalries and animosities among the different Amerindian groups. He also uses the social conventions of traditional ideology that value motherhood to highlight her function as first mother, a view that reinforces his patriarchal society's accepted concept of gender roles. Gorostiza does not deny any of the charges against her but asks us to see them from her perspective, a new attempt in Mexican literature.

Although he absolves her of the historical role of victim, it is ironic that the playwright's own presentation of her character victimizes her no less seriously by succumbing to gender stereotypes of feminine behavior. The playwright's thematic needs lead him to betray the character's inner plausibility in much the same manner that the sensibilities of the author of *Xicoténcatl* led him to treat his sixteenth-century characters as nineteenth-century romantics. One brief example from act 3 shows Gorostiza's perhaps unconscious adherence to the views of patriarchy regarding women.

We should remember that Cuauhtemoc heard La Malinche unveil in discourse what her body still kept hidden, the fact of her pregnancy. He accepted the idea that the child represents a restitution to the American land of its "stolen produce" (an image I take from Usigli's text). Cuauhtemoc also symbolizes the negative reaction to her relationship with Cortés in that he prophesies that she will be punished through the centuries for her behavior. Cuauhtemoc's stoic acceptance of the disclosure of her pregnancy—after all, it is the sign of the defeat of the Indian world that he represents—is contrasted with La Malinche's hysteria at his disclosure of more mundane news. In her reaction, she becomes a literary commonplace—in short, the wronged and jealous woman. The uncovering of her inherent identity as woman/land takes place at the moment of discovery of Cortés's secret: his wife is coming to Coyoacan. La Malinche hears this and reverts immediately to stereotype:

Malinche: (alarmed) His wife? Was it said that his wife is coming here?

Cuauhtemoc: (pretending) I wasn't listening . . .

Malinche: Yes! They said that she has arrived in Texcoco and
she is headed for Coyoacan. Why didn't he tell me anything?
Why this betrayal and this deceit?

Cuauhtemoc: (trying to calm her) I never heard him say he was
married. . . . (conciliatory) He himself will be able to explain it
to you. Perhaps you've heard wrong. In any case, he will have his
reasons to give you.[54]

This exchange merits several comments. First, we see how La Malinche reacts immediately with alarm and fear when she discovers
the imminent arrival of the wife of her lover. Gorostiza sets up the
eternal triangle that is well rooted in Mexican culture; ironically, he
characterizes La Malinche as the wronged woman in the love story,
an unconscious parody, perhaps, of her role as the wronged woman
in national history. Her discourse elicits further comparisons of her
functions, for she associates with Cortés the same words that are applied to her: "betrayal" and "deceit." Because of the correlation, however, her own exploits in the historical arena become trivialized to
the same plane of romanticized passion that is the stuff of the *folletín*,
or comic book romance, accentuating her victimization within the
text and without.

The presence of Cuauhtemoc as her confidant, despite the lack of
a logical or historical reason for his being there, is justified thematically since he links the two scenes and the two images of La Malinche: as all-sacrificing mother and as jealous lover. His reaction to
the news is as implausible as La Malinche's except insofar as both
react within the paradigm of patriarchal models of gender relations.
Regarded in the play as the enemy of Cortés, he now becomes his
defender, the calm, reasoning voice that looks for excuses for the behavior of the man in the triangle. For in this scene, Cuauhtemoc no
longer represents Indians or Indian males but is Man to La Malinche's Woman. Cortés's betrayal was after all a male infidelity to the
opposite sex, and according to the masculine code it must be defended. Hence his calmness, his search for reconciliatory remarks,
his appeal to reason, that realm of the masculine. In the dominion
ruled by the sexual code, Cuauhtemoc and Cortés are compatriots
while La Malinche is the outsider. Sexual bonding is stronger than
race or religion.[55] The irony of this presentation should not be lost,
although it may well have been missed by Gorostiza and the patriarchal audience.

The subtext that is at work here relates to male-female relations of the twentieth century and reveals the male author's inherent sense of male bonding. The verisimilitude of the interactions has nothing to do with the social mores of the conquest period but everything to say about the patriarchal code that governs behavior in Mexico. As a character La Malinche has been betrayed by her author, for he has made her conform to a paradigm of stereotyped female behavior when until that point she had endeavored to rise above any narrow constraints. Has she not struggled and fought and suffered, too, beyond the role of passive, weak-willed Woman? Has she not borne the child that symbolizes victory? From ascension and redemption through motherhood, she has been made to topple, again, by showing not her purity and self-sacrifice but her petty jealousy and selfishness. Her greatest fault and infidelity has been uncovered, perhaps more than in other texts: stripped bare, she is Woman. Gorostiza brings out through the semiosis of the stage the greatest guilt of Woman, that which caused the exile from paradise: every mother is necessarily a woman, whose fidelity is not to the child alone but is based on multiple loyalties. Her fall from the pedestal of motherhood on which she was placed in this text is not a result of actions, but of her reactions to male-engendered acts. Her domination by the masculine is complete and all-encompassing.

It is ironic, therefore, that consciously or not, Gorostiza provides the audience with the traditional trajectory of behavior toward La Malinche and the Indian female: to expropriate what is valuable—her progeny, her reproductive labor—and to ignore her human needs. Paternity, parturition, and property are once again united to advance the interests of the patriarchy. Whereas Novo virtually ignores La Malinche, and both he and Usigli find it necessary to substitute Cuauhtemoc for the role of *pater* in the formation of *patria*, Gorostiza makes it his enterprise to reevaluate the historical father Cortés along with the mother. In every case the reproductive labor of La Malinche/American woman is appropriated by the male. It is important to bring into consciousness the effect of a patriarchal reading even for an author clearly sympathetic to the female protagonist.

Although Gorostiza is clearly sympathetic to his female protagonist, his presentation conforms to the parameters established by the traditional versions of the Malinche paradigm, in which her functions were necessarily a fulfillment of patriarchal needs. Gorostiza together with Novo and Usigli maintains the tightly bound image of a patriarchal Malinche that crystallized the thoughts and emotions of a nation and has remained constant over the course of time. The image that serves the regime can be liberated, however, as substantiated by the presentation of La Malinche in *Todos los gatos son pardos* (1970; All cats are gray), an elliptic tale based on the adage that in the dark all cats look gray. Fuentes's portrayal reveals how the change in time and sociopolitical milieu has affected the critical consciousness of an author's reading of this recurring signifier in Mexican culture. Whereas Gorostiza, Usigli, and Novo appear to have in common the project of national unification within the paradigms of the patriarchy, Fuentes wrote his play after the national tragedy of Tlatelolco and the recognition it brought that the old paradigms are oppressive structures that lead to destruction. Fuentes's role as a myth-debunker is well known. As Lanin Gyurko observes, Fuentes "relentlessly explores and burlesques some of Mexico's most cherished national myths."[56] In *Gatos*, Fuentes begins the reevaluation of national myths at their origin.

In his provocative essay with the oxymoronic title "Remember the Future" (1986), Fuentes hypothesizes that one of the reasons the Aztec world succumbed to the Spanish conquistadors has to do with the fact that Aztec civilization "lost its future because it lost its past."[57] He does not believe it possible for a nation to have a future if it denies its past. For that reason, if Mexico continues to accede to the Spanish design, which attempted to efface the Indian past, then Mexico will have no future. Fuentes envisions the path to the future and the recouping of the Indian past through the role of "words and woman," both embodied in the figure known as La Lengua—La Malinche. In this essay he revises the contemptuous and disdainful view of La Malinche that he had presented in *Tiempo mexicano* (1971; Mexican time), where he stated that La Malinche "generates betrayal and corruption in woman."[58] In the 1986 essay he comments that "she defeated the Indian monarch; she also defeated the Spanish conquistador by giving birth to his child, the first Mestizo, the first Latin American, who would speak Spanish with an Indian accent." The idea of his essay had been already dramatized in *Gatos*.

Lanin Gyurko, among the first critics to focus on the figure of La Malinche, has commented on the positive role Fuentes gives to her: "Rather than as a traitress, La Malinche is evoked as a protector and defender of her own people. She is presented as a shrewd woman who utilizes her privileged position as a confidant of Cortés in order to sway the Spanish conquistador toward assuming a moral responsibility for the Aztecs."[59] Fuentes thus continues important aspects of Gorostiza's Malinche in that both favor her positive qualities with regard to nationhood. Fuentes stresses her initial attempts to encourage Cortés to assume the role of Quetzalcoatl, the god of creation, love, and social justice, and thus protect the Indians from abuse and Spanish oppression—a project that fails. Moreover, he develops La Malinche as a figure estranged from both cultures, that of the Indians and that of the invading Spanish, so that she assumes an identity independent from the traditions of both groups in order to symbolize the creation of a new nation that, significantly, will be based on new paradigms of behavior. This positive agenda, as we shall see, still remains only a potentiality and not an actuality, both in the text and in Mexican society.

Fuentes uses the semiotic system to emphasize the positive role of La Malinche by having her figure initiate the discourse of the play. She is the first to take the stage; the first words are hers and they are self-referential: "Malintzin, Malintzin, Malintzin, Marina, Marina, Marina . . . Malinche, Malinche, Malinche. . . . Three were your names, woman: the one your parents gave you, one given by your lover, and one given by your people. Goddess, lover, or mother, I lived this story and can narrate it. . . . Malintzin, Marina, Malinche: I was the midwife of this story because I was first the goddess who imagined it, then the lover who received its seed, and finally the mother who gave birth to it. Goddess, Malintzin; whore, Marina; mother, Malinche."[60] Fuentes's Malinche begins as an active, assertive, and mature woman, with a plan of action, the word as well as woman. Throughout the play, her discourse associates her with the positive vision of Quetzalcoatl, while both Cortés and Moctezuma, in contrast, are presented unsympathetically, and both wind up as outcasts in their respective cultures. Furthermore, Fuentes, like Usigli, spreads the blame of *malinchismo*. I agree with Gyurko that "the greatest traitor, the true 'malinchista' of this drama, is the Aztec leader who not only did not offer resistance to the invaders but who actually prostrated himself to them, treating them as gods."[61]

Although La Malinche also refers to Cortés as a god, she seeks to exploit him and use him to establish a new kingdom, not for Spain but for themselves, with Cortés in the role of Quetzalcoatl. She herself expresses this idea, attributing to her own discourse the plan to convert Cortés into a god: "You are a commoner and a mortal; you will be, through my mouth, a god and immortal."[62]

La Malinche almost succeeds in controlling Cortés as an instrument of her own will to formulate a new nation that would eliminate both the bloody sacrifices of the Aztecs and the brutality and oppression of the Spaniards. This image of La Malinche as a spokesperson for authentic national ideals and not a betrayer of Indian values is a marked departure from the tradition. Nevertheless, Fuentes's Malinche resembles Gorostiza's in the way she conforms to the role imposed upon women by a patriarchal culture.[63] She cannot put into action her vision of a new Mexico without the aid of a male figure, as we see whenever she speaks to Cortés to try to impose upon him her political views. Although she uses the imperative mode, she needs him to accomplish the action: "Don't assassinate the good of my people, sire . . . try to understand us, to give us an opportunity; don't erase our dreams of land with your sword, don't destroy our fragile identity; take what is built here and build by our side; allow us to learn from your world, just as you may learn from ours."[64] This Malinche is not a traitor to the Mexican people but one who hopes to preserve the values and identity of the *patria* as it fuses with the new influences. As Merlin Forster notes, La Malinche is "the only one of the three principal characters who really senses the importance of the events in which they are all taking part."[65] Fuentes's Malinche does not wait for the judgment of history to condemn both Moctezuma and Cortés; she is also the only one to recognize before the conquest is completed that neither side offers salvation. For example, she rails at Cortés, accusing him of being no different from Moctezuma: "You have bathed us in blood and brought us terror and slavery. . . . You have imposed your tyranny instead of Moctezuma's."[66]

Her realization that Cortés represents no real alternative to the oppression of Moctezuma ironically is also expressed by both Cuauhtemoc and Cortés. As synecdoches of possible change for their respective cultures, both leaders verbalize the idea of the repetition of the oppressive structural configuration that shapes both the Aztec and the European worlds. Cortés says to Father Olmedo: "Empires have merely passed from one hand to another, from Alexander the Great to Charles V." Cuauhtemoc echoes the same words, directed to Moctezuma: "Empires have merely passed from one hand to another."[67] Moctezuma or Cortés, all oppressors are alike; or, as Fuentes puts it metaphorically, in the darkness of despotism, "all cats are gray."

Despite the finality of this realization, Fuentes tries to associate the oppressive structures with the empires that are represented by the male figures of Cortés and Moctezuma. La Malinche, in contrast, presents a different pattern of action, which she had hoped, erroneously, to impose upon Cortés. Fuentes posits for La Malinche a second chance to bring to Mexico the reign of Quetzalcoatl (peace, justice, and love) through her role as the mother of the new nation.

In the ninth and final scene of the play, La Malinche speaks as if she were giving birth to the child she had desired, "a child made of our two bloods,"[68] as she tells Cortés at the close of act 2. As she addresses her child, she again speaks to this male figure in the imperative mode, as she had spoken to his father, and again it is to beseech him to do what she has been unable to do alone: "Come forth, son of betrayal . . . come forth, son of a whore . . . come out, son of La Chingada . . . adored son of mine, come out onto the land that no longer is mine or your father's but yours . . . come forth, son of two enemy bloods, come to recover your accursed land."[69] In contrast to her position in the other plays, here La Malinche is alone on stage, unencumbered by the "cats"—the two men of opposing races who are of similar ideology. She engages in a very long, impassioned monolog to her son, the future Mexican, born of the fusion of two worlds, two cultures. From the imperative she switches to the future tense, as she envisions in the child the figure that Moctezuma awaited and the one she had hoped to create in Cortés, the reincarnation of Quetzalcoatl: "You alone, my little son of La Chingada; you must be the plumed serpent, the winged land, the clay bird, the screwed and doubly screwed son of Mexico and Spain; you are my only legacy, the legacy of Malintzin, the goddess; Marina, the whore; Malinche, the mother."[70] When she addresses the child of synthesis, she invokes its presence, but the figure does not appear as an icon on stage; it is created only as a verbal construct. In order for La Malinche's legacy to be born, to see the light of day, a new sociopolitical structure has to form; the past cannot be the pattern for the future, as it has always been considered fatally and forever in Mexico.

Although La Malinche's inheritance is considered a positive ideal, Fuentes the playwright nevertheless gives his spectators an ambivalent message about the reality and feasibility of this ambition. He deconstructs his own discursive enterprise or perhaps the enterprise he associates with La Malinche, making her role once again that of the outsider, the victim—this time of the author's message, just as had occurred with Gorostiza. For as much as Fuentes might wish that the past need not predict the future and that the authentic national ideas he associates with La Malinche be born for Mexico, through structure, imagery and temporal manipulation he indicates the eternal return of cultural patterns.

The ninth scene does not end with the appearance of the child of La Malinche's wishes. Rather, Fuentes brings the final scene out of the time of the conquest into the present, but not through allusions and prophetic speeches in the manner of the plays of Usigli and Gorostiza. Instead, his technique recalls that of Novo, albeit in inverted form. Whereas Novo had used masks of the conquest figures to cover the forms of the contemporary actors, Fuentes introduces on stage in the final scene the characters of the conquest in modern dress. The characters with parts in the conquest take on new roles as recognizable contemporary figures—soldiers, police, workers, beggars, university students. Fuentes suggests semiotically that, though covered by the clothes of modernity, the roles of exploitation and oppression enacted in the conquest have not changed.

The patriarchy that structures Mexico from the past to the present has silenced the discourse of change embodied in La Malinche and prevented the synthesis she represents from gaining a presence on the stage of the world. At the end, she can only cradle the body of the young university student killed by the police, an action included in the play as emblematic of Tlatelolco. The vision of La Malinche that Quetzalcoatl will rule in Mexico remains a future event.

Perhaps in response to his own frustration at being able to verbalize the ideal without bringing it into existence, Fuentes leaves his audience with a final paradox. Quetzalcoatl appears as an icon on stage, symbolically positioned on high, at the same time as dead buzzards rain down, a reenactment of one of the prophecies announcing the coming of Quetzalcoatl, an omen related in the chronicles and described in scene I of the play. As we know, only the false Quetzalcoatl/Cortés appeared after that omen. Does not Fuentes reproduce, in this circularity of the images, his belief that the past continues to infuse and give shape to the present? Is he implying that modern Mexico is a mere commercial and technological façade covering the fatalistic structures of the past, which inevitably and irrevocably reassert themselves, as he told us in *Aura*?[71] Is Mexico ready for the real Quetzalcoatl proposed by La Malinche, or will another false prophet appear? How to break the pattern? The Indianism of Usigli or Novo, the praise of *mestizaje* of Gorostiza and Fuentes—such ideological constructs are ineffectual instruments for changing the structure of a society that exploits the Indian, the mestizo, the female, all marginalized beings at the periphery of the power system.

One way to break the stranglehold of a recurring pattern from the past is to repudiate the paradigms of behavior associated with the traditional national myths. Fuentes contributes to this positive national agenda by presenting a new configuration of the Malinche role. By distancing her from the male figures, Fuentes uses her as an instrument of destruction against the patriarchal paradigms that Moctezuma and Cortés together represent.

Fuentes shows in *Gatos* that he is no longer the producer of the patriarchal voice found in such texts as *La muerte de Artemio Cruz*, for example. If in his treatment of La Malinche he does not yet bring her role into the realm of feminist discourse, he at least attempts the deconstruction of the patriarchal feminine figure of La Malinche that had appeared on stage in earlier representations of the conquest theme. As *Gatos* shows, the sociopolitical drama that took place at Tlatelolco in 1968 transformed the nature of historical representations on the Mexican stage. The plays to be analyzed in chapter 7 reveal a new ideological perspective in the treatment of the conquest and offer still other interpretations of La Malinche that further modify the palimpsest.

CHAPTER SEVEN

Re/visions of the Cultural Metaphor

JUST AS Fuentes's Malinche serves to bridge two different cultures, Fuentes's play serves as a bridge to the next group of plays, which deal with the conquest in a new way. His uncoiling of the tightly bound images of La Malinche leads the way to its further decoding by Rosario Castellanos in *El eterno femenino* (1975; *The Eternal Feminine*), Willebaldo López in *Malinche Show* (1977), and Sabina Berman in *Aguila o sol* (1984; Eagle or sun). They demonstrate their new perspective by using satire, farce, and parody to criticize the authoritarian, patriarchal structures that have maintained the traditional restrictive paradigms we saw reflected in the earlier portrayals of La Malinche. In contrast to Fuentes's lack of humor and the seriousness of tone he maintains throughout *Gatos*, the plays of Castellanos, López, and Berman are witty, humorous satires.[1] It has been suggested that satirical humor evolves "out of the need to analyze reality, to criticize oppressive institutions, to affirm a people's sense of worth, and to facilitate structural change," the aims of the plays to be discussed next with regard to their presentation of the myths of the Mexican nation.[2]

It is interesting that both Castellanos and López re-create the figures of the conquest but do not follow the tradition of Usigli, Gorostiza, and Fuentes, in which the historical context is re-created, nor that of Novo, in which contemporary figures wear the masks of the past. Rather, in both *El eterno femenino* and *Malinche Show*, the named historical figures are brought on stage as revenants—figures resuscitated from death—through processes related to advances in "technology." They share the use of the apparatus of science fiction as a device to enable the historical figures of the conquest to meet with contemporary characters. In contrast with Elena Garro's use of magical realism in the short story "La culpa es de los tlaxcaltecas" (The Tlaxcalans are to blame), in which the past and present are seen as one continuum, in these plays the idea of temporal continuity is questioned and deconstructed to show its falseness for contemporary Mexican society.

Castellanos and López use the device of revenants on stage to highlight the coercive power of recurring cultural paradigms. As they explore the theme within the conventions of fantasy, they emphasize that the accepted cultural conventions are as artificial and as destructive as the imaginary technology they invent.

Although Castellanos, like Fuentes, has expressed the ideas she re-creates in her play in essay form, the special qualities of the dramatic genre enable her to approach the spectator more directly. As Arthur Miller reminds us, drama is "dynamic, it is always on the move as life is, and it is perceived like life through the motions, the gestures, the tones of voice, and the gait and nuance of living people."[3] The conventions of drama enable Castellanos and López to resuscitate the historically dead characters and present them with credibility by means of living actors so that the spectator perceives their existence to be the same as that of the so-called real characters.

Castellanos makes use of another literary convention when she places her fantasy within a realistic frame.[4] In this play written about women, the frame is a space dedicated to the formation of the image of patriarchal woman, the beauty salon. The protagonist's name, Lupe or Lupita, is a reference to the Virgin of Guadalupe, icon of Mexican national identity and the opposite pole with respect to the bad woman represented by La Malinche. Lupita goes to the salon to get her hair done in preparation for a special event, her wedding day. The prosaic aspect of the activity is transformed by its being related to a liminal period considered a rite of passage for patriarchal woman: the marriage ceremony. In calling the mariage ceremony a liminal period, I refer to Victor Turner's sense of the term, as a complex and dramatic transition period in which one is moved in accordance with a cultural script.[5] According to Turner, the period of transition enables one to generate new myths, symbols, paradigms, and political structures; Castellanos attempts to create changes in the patriarchal hierarchy by first deconstructing the institutionalized myths and paradigms associated with marriage and its corollary roles.

A salesman, the only masculine figure in the realistic frame, enters the beauty salon in order to sell a new technological apparatus, described as a symbol of progress from the USA.[6] The device fits into the dryer in order to stimulate carefully programmed dreams especially designed to protect women from their greatest danger—thinking. Lupita is chosen to try out the device in recognition of her liminal state: "It's a very special occasion: she's coming today to have her hair done for her wedding."[7] The dream chosen to prepare her for the new phase of her life is "What Does the Future Hold for Me?"[8] The salesman proudly declares that the script was carefully created not by any human but by "a machine, a computer, an electronic brain, something that never makes a mistake."[9] His masculine confidence in science is soon belied when the apparatus malfunctions and produces not the dreams prescribed by the patriarchal script but images that show the nightmare of gender relations for the Mexican female. In the dream sequences married life is satirized to show the hypocrisy upon which male-female relations are based. Lupita awakens with horror at the images of her dream, calling them "a horrible nightmare."[10] Despite her protests, she is convinced to sit under the dryer once more, which motivates the scenes of act 2.

The electronic device is reprogrammed, and this time Lupita's dreams revert to images from the cultural script of Mexican history. This second act satirizes the traditional legends of Mexican history. In returning to historical women who have been reified, Castellanos reverses the process of tropism during which the individual instance is raised to the level of general validity, thereby forcing the immobile and immortal images of institutionalized myths to regain their mobility and dynamism. The figures who return to life in the second act are seven key women who have influenced the social code for contemporary female behavior. Each woman comes from a different temporal period and has been immortalized/immobilized in history to represent behavior patterns that are to be either emulated or rejected, beginning with the biblical Eve, infamous as the instigator of humanity's fall from paradise. The legendary Mexican figures start with La Malinche of the conquest; Sor Juana Inés de la Cruz, the baroque poet; Doña Josefa Ortiz de Domínguez, a patriot in the period of Mexican independence; the Empress Carlota; Rosario de la Peña, for whom the poet Manuel Acuña was said to have committed suicide; and Adelita, a name made famous in *corridos*, songs composed about the Mexican Revolution.[11] Sor Juana, who embodies the most literate and outstanding intellectual woman of Mexico, asserts that these consecrated images are nothing more than the result of a version she calls "stereotyped, official" ("estereotipada y oficial"). She declares that the women have suffered distortions of their images at the hands of others. They will present themselves "as what we were. Or at least, as what we think we really were."[12] The treatment of La Malinche, first woman of Mexican history, serves as a synecdoche for Castellanos's treatment of these other mythic women.

Castellanos's version of La Malinche inverts the popular interpretation of her as the first *chingada*, the incarnation of sexual openness that led to the rape of America by the foreigner. It also deconstructs the romantic interpretation that she betrayed the Indians because of her great love for Cortés. In Castellanos's version, rather than sexual relations being her forte, La Malinche reveals herself to be more knowledgeable than Cortés about power relations and how to move a political agenda, recalling Fuentes rather than Gorostiza or Usigli. With this interpretation Castellanos counters the traditional portrayal of La Malinche that she describes in her essay on feminine images, "Once Again, Sor Juana."[13] When La Malinche re-enacts the scenes with Cortés, she tries to liberate herself from the masculine, patriarchal paradigm that has imprisoned her for so long. For example, the chronicles refer to the episode of the burning of the ships to show that Cortés was a tactical genius whose bravery contributed to the conquest. In the dialog presented by Castellanos, we witness an inversion of the traditional roles. La Malinche is the valiant and perspicacious one, while Cortés only knows how to complain about the sad circumstances in which he finds himself and blame others for his troubles. While Castellanos's text states that the burning of the ships occurred, the context of the event changes from an ingenious plan to an accident. Furthermore, La Malinche is the one to invent the strategy that saves Cortés's skin:

> Cortés: Oh, what I wouldn't give to have in my hands for a minute, only one minute, that sailor who started smoking in the hold of the ship and then fell asleep! . . . Not one trace remained of any of the ships.
> Malinche: . . . Why don't you take advantage of the circumstances to have the rumor spread that you, you yourself, burned the ships?
> Cortés: I? What for?
> Malinche: In order to cut off the return to Cuba. There are many cowards and one or two traitors in your army who would like to return. Now they can't do it and they have no other remedy than to face up to facts.[14]

Castellanos thus transforms the famous episode of the burning of the ships into a humorous event and deconstructs the tradition that considers Cortés a skilled tactician.

Castellanos presents her own version of another key motif that is part of the conquest mythology and has been treated by other playwrights in a serious manner. Again, in the exchanges between Cortés and La Malinche, it is La Malinche who appears wise and alert, while Cortés seems easily manipulated. Cortés asks her for help in taking off his armor, which is heavy and uncomfortable in the heat. La Malinche refuses to do it, and dares to say no to her master:

> Cortés: How dare you to say "no" to me? You are my slave, my property, my object.
> Malinche: I am your tool, I agree. But at least learn to use me for your benefit.[15]

La Malinche then explains that the armor gives him the aura of a god and that he would benefit greatly from keeping it on:

> Malinche: If you take it off, the Indians will see what I have seen and do not tell: that you are a man like any other. Perhaps weaker than some others. In your armor you seem like a god.
> Cortés (flattered): Give me a mirror. (He looks at himself and agrees.) True. And this role of a god fits me to a T.[16]

This Cortés who looks at himself adoringly in the mirror and is easily taken in by a little flattery resembles the stereotype of feminine behavior more than that of the astute conquistador depicted by López de Gómara, among others. Even the Mexican historian Justo Sierra, in his well-known essay *The Political Evolution of the Mexican People,* compares Cortés with Caesar.[17]

The irony and parody involved in Castellanos's treatment of Cortés and La Malinche can be further appreciated by comparing the comment of the North American translator of Gómara's work, Lesley Byrd Simpson, who says in the prologue: "Cortés' policy toward the Indians is an astonishing blend of ferocity, flattery, double-dealing and magnanimity, and is, moreover, immensely successful."[18] Castellanos has kept the signifieds, or meanings, but attributes them to the female signifier, or visual image on stage. By inverting the roles and the signifieds associated with the signifiers, she adopts a more revolutionary stance than that of Fuentes. She attacks the tradition and the system that maintains it.

Castellanos places herself within the revisionist mode of Mexican history that questions the sacred myths. Her ironic treatment of the figures of the patriarchy shows that they are not sacred and immutable figures but are vulnerable to change. It is Sor Juana who interprets the meaning of the presentations that differ from the history books: "What you have seen is only an entertainment. It's, perhaps, just one version."[19] Sor Juana acknowledges that the history books are the creations of instituted authority, which has had the power to insert into discourse the images of patriarchal ideology. The theoretical base of Sor Juana's comment and, by extension, of the play itself can be found most clearly in Michel Foucault's succinct explanation that power and discourse serve each other: "It is in discourse that power and knowledge are joined together."[20] Each scene shows that the coercive power of patriarchal ideology has not changed through the years, though the signifiers used to present the signified may differ depending on the century. Thus when Carlota explains that she and Maximilian went to Mexico with a mission in order to "redeem, reconcile, unite and civilize the Mexican people," La Malinche's retort reminds us how the oppressors keep repeating an unchanging, constant script: "Exactly the same thing that Hernán Cortés's propagandizers said."[21] When Adelita proves that the generals from opposing sides in the Mexican Revolution were equally corrupt and self-interested, Sor Juana, ever the voice of irony, concludes: "But the history books say that the Revolution was a success."[22] Adelita's response shows that the temporal changes have not brought progress: "If it had triumphed, would this girl be here? Would there still be girls like her, with parents like hers, with sweethearts like hers, with a life like hers?"[23] Adelita expresses the theme that the status of women has not been altered through the years, neither by the revolution nor by social change.

The dream sequence functions thematically by bringing together women from all the periods of Mexico's national history. Their accounts confirm on the one hand that the paradigms that have conditioned women have not changed through the centuries despite the progress of science and technology. On the other hand, the disparity between the women's versions and the official story also confirms that the established myths are mere "versions" and can be and should be subject to change.

Like the Castellanos play, Willebaldo López's *Malinche Show* highlights the coercive power of both technology and recurring cultural paradigms. López uses another innovation within the fantasy genre to bring out the historical situations that set the paradigms for behavior. Unlike Castellanos's small, flealike device, his technological tool fills the stage as a huge, monsterlike machine with many parts. Two armlike protuberances hold up the figure of La Malinche, not a puppet or an avatar but the original woman from the sixteenth century, who has been brought to life, along with Cortés, because of her importance to the economic plans of the country. She has been made the star of a TV show designed to convince the Mexican masses to participate in modern consumer society and forget the troubles of their reality. Reality is equated with economic misery and is juxtaposed to fantasy, defined as "another world foreign to one's own" where one is distracted by the pleasing images offered by mass communication media.[24] Since La Malinche has been defined in Mexican mythology as the woman who allowed the other world to enter Mexico, she is the spokesperson or tool of the exploitative forces encouraging Mexicans to enter into the "other world" of foreign fantasy.

The three people who work the machines and attempt to control La Malinche's activities are called *Prestanombres*, "Name-lenders," a neologism defined in the text by La Malinche as the people who "lend their name and in that underhanded way cause clandestine stockholders to buy shares in our country."[25] It is ironic that these shills are defined by La Malinche in a way that recalls the meaning of *malinchismo* given by Paz in *El laberinto* and analyzed in chapter 5. The modern-day *malinchistas*, or "name-lenders," are shown to be just as much governed by others in their actions as they wish to control La Malinche; they are stand-ins for the Triumvirate, who are the virtual masters. The power of the real rulers is shown semiotically when they are positioned above the stage on the upper part of the machine. A parody of the Trinity, the unholy threesome is composed of a gringo, a nun, and a European who varies the language he speaks (German, Italian, French, etc.), thereby symbolizing the major European forces that influence the culture and economy of Mexico.

The question that comes to the spectator's mind is, Why keep La Malinche and Cortés alive? Why not use metaphors or avatars as other writers have done? As will be discussed in chapter 9, Emilio Carballido in *Ceremonia en el templo del tigre* ("Ceremony in the temple of the tiger") names the Indian servant Marina to indicate her status as sexual object and to recall the conquest as a subtext for the contemporary interactions. And Elena Garro's *Los recuerdos del porvenir* (*Recollections of Things to Come*) and "La culpa es de los tlaxcaltecas" (The Tlaxcalans are to blame) use the characteristics associated with La Malinche as a subtext to comment on male-female relations in Mexico. Similarly, the texts of Carlos Fuentes have been analyzed in detail for the many avatars he includes that show how the historical past remains a vital part of the Mexican present. For López, however, as for Castellanos, the deliberate rupture of the conventions of reality is purposeful and thematically meaningful.

By having the historical figures on stage represent themselves in their symbolic roles, López reverses the stylistic process of tropism, and in that way he shows the metaphor made literal. Their iconic presence on stage indicates that their patterns of action continue to exist in Mexico today; La Malinche, who functioned in the sixteenth century as "the country's open door to the worst intentions that come from abroad," continues to act in her TV show as "the mother of the investing invaders of the country."[26] Similarly, Cortés was the foreign invader in the sixteenth century who raped the country with no regard for its well-being, a pattern of action he continues to approve of for the contemporary Spaniards in Mexico.

In the same way that López reverses a traditional stylistic process by making a metaphor literal, he applies the pattern of reversal to character development, theme, chronology, and structure in order to upset and invert the established paradigms. It is interesting to relate López's evaluation of the paradigm to the 1975 song by Gabino Palomares, "La maldición de Malinche" (The curse of La Malinche). According to Mirandé and Enríquez, "three stanzas from the song illustrate a self-indictment by Mexicans in this century for opening their doors to foreigners, yet the curse that originates in Malinche is ultimately seen as infecting the culture, so that she is once again held accountable for the chains Mexico has assumed in inviting foreigners into its land."[27] The words of the song offer insights into the popular version of the Malinche paradigm: "We remain with the evil curse / to offer to the foreigner / our faith, our culture, / our bread, our money . . . / Today in the twentieth century! / Blondies continue to arrive, / and we open our houses to them / and we call them friends. / O curse, from La Malinche! / sickness of the present / when will you leave my land? / when will you free my people!"[28] The message of popular culture is clear and time-worn, as the frequent use of the word *malinchista* proves,[29] yet López transforms it in his play. He begins with the popular images of La Malinche and Cortés in their roles as oppressors in collusion only to deconstruct the system of conventions upon which the stereotypes are built. His treatment is original in the way he uses reversals to accomplish his positive agenda of deconstructing the tightly controlled images of the patriarchal paradigms.

Thematic and character reversals are seen when La Malinche rebels against her use as a *malinchista* and becomes instead the conscience of and spokesperson for nationalist Mexico. She explains to Cortés the current situation: that a multitude of strangers are taking everything out of the country and leaving the natives with nothing; ironically, he is disturbed to find out that groups other than the Spaniards are being allowed to conquer the country. Although La Malinche is still the interpreter for Cortés, thematically she represents not the interests of Cortés and the foreigners but the nationalist perspective. The signifier "La Malinche" breaks away from the fixed signified that the patriarchal triumvirate has worked hard to maintain. Other examples in the text reinforce the distance between signifier and signified that is necessary to contravene the fixed paradigms of behavior.

As proof of the multiplicity of perspectives, one action is shown to have different interpretations. In a poignant scene La Malinche asks Cortés to kill her because she no longer wishes to go on serving as a symbol of exploitation. Yet the Female Name-lender interprets the exchange as a case of attempted suicide for love, transforming the signs into a repetition of the foreign Romeo-and-Juliet paradigm that distorts the action; these comments make the audience aware of the faulty process of image-making.

The configuration of spatial relations, the proxemic code, also serves to destroy ready acceptance of the patriarchal paradigms. During the interchange in which La Malinche introduces the topic of exploitation, both she and Cortés address the audience constantly while they talk. The direct address to the public involves the spectator as a judge in the action and as an accomplice in the rejection of the pattern under scrutiny. For example, La Malinche tells Cortés that the Name-lenders allow the foreigners to "carry away our treasures, leaving the majority of Mexicans in misery. (Facing the Public.) Right?"[30] By prodding the audience to acknowledge the adverse effects of the activities of the Name-lenders, La Malinche tries to distance them from the Name-lenders and what they represent. At the same time, López also encourages the audience to recognize the change in La Malinche's perspective—her distance from a so-called *malinchista* outlook. Thematically López's Malinche echoes an attitude expressed by Novo's Malinche in the dialog "Malinche and Carlota," since she disdains the North Americans and other new-breed materialist conquerors in comparison with the Spaniards. López, however, takes advantage of dramatic techniques in order to manipulate his audience to imitate the behavior of the new Malinche.[31]

In addition to thematic reversals, temporal inversions occur when the movement of the first act leads to the resurrection of Cuauhtemoc, the Indian leader whom Cortés defeated. In contrast to the historical events, which dictate that the Indian disappear after the conquest, he reappears from the depths of the underground at the end of act 1 and continues to interact with his conquerors in act 2. Cuauhtemoc wants to take advantage of his presence as a revenant to mistreat Cortés in the same way as the Spaniard had handled him. Though their interchange is humorous, the comical effects do not hide the thematic intention of his appearance, which is to contradict the fixed paradigms of behavior established in the world of verifiable reality. The fixed, authoritarian world as a system of representations is made suspect, its artificiality is emphasized, and its necessary predictability is made questionable.

In the final scene of *Malinche Show* the rebellion of La Malinche against the advances of science and technology seems to have been accomplished when she finally succeeds in dying. Yet it is not the end of the play, for López takes the opportunity to warn his audience that the "sons of La Malinche" made famous by the essay of Octavio Paz have been programmed to continue her role. A Martín Cortés is brought on stage, said to be just one of the many Mexicans found outside the studio, the synecdoche for all the mestizos born after the union of La Malinche and Cortés. He takes the dead Malinche and dresses her up so that he can continue using her as a way to promote *malinchismo* for his own benefit. The utter cynicism of Martín's exploitation of his own mother is another warning against the coercive nature of the cultural paradigm.

López, like Castellanos, shows that temporal change has not brought cultural change. They both use historical figures in a contemporary context to illustrate that the paradigms that have conditioned Mexican culture have not changed through the centuries despite the progress of science and technology.

While Castellanos and López deconstruct the old role models and critique patriarchal ideology, Sabina Berman carries invention even further in her parodic text *Aguila o sol*. In the prologue of the published version she mentions her intention to digress from the official history presented by the discourse of power by basing her play on documents generated by those who are generally excluded from the discursive enterprise: "The play is based on the indigenous chronicles of events as anthologized by Master León Portilla in *La visión de los vencidos* [*Broken Spears*]. Thus, it is the point of view of the conquered peoples that is expressed."[32] In accordance with her aim to demythify the official version of the conquest, established cultural roles and structures of belief are challenged; nothing is sacred, and the dramatic discourse mocks all those who exercise power— the conquistador, of course, but Moctezuma and his entourage as well. Through her inversion of the relationships between characters, Berman suggests the inversion of the cultural equation that valorizes the European and denigrates the indigenous role.

Like Castellanos, Berman chooses for her subject matter well-known and familiar texts that she transforms through parody and satire. The playscript states that the history to be presented focuses on the crucial events from the time the Spaniards are first sighted by the Aztecs until the death of Moctezuma, events described in chronicles and history books as well as numerous literary texts. Berman creates a "mestizo" or heterogeneous style by mixing together on stage social realism, surreal dreams, and street theater, together with techniques of satire and farce. The lack of a totalizing unity is not a flaw but one of the drama's important traits, revealing the conflicts at the heart of the enterprise of the conquest itself as well as the subsequent national identity forged by the colonial power.

In one of the scenes called *teatro callejero* (street theater), two comics discuss the support given by the Tlaxcalans to the Spaniards, an important alliance that historians have considered crucial to the victory of the Spaniards.[33] While the content of the scene reflects the documentary material, the presentation is humorous and offers a good example of Berman's use of mestizo elements. The dialog is a mix of contemporary slang and sexual innuendo, an anachronistic linguistic pastiche that breaks with temporality and the accepted cultural paradigms considered "eternally" valid for Mexico:

> Comic 2: Keep going. What did the Tlaxcalans do?
> Comic 1: Well, they all had to crouch down before the white men. It was, like, say, a meeting of "an egg" (force) and a "support" (chicken).
> Comic 2: Wow! A meeting of force (egg) and support (chicken)?
> Comic 1: Sure, each Tlaxcalan had to bring to the "blondies" (foreigners) an egg and a chicken; tortillas, some nice eggs, some chickens, some hens; they gathered up a huge pile of provisions.
> Comic 2: Eggs/Balls! That's what's missing from those S.O.B.s[34]

The humor of the dialog is based on a play on words that sound similar in Spanish and have sexual connotations. In the Spanish text, *huevo* (egg or force) and *apoyo* (support) appear, serving on one level as references to military strength and force, since *huevos* colloquially refers to male sexual parts (testicles, or balls) and virility. In Mexican Spanish, *apoyo* and *a pollo* (help and chicken) sound alike, so the homonym for *apoyo*, *a pollo* (chicken), is also heard at the same time, supporting the simple meaning of *huevos* as food. Thus Comic 1 says that the Tlaxcalans met with the Spaniards in a gathering of *huevos y apoyo* (either eggs or force, and support or chicken). When he repeats the information a second time, he changes the signified but not the oral signifiers, giving the audience a chance to understand both sets of signifieds. By using humor and sexual innuendo to refer to the help the Tlaxcalans gave to the Spaniards, the comics censure their actions in providing food and comfort to the conquistadors.

If we examine Berman's stylistic technique in the light of Mikhail Bakhtin's discussion of comic representation, we can explain the processes of her humor: "Laughter has the remarkable power of making an object come up close, of drawing it into a zone of crude contact where one can finger it familiarly on all sides. . . . Laughter demolishes fear and piety before an object, before a world, making of it an object of familiar contact and thus clearing the ground for an absolutely free investigation of it."[35] Bakhtin emphasizes that laughter removes the object—here the alliance between the Tlaxcalans and the Spaniards—from its traditional context and places it on the comic plane, where it is broken apart. What takes place is "a comic operation of dismemberment."[36] The comic operation of dismemberment is also accomplished in the dialog by the reference to "huevos," in which the Spaniards and their allies are emasculated to expose their true nature, the falseness of their patriarchal power. The use of popular speech (the diminutive -*ito* applied to all the food items, *montonsote,* and so on) also contributes to the humor because of the incongruity between this popular version and the established tradition of historical narratives.

As the pun on *apoyo* illustrates, Berman focuses directly on the instability of linguistic signs as a way of demonstrating a lack of reliance on and mistrust of all verbal constructs, historical documents and the patriarchal tradition included. Like Castellanos and López, Berman attacks the tightly bound paradigms of traditional discourse in the way she presents the principal players of the encounter.

For example, when Cortés first appears, his initial comment offers a provocative revision of his historical role as the first speaker of Spanish in Mexico, if not literally then in synecdochic terms: "Cat for a hare, you dirty black traffickers? Me pee in pants? Maybe give out licorice ice."[37] The audience/reader's expectation is for Cortés to speak in a language understandable by the audience, since a concomitant feature of colonialism, as Frantz Fanon reminds us, is the imposition of the language of the dominant culture on the colonized peoples.[38] It is not Cortés, however, who is intelligible to the audience, but the Indians. Cortés is presented as speaking a form of pidgin Spanish, a bastardized version of *castellano* that includes foreign words and even words that originated later than the conquest. The inclusion of signifiers from many time periods and from countries whose imperialist policies affected Mexico—France, Italy, Germany, and the United States—reflects the realities of foreign political, economic, and cultural influences that still operate. As further

examples of his speech will show, Berman's presentation of the conquistador functions in total disagreement with the historical version
of his behavior.

Because Cortés never utters a complete and logical sentence, the
only way his ideas are made known is through the interpretive skills
and imagination of La Malinche. For example, when Cortés says,
"Morgn morgn cascarita: hispanuss versus mexicanus," La Malinche is needed to tell the Indians—and the audience—the meaning
of his words: "He wants to compare you. Tomorrow there will be a
tournament on the beach. You will fight in pairs: white man against
Indian."[39] It is ironic that La Malinche as translator is also required
by the Spanish-speaking audience, whose mastery of Spanish in
Mexico is the legacy of the colonial heritage. Nevertheless, Berman
re-creates the real problems of communication brought by the encounter of two different civilizations. By means of this linguistic
game, moreover, she encourages our identification with the conquered Indians and not with the conquerors.

Berman's parodic approach with regard to the patriarchy is also
evident in the presentation of the first encounter between Moctezuma and Cortés. Moctezuma has already been presented on stage
as the monarch whose fear of omens and belief in prophesy led him
to misread the signs and assume that Cortés was the returning god
Quetzalcoatl. The error of his belief is immediately shown when
Cortés acts like a babbling fool:

> Moctezuma: Come and rest; take possession of your royal es-
> tate: give repose to your body. Please enter your home, our dear
> Lords!
> Cortés: Soothing, writhing snakes, flying feathered friends.
> Malinche: He says, "Have confidence, Lord Moctezuma. Fear
> nothing."
> Cortés: Cuore mío! Oh, cuore mío!
> Malinche: "In truth we love you; we love you deeply."
> Cortés: A little poker? I pass. Me bluff? See, five aces, I mean
> four: check my sleeves.
> Malinche: He says, "Now that he is in your home, you both
> may speak freely. Have faith."[40]

The contrast between Moctezuma's warm, welcoming speech and
Cortés's reaction is as incongruous as it is indicative of the conquistador's identity as the false prophet of love and brotherhood.
Cortés's incoherence on the one hand and Moctezuma's incompre-
hension of the political reality on the other show that both patriar-

chal leaders are empty signs: they do not signify the authority and command with which history has invested them. It is the "borracho," the drunkard, who states the political reality of Moctezuma's empire: "The Aztecs have sucked the blood of the other peoples, they have grown in size in order to crush others."[41] Moctezuma is shown to be as imperialist as Cortés in his treatment of the people of Mexico.

While Moctezuma and Cortés are divested of their authoritative roles, Berman also treats La Malinche in a nontraditional way. For her as for Castellanos, La Malinche does not appear in her traditional role as the submissive woman in love with Cortés. Although she acts as translator for Cortés, she does not appear to be a traitor to her people, since, as we have seen, the Indian chiefs are not worthy of loyalty or respect. In *Aguila o sol*, it is Moctezuma who exhibits the behavior traditionally associated with La Malinche: *malinchismo*, deference to the foreign and rejection of anything native.[42] In his subservience to the Spaniard, he is the true colonial: "Moctezuma: Mexicans, Tenochcans, Tlatelolcans, we are not as competent as the strangers, don't fight, Mexicans."[43] Moctezuma's judgment regarding the "competence" of the Spaniards offers a good example of dramatic irony, for it has just been negated in the previous scene. His submission to the Spaniards occurs after the scene entitled "El tesoro" (The treasure), in which the Indians describe the Spaniards as being excited as monkeys when they see gold. The Indians consider the worst part of the crazed behavior of the invaders to be their rejection of the esthetic beauty of feathered objects; instead, the Spaniards take the golden jewelry and works of art and melt them down to make bars. They are clearly shown to be uncultured philistines and barbarians, in contrast with the conquered Indians. By inverting the roles and signs associated by tradition with the behavior of the Indians, La Malinche, and the Spaniards, Berman suggests that the imperialist patriarchal system that maintains those codes can also be subverted. Thus Berman, like Castellanos, situates her text in the revisionist mode that questions the myths and motifs of the patriarchal images. Both dramatists show that the people associated with power are transformable and assailable, that their form of discourse is not a given truth but only an interpretation open to alteration and modification. The disparity between their parodic versions and the official story also confirms that the established myths are mere "diversion," in Sor Juana's terms, and can be and should be subject to change. The purpose of this return to the past is to come back to the present with the clarity and strength needed to demystify the myths that have locked in stone any real change for Mexican society.

In his text on colonialism, Frantz Fanon asserts that the native has to affirm his/her own culture and recover a usable past,[44] precisely the enterprise of Rosario Castellanos in *El eterno femenino* and Sabina Berman in *Aguila o sol.* They wrest the past from the discourse established by the patriarchy as it was constructed by the forces of colonialism in order to use their reconstruction "with the intention of opening the future, as an invitation to action and a basis for hope."[45]

CHAPTER EIGHT

Re/formation of the Tradition by Chicana Writers

THE MEXICAN WRITERS discussed in chapter 7, who have contributed to the contemporary re/vision of the Malinche paradigm, were cognizant that the transformations that occurred in the image of the historical figure were due to the influence of a patriarchal society's image of women. Their focus was not so much on the betrayal by La Malinche of the Aztec *patria* but on her role as a victim in an uncomprehending patriarchal system. Castellanos, López, and Berman reveal that the historical experience of oppression related to discourse is rooted in the polemical role of La Malinche, which has continued to influence contemporary behavior patterns. It is not unexpected, then, that the descendants of the historical Malinche, who are found both in Mexico and in the United States, as Chicanas, today identify with La Malinche's role or are *made* to identify with her. Chicanas in particular are likened to her by males who see them consorting with Anglos or accepting Anglo cultural patterns. Instead of responding passively to this potentially detrimental identification, Chicana writers have been invigorated and often transformed by the encounter with the Malinche paradigm, from both theoretical and thematic perspectives. Since these writers connected to Mexican culture share with my study a common goal—to analyze the contributions of a historical woman and to evaluate her literary image—their work can be considered as part of the ongoing reevaluation of Mexican official discourse in its broadest sense.

That the response of Chicana writers to the sign of La Malinche is rooted in a broad Mexican cultural heritage can be seen when their work is compared with that of Mexican writers. Because the themes and forms introduced by Rosario Castellanos provide both a context and a conceptual springboard from which to study the Chicanas' re/formation of the Malinche paradigm, I shall first explore Castellanos's poem "Malinche" as it gives voice to a silent woman:

Malinche

From the throne of command my mother declared: "He is dead."
And threw herself
into another's arms: the usurper and the stepfather
who did not sustain her with the respect
a servant renders to the majesty of a queen
but groveled in their mutual shame of lovers and accomplices.

From the Plaza of Exchange
my mother announced: "She is dead."

The scale balanced for an instant,
the chocolate bean lay motionless in the bin,
the sun remained at midpoint in the sky
awaiting the sign
which shot like an arrow,
became the sharp wail of the mourners.

"The bloom of many petals was deflowered,
perfume evaporated,
torch flame burned out.

A girl returns to scratch up the earth
in the place
where the midwife buried her umbilicus.

She returns to the Place of Those Who Once Lived.

She recognizes her father, assassinated,
ah, by poison, a dagger,
a snare before his feet, a noose.

They take each other by the hand and walk,
disappearing into the fog."

Thus the wailing and lamentation
over an anonymous body: a corpse
that was not mine because I was sold
to the merchants, on my way as a slave,
a nobody, into exile.

Cast out, expelled
from the kingdom, the palace, and the warm belly
of the woman who bore me in legitimate marriage bed
who hated me because I was her equal
in stature and rank,
who saw herself in me and hating her image
dashed the mirror against the ground.

I advance toward destiny in chains
leaving behind all that I can still hear,
the funereal murmurs with which I am buried.

And the voice of my mother in tears—in tears!
She who decrees my death![1]

While Castellanos in *El eterno femenino* added other Mexican women to her critique of the patriarchal tradition that has been perpetrated upon its people, in "Malinche" she focuses on the paradigmatic characteristics of betrayal and victimization associated with La Malinche. She deconstructs the paradigm, however, so that La Malinche is shown to be the one who is betrayed and victimized instead of the perpetrator. The form of the poem, a first-person monolog, suggests that by telling her story herself, the woman not only initiates discourse but also initiates the process of self-definition that leads to a challenge of the dominant patriarchal system. As Yvonne Yarbro-Bejarano has pointed out, the process of self-definition involves moving from the margin to the center, an assumption not readily belonging to the Mexican woman or the Chicana who is her descendent. The Chicana writer, says Yarbro-Bejarano, "finds that the self she seeks to define and love is not merely an individual self, but a collective one. In other words, the power, the permission, the authority to tell stories about herself and other Chicanas comes from her cultural, racial/ethnic and linguistic community. The community includes the historical experience of oppression as well as literary tradition."[2] Although Yarbro-Bejarano is primarily concerned with the role of Chicanas as subjects of their own stories as a way of challenging the dominant culture's definition of women, her comments are also germane to the problem of the Mexican woman's role in the literary world. The "urgent need to dominate the written word in order to smash stereotypes and rewrite history from the perspective of the oppressed"[3] that Yarbro-Bejarano finds in the poetry of Chicana writers begins in the history of La Malinche, the Tongue, who experienced one of the greatest forms of betrayal and victimization when her own words were used against her.

A re/vision of La Malinche is generated in "Malinche" by having her initiate discourse about the first crucial event of her life, the circumstances leading to her exile. Castellanos gives voice to La Malinche in the guise of a young child who has suffered the deepest deception of all when her own mother abandoned her by sending her away from home to become a slave in a strange land. La Malinche expresses a double deception, for the body of another—"an anonymous body"—was substituted for her own at the same time that she was deprived of her identity: "I was . . . on my way as a slave, a nobody." She lost both her father, through his assassination, and her mother, through the subterfuge involved in her feigned death. Her mother not only replaced the father figure with another (the usurper and stepfather) but substituted another child's body for her own, over which tears were shed and lamentations wailed. It should be noted that one of the subtexts recalled is the motif of the crying mother—La Llorona—a well-known figure in Mexican folklore who is associated with the Malinche paradigm; La Malinche is said to be crying for her children subjugated by the Spaniards.[4] Castellanos's text ironizes the figure of the crying mother, for La Malinche's mother acts falsely in her lament for the death of her child, while La Malinche cries here for the lost child that is herself. Castellanos indicates to the reader that La Malinche herself begins her trek on the path of history as a victim of persecution.

Despite the poem's narow angle of vision—one scene in the early life of young Malinche—inherent in this initial scene are the essential elements of her life story of continual cultural replacements and substitutions, of perfidy and hatred, of loves lost and gained and lost again. Her solitary state as a slave unwillingly cut off from her people is captured in the line "I advance toward destiny in chains"; it is a line that also encapsulates the destiny of La Malinche in Mexican history as the woman captive to a foreign, estranged vision, be it European or patriarchal. The fact that her mother, a member of her own gender, initiated the betrayal proves that neither superficial gender nor class associations are as important as shared ideology, a theme in Garro's "La culpa es de los tlaxcaltecas," which will be treated in chapter 9. Castellanos's Malinche attributes to her mother a hatred of her because of their equal status:

> [she] who hated me because I was her equal
> in stature and rank,
> who saw herself in me and hating her image
> dashed the mirror against the ground.

Castellanos offers a perceptive observation concerning self-hatred among women and the results of that hatred; she identifies two detrimental behavior patterns—they may either eliminate other women or encourage their sisters to follow the same debilitating pattern of behavior.[5]

Those who accept this hatred of La Malinche repeat the pattern of her mother. In contrast to the established pattern, Chicana writers have shown that they resist this negative tradition. They do not hate her image but attempt to give voice to the maligned daughter as she faces the other cultures into which she was thrust.

Just as Mexican women must deal with the presence of the Malinche paradigm, Chicanas view themselves as symbolic daughters of La Malinche. In the words of Cherríe Moraga, "As a Chicana and a feminist, I must, like other Chicanas before me, examine the effects this myth has on my/our racial/sexual identity and my relationship with other Chicanas. There is hardly a Chicana growing up today who does not suffer under her name even if she never hears directly of the one-time Aztec princess."[6] The revisionist works of Chicana writers are significant on two counts. They began to react to the negative presentations of La Malinche as a direct defamation of themselves as women who bridge two cultures in their role as a hyphenated peoples—Mexican and American. La Raza and the gringo culture of North America are the two opposing forces that influence the Chicanas' perspective. Their approach to the sign of La Malinche as part of their cultural heritage has been multifaceted. They have analyzed and evaluated the contributions of the historical Malinche in essays, and they have incorporated the figure into their creative works as another way to make her their own, to transform her into their own image instead of accepting the image of La Malinche constructed by patriarchal cultural forces. Culture and gender shape experience, these Chicana writers remind us; the actions of La Malinche were influenced by those two key factors, just as our readings of her actions are affected by our own culture and gender.

For many of the Chicana writers, their own political and social concerns and their questions regarding ethnicity are derived from La Malinche's experiences. Her body becomes the locus of origin of the contemporary Chicana. Her participation in the deeds of the conquest as an active and vital figure needs to be understood as a way of rejecting the destructive implications of previous interpretations and recovering the ambiguities and possibilities inherent in the figure that a changing feminist perspective brings forth. Her contribution to history within a sociopolitical context corrected for distortions is the goal of many feminist writers, whose representations of La Malinche have radically altered the configuration of the image.

Representative of the revisionist attitude is Adelaida Del Castillo's essay "Malintzín Tenépal: A Preliminary Look into a New Perspective."[7] Her position is one that most Chicana writers would support: that any attack on La Malinche also defames the character of Mexican and Chicana women. Although Del Castillo follows the data concerning La Malinche's life story as related by Bernal Díaz, she continues the perspective offered in Castellanos's poem in the way she conveys a personal reaction to the human aspect of Doña Marina's life story. She refers to the fact that the young girl called Malinal went from being a princess to a slave among merchants: "It is now that we can begin to understand that La Malinche, the young Aztec princess, was, in fact, betrayed, dethroned, and sold into slavery by her own mother—it all had the simplicity of an evil fairy tale. . . . To be sure, it must have been a very painful, traumatic and confusing experience to have [undergone] the drastic transition of Aztec princess to Mayan slave." In contrast to Bernal Díaz's tone, she adds that in all La Malinche's endeavors, she acted as a real woman, "not as a goddess in some mythology, but as an actual force in the making of history."

Del Castillo also attempts to temper the negative attitude toward La Malinche by noting that she was in a position to help the Indians through her direct influence on Cortés: "She resourcefully mitigated possible violence between indio and Spaniard through her own persuasion—effective use of her precocious intelligence and role as a bridge figure. She alone . . . could determine and give validity to the negotiations and treaties which went on between the Spanish aggressors and her indio world." Del Castillo also counters the accusation that Doña Marina was a traitor to the nation: "One wrongly assumes that there was a 'patria' similar to the patrias of today. The fact is, there were many Indian nations within the Aztec Empire and these nations were always attempting, through one rebellion or another, to regain their former independence." The major contribution of her perspective, however, is her portrayal of Doña Marina as a religious activist. She quotes both Fray Cristóbal de Alameda, who writes of Marina's easy grasp of the Christian faith, and Bernal Díaz, whose description of Marina's reunion with her family stressed the importance to her of her new religious faith and the rejection of the bloody Aztec rites. While I have considered the possibility that the citation attributed to Doña Marina may be more the Spanish interpretation of her beliefs than those of the woman herself, Del Castillo accepts her expression of feelings as valid and elaborates on this point to the extent of considering La Malinche a religious martyr who has been either ignored or defamed. Del Castillo says that it was religious faith that motivated the actions of Doña Marina: "A careful look at what is known about her and her times seems to indicate the immense probability that Doña Marina's participation in the conquest of Mexico was a manifestation of her faith in a godly force—the prophecies of Quetzalcóatl. It is because of this faith that she sees the destruction of the Aztec empire, the conquest of Mexico, and as such, the termination of her indigenous world as inevitable." Del Castillo rejects the romantic's idea of love for Cortés as the motivation for Marina's actions and stresses belief in a godly force, which gave her the physical and spiritual stamina to withstand the hardships and atrocities of the conquest. Just as the Spaniards were motivated by a divine imperative, so, too, was Doña Marina according to Del Castillo's version. Del Castillo attributes her death to that other scourge of the Indians at the time, smallpox, and places her age at twenty-two, which is a supposition, since we have no conclusive documents.[8]

Del Castillo also explores the reasons for the misinterpretation of La Malinche's role in the conquest and her transformation into the embodiment of female negativity for Mexican culture. She suggests that it is related to "an unconscious, if not intentional misogynistic attitude toward women in general, especially toward self-assertive women, on the part of western society as a whole." This Chicana writer brings out the interesting point that popular Mexican heroines—the revolutionary war's Adelita, Juana Gallo, and La Valentina—are admired not as feminine activists "but because their behavior is interpreted as being imitative of masculine behavior . . . [they] became 'machas' which Doña Marina never did." According to Bernal Díaz, however, Doña Marina did possess so-called masculine attributes when it came to her ability to participate in the rigors of battle, a characteristic, I have suggested, that anticipates the *soldaderas* (see chapter 2). Del Castillo's point, nevertheless, is well taken—that women who are viewed both as feminine and as activists are not acceptable; she quotes Carlos Fuentes in *Tiempo mexicano*, who helps condemn La Malinche by stating that she "generates betrayal and corruption in Woman."[9] Del Castillo castigates the assumptions of Fuentes: "Fuentes implies that if women are rotten creatures, it's not their fault; we're not even acknowledged as creatures responsible for our own actions. Blame Malinche. She generates the evil! In the end, only a woman could be responsible for others' faults. Carlos Fuentes' rationale is not atypical of the kind of misogynistic reasoning which portrays women as being 'innately' evil and, thereby, justifiably in need of male domination." She also takes to task the American novelist Margaret Shedd for depicting the woman in her novel *Malinche and Cortés* as a "rampant nymphomaniac" and referring to her frequently as a whore.

Del Castillo's contribution to the paradigm is her portrayal of the actions of La Malinche within a religious context, picking up on the aspect of Bernal Díaz's presentation that stressed the importance of

Christianity. More important, she reminds her contemporary readers that the woman underwent many traumatic experiences in her own life before being transferred as a slave to the new group, but that her intelligence and beauty made her a valuable asset to the Spaniards.

In "The Concept of Cultural Identity in Chicana Poetry," Elizabeth Ordóñez highlights the importance of the Malinche figure for Chicana poets: "As the symbolic progenitor of the mestizo people, La Malinche has either been officially reviled or compassionately respected; but always as object, as receptacle of the seeds of La Raza. It was left to the Chicana writer to assume the function of historian and myth-maker; to wrest the figure of La Malinche from her captivity within the confines of patriachy's historical and mythical discourse; and to restore to La Malinche her integrity and her voice."[10] Ordóñez illustrates her comments with references to specific works by Chicana poets who began to publish in the early seventies. Some of the writers who make use of the Malinche figure include Lorna Dee Cervantes, Lorenza Calvillo Schmidt, Inés Hernandez, and Adaljiza Sosa Riddell, who succinctly summarizes the burden in her phrase "Damn! How it hurts to be Malinche!"[11] Like Berman's Malinche in the play *Aguila o sol*, both poets move freely between the world of La Raza and the other world, although for the Chicanas it is a decidedly gringo world. They face their personal problem of acculturation or divided loyalties by making La Malinche a symbol for the problem.

Despite having borne the brunt of negativity for so long, La Malinche is now being considered as a remarkable woman with strong personal character and positive attributes. The move to resurrect her as a model of inspiration rather than condemnation continues. The new readings have modified the preexisting works, allowing us to view them anew, readjust the givens of the old interpretations, and create a new cultural inheritance.

Among the poets who feel compelled to reassess the Malinche figure, Lucha Corpi has written a series of poems entitled *Marina*. Born in the state of Veracruz, she writes in Spanish although she now lives in the United States; thus she reverses in a way the situation of La Malinche, who used the language of the invader in her own country. Corpi comments that her discovery of Marina came as she learned to explore the uses of poetry, so that her "image, both tragic and glorious, has walked ever since through the corridors of my life."[12] It is noteworthy that Corpi refers to the figure as Marina, using the Hispanic form of the name; perhaps she avoids the sign Malinche because of its obvious association with *malinchismo*.[13]

The first poem of the series is entitled "Marina Madre" (Marina Mother) and in some ways offers a gloss on the portrait offered in Castellanos's poem in its references to the early scenes in the life of the Amerindian woman. In addition, it contradicts the entire negative tradition that equates her birth with evil omens and anticipations of betrayal. Corpi writes, "With the blood of a tender lamb / her name was written by the elders / on the bark of that tree / as old as they."[14] The poet substitutes for the image of scapegoat that of the sacrificial lamb that La Malinche becomes, replacing the negative signs with more culturally positive associations. To replace the motif of *vendepatrias*, "traitor," Corpi shows that La Malinche was acted upon first when she was sold: ". . . she was sold . . . from hand to hand, night to night, / denied and desecrated, waiting for the dawn."[15] The passive form and the series of suspension points that continue the verbal idea, as well as the metaphoric phrases that follow, succinctly capitulate the history of La Malinche from the time of her first betrayal until now, in which she is still awaiting the dawn of deliverance from her negative reputation. Corpi's Marina, however, does not address the reader directly in the first person, in the manner of Castellanos, but is described by a narrator, which lends an air of objectivity to the presentation. Nevertheless, like Castellanos, Corpi shows that the subsequent events in which Marina was enmeshed had their origin in the initial act. In addition, Corpi goes beyond the chronology of the conquest and the limits of the single character in the way she forms allegorical phrases referring to the lives of Mexican women in general. "Her womb sacked of its fruit" ("Su vientre robado de su fruto") stands as a solitary line in the poem and recalls Usigli's synecdochic presentation of her as a reproductive unit, yet suggests the tragedy of her condition by the way the words "vientre" and "robado" are juxtaposed without the conjugated verb—without action on her part. In this one line Corpi verbalizes another of the tragedies inherent in the Malinche paradigm, the way she represents the Indian women whose reproductive labor was appropriated by the patriarchy with no regard for their own benefit or consent.

The last stanza is another fine example of Corpi's synthesis of the paradigm. She manipulates the deixis of the poem—especially its subject pronouns—to convey the allegorical nature of the relationships involved in the paradigm: "You no longer loved her and he denied her, / and that one who as a child cried out to her 'mama!' / grew up and called her 'chingada.'"[16] Although "that one" (the demonstrative pronoun "aquél" in the Spanish is a clear reference to the "child" of La Malinche, the subject pronouns "you" and "he" are more open to interpretation. "You" would be the addressee of the poem, the one who rejects La Malinche. Is the person addressed who no longer loved or wanted her a sign for her mother and the Indian culture from whose context she was wrested? Or could it be Cortés, who stands for Hispanic culture and who also rejected her when her help was no longer necessary? It is also possible that if "you" is her mother, "he" refers to Cortés, for he negated the importance of her presence in his letters just as he denied her emotional significance when he married her off to Juan Jaramillo. Historically "he" as the Mexican nation also negated her contributions. Rodríguez-Nieto translates "he" as "the elders," a phrase that recalls the Indian hierarchy. The interchangeability of the identity of "you" and "he" points out that each group acted in a similar way. Both the Indians and the Europeans have repudiated La Malinche. The "aquél," the third party, is the mestizo child, who accepts her role as his mother; but after she has contributed to his formation he rejects her as well by identifying her as the passive, sacrificial figure who is a sexual object, "la madre violentada" (the violated mother), as well as "la madre primera de nuestra nacionalidad" (the first mother of our nationality), as Alfonso León de Garay expressed it and as it was dramatized by Willebaldo López's Martín Cortés in *Malinche Show* (see chapter 7).[17]

No realistic motifs are included in this poem that initiates the Marina cycle, except for the title and the last word—the former a clue to her specific identity, the latter to her role as a symbol of woman betrayed and victimized. The three remaining poems follow the same pattern of suggesting the subtext by including "Marina" in the title and using only pronouns instead of proper names to refer to the various characters in her life story. By this technique Corpi succeeds in showing that the Malinche figure is indeed the subtext for the life of most Mexican/Chicana women.

In "Marina Virgen" ("Marina Virgin"), the second poem, Corpi deconstructs the negative images incorporated in the paradigm by juxtaposing "la chingada," the name with which she ended the first poem, with that of the virgin. As we have seen, La Malinche is generally considered the polar opposite of the Virgin of Guadalupe, but in the title Corpi brings these conflicting images together. The poem elaborates on the image of Marina emphasized by Adelaida Del Castillo, her role as a Christian. In the first stanza "she"—the reader assumes that all references are to Marina—is depicted as willingly accepting the Christian religion and relating the new religious practices to her love for the "you" to whom the poem is addressed. Again, the reader assumes that "you" is Cortés or, through synecdoche, the

Hispanic culture to which he introduced her. Corpi associates these two characteristics, the acceptance of the new faith and the submission to the new love, as signs of her "sin," which is mentioned in stanza 2: "Then [she] covered her body / with a long, thick cloth / so you would never know / her brown skin had been damned."[18] Her acceptance of the foreign tradition as the dominant force is also seen as part of her sin, for in trying to cover her "brown skin" she tries to assume a new identity. The dichotomous nature of Marina's submission to the new religion is thus expressed, for her acceptance also meant the rejection of another religion. The revalorization of Indian culture after Mexican independence from Spain strengthened the diatribe against La Malinche and her sin of *malinchismo*, of acculturation. Corpi not only releases the image of Marina from the sin of sexual promiscuity by calling her "virgin" in this poem; she also associates her true nature with the land in the final stanza: "Once, you stopped to wonder / where her soul was hidden / not knowing she had planted it / in the entrails of that earth / her hands had cultivated— / the moist, black earth of your life."[19] In a reversal of androcentric tradition, the cultivated land is now identified not with the body of the woman but with the man, "the moist, black earth of your life." She is the active figure who "worked the land." The symbolism of the poem also deconstructs the image of the Indian woman whose "fruit" is stolen from her ("her womb sacked of its fruit" from the first poem, which expresses her victimization in traditional imagery). In this poem, which begins with the phrase "of her own accord," she plants of her own volition. While a sacrificial tone is also part of the poem, nevertheless the victim's role is mitigated here because it was on her own accord and with love for the addressee that she acted the way she did. She acts not as the Mexican Eve, selfish and rejecting, but more in accordance with the positive pattern of the Virgin, who embodies the most virtuous feminine attributes: forgiveness, succor, piety, and virginity, as well as saintly submissiveness, as Mirandé and Enríquez remind us.[20] Marina does not take on all these traits, for she is not passive or submissive in a saintly manner. However, to shift the image from the paradigm of Eve to that of the Virgin is to purge the figure of her traitor's role. Marina's transfer of interest—the meaningful "change of organization" that Ireneo Paz employed to convey the transfer of emotion/power from the Indian to the Spanish system—is recast here not as disloyalty to "patria," the fatherland, but as a reconfiguration of *patria* and *"pater,"* in the way Celestino Gorostiza suggested in his play *La Malinche.* Her love, like the unselfish love of the Virgin, led her to plant her soul in the earth of his body, a metaphoric expression of her sacrifice, so that her union with him changes from an act of "submission" to a deed that would bear fruit—the mestizo nation.

This positive view of Marina's actions is not part of popular culture, as Corpi recognizes in the third poem, "La hija del diablo" ("The Devil's Daughter"). The title stands in contrast to the previous "Marina Virgen"; agricultural and religious imagery previously combined for a positive interpretation is here used to show the negative reactions to her role.

> When she died, lightning struck in the north,
> and on the new stone altar the incense burned
> all night long. Her mystic pulsing
> silenced, the ancient idol
> shattered, her name
> devoured by the wind in one deep growl
> (her name so like the salt depths of the sea)—
> little remained. Only a half-germinated seed.[21]

This brief poem captures the effects of time that transformed her life—symbolized by Corpi as "mystic pulsing"—into the work of the devil. By focusing the denunciations of La Malinche on the events that followed her death, Corpi acknowledges that during her lifetime both the Indians and the Spaniards thought highly of her and respected her words and deeds. At first her death caused mourning—lightning struck and incense burned; but in time her name was denounced and cursed by all (the "one deep growl"). Corpi shows that the signifier "Marina" was given many signifieds, loaded with as many meanings as the profundity of the sea to which the sign is also related. Yet by ending the poem with the image of a half-germinated seed, Corpi suggests the very revisions that her own poem instantiates. The seed that was left to grow may be a reference to the mestizo progeny of La Malinche, who are still waiting to assume their role in Mexican society, and also, in accordance with the polysemous nature of the sign, a reference to the Chicanas who would be the future generation to evolve from her inheritance, too. The adjectival phrase "half-germinated" is placed alone in the original Spanish, with a space after it, to be filled when the seed completes its development. Corpi's poem represents the advanced stage of the germination process that will end the silence surrounding Marina's "mystic pulsing."

Corpi identifies the Marina of her poems in the series of metaphors that comprise "Ella (Marina ausente)" ("She [Marina Distant]"):

She. A flower perhaps, a pool of fresh water . . .
a tropical night,
or a sorrowful child, enclosed
in a prison of the softest clay;
mourning shadow of an ancestral memory,
crossing the bridge at daybreak,
her hands full of earth and sun.[22]

Although Corpi entitles the poem as if Marina were absent—either temporally or, as the English title implies, physically distant—yet in fact this and the previous poems bring to the present—both temporally and in terms of our consciousness—the identity of "she." As I have suggested, the texts function as a recompilation of a majority of the images and metaphors included in the palimpsest of the Malinche paradigm: from love to betrayal, the religious and the sexual, reproduction to repatriation. The dichotomy of her image as either the beautiful tropical flower or a sad child imprisoned in an earthbound cell points to the polarity inherent in the sign.

Corpi, like Fuentes and Berman, presents her as a bridge figure. Although the Indian past that she embodies is a mournful memory, Corpi sees Marina's contribution as one of promise and future, for she walks across the bridge from the past to the future, *mañana*, her hands filled with earth and sun—the benefits of nature. The sorrowful child in the clay relates her to the seed about to germinate, the mestizo/Chicano child of her lineage to whom the future belongs. The image of a perfidious Malinche is distant, absent from this poem which looks to the future not as a repetition of the past but as the dawn of a new day, a new way: a new identity for "ella."

We should note that the narrative voice of Corpi's poems is not that of Marina but of another, perhaps her spiritual daughter. In contrast, Carmen Tafolla gives the burden of discourse to her Malinche in the poem "La Malinche," in which the "I" is a proud and self-assured self-conscious narrator. Her use of English and Spanish in the poem, not uncommon among Chicana writers, reminds us here of the language skills of La Malinche. Mastery of the language of the oppressor need not signify being mastered, however, for Tafolla's Malinche interprets her acculturation as a positive and visionary act, daring and decisive. Whereas previous poets recalled the pain of being labelled *malinchistas* for their love of men outside La Raza, Tafolla's perspective recognizes that La Malinche's role makes her the spiritual mother of the Chicana.

While it is not my purpose to comment on all the poems in which

Chicana poets refer to La Malinche, it is essential to note that for the new generation of writers the Malinche figure has become important in a positive and active manner. As a fitting end to this overview, Carmen Tafolla's "La Malinche" may best express the revolutionary voice of the reincarnated figure; we note not only the powerful ideas but their presentation in a poem whose form is indicative of the regenerated, remodeled, future-oriented woman:

For I was not traitor to myself . . .
    I saw a dream
        and I reached it.
            Another world . . .
                la raza.
                    la raaaaaaa-zaaaaaa . . .

Like Corpi's line of open space, Tafolla's use of suspension points and open vowels opens the poem and gives voice to the idea of a future that is new, not the ever-repeating pattern that was considered to be eternally the self-inscribed reality of La Malinche as Mexican woman.

Just as Chicano males would want to see their machismo in a positive light, as a source of ethnic pride and endurance in the face of discrimination, so, too, would Chicanas want to reinvent *malinchismo* as the way to bridge two cultures, not a selling out but a giving, a sharing of positive values with two cultures.

By appropriating her name for the concept of acculturation—*malinchismo* is after all a term to describe the submissive deliverance of nationhood—Mexicans and Chicanos emphasize the cyclical nature of the phenomenon, as well as relating the idea to the belief in the crucial role of women in the betrayal of one's culture. Other Chicana writers offer different perspectives, but the unifying theme is their attempt to valorize the active aspect of La Malinche while putting into historical perspective and context her support of the enemy Spaniards. The problem for feminists in part has been how to balance the idea of La Malinche as slave on the one hand, obeying the wishes of her master, and as independent, active translator on the other, who searched for the right words to bridge the gap between two cultures, who served as a link for two cultures, becoming the mother of the new race of mestizos. Despite having borne the cultural brunt of negativity for so long, La Malinche, the historical figure, was a remarkable woman with personal strength of character, intelligence, and beauty. As a literary image she has suffered in her representation according to the needs of the national agenda. The move to resurrect her as a model of inspiration rather than condemnation reflects a transformation in the consciousness of contemporary readers/writers. Their new readings have modified the preexisting works, allowing us to view them anew, to readjust the givens of the old interpretations and create an enriched cultural inheritance that allows for positive female images.

CHAPTER NINE

The Malinche Paradigm as Subtext

PREVIOUS CHAPTERS dealt with various configurations of La Malinche within texts set in the conquest period. The extent to which La Malinche has become part of the Mexican consciousness can be verified further in the number of works that have no ostensible relation to the historical period of the conquest yet use the paradigm as a subtext.[1] When a woman is used as an object of exchange or is raped by an "invading" male figure and then abandoned or willingly consorts with newcomers and betrays her people or accepts a different culture and rejects her own or is blamed without reason for the evils that befall her people—such elements of characterization relate the woman to the popular configuration of the Malinche paradigm. Although not every tale of talent sacrificed, loyalty misplaced, or idealism betrayed need be construed as a reference to La Malinche, I leave it to readers to judge to what extent other Mexican and Mexican-American texts contain familiar accents.

It is tempting to attribute to the powerful resonance of the paradigm the numbers of fictional representations of women who are physically abused by conquistador figures and then abandoned. Within such a reading, Catalina Bernal in Fuentes's *La muerte de Artemio Cruz* (1962; *The Death of Artemio Cruz*) could also relate to the Malinche paradigm, since she is virtually handed over to the conqueror Cruz by her own people (her father Don Gamaliel Bernal), and after Cruz uses her services to attain what he wants, he abandons her, in effect, and goes on to his next conquest. Artemio Cruz himself can be read as a *malinchista* in the way he sells out his ideals in order to reap material gain.[2] In his epic novel *Terra nostra* (1975), the central character Celestina recalls the Malinche image in one of her metamorphoses, as Fuentes continues to explore problems in Mexican national identity. Perhaps more obviously based on the presuppositions embodied in the Malinche paradigm is Fuentes's play *El tuerto es rey* (The one-eyed man is king) published with

Todos los gatos in 1971, in which there appears a reference to a character called Marina. The name stands out as a possibly realistic motif in the otherwise absurdist, nonreferential play composed of polysemous characters and signs. In his study of Fuentes's plays, Merlin Forster wonders whether the name is a reference to the Marina of *Todos los gatos*.[3] It is not that every use of the name Marina is automatically an allusion to the historical figure, but in *El tuerto*, Marina is the woman abandoned by Duque when he comes to work for Donata. By using Marina as the sign for the woman Duque leaves, Fuentes makes use of the audience's presuppositions concerning the Malinche paradigm. These influence the way we relate to the sign itself and to the text in which she appears. Marina as the woman in Mexican history who depends on the male only to be abandoned by him is the first element in the paradigm evoked by the sign. Other motifs can be called upon as associations in the text may warrant. As Duque says, "Memory will serve as a portent."[4] The first Marina has prepared the path for subsequent ones. In this chapter I shall focus on selected texts in which the Malinche paradigm is embedded as a presupposition that influences male-female behavior and the configuration of female images in general.

Like Fuentes, Elena Garro is recognized as a writer who textualizes the Mexican preoccupation with the circularity of time, the idea that present events are merely a repetition of past actions and that the future is destined to be a repetition of the present. The title of Garro's novel, *Los recuerdos del porvenir*, indicates that the future can be remembered because "the future was the repetition of the past."[5]

In *Los recuerdos* and "La culpa es de los tlaxcaltecas" (The Tlaxcalans are to blame), Garro relates her concept of time to the image of women in Mexican society. Although she does not mention overtly the name of La Malinche, her characterizations of the women and their actions relate them to the first woman of Mexican literature. By using the Malinche paradigm as a subtext, Garro explores how women have been confined to a paradigm of behavior that compels them to repeat the history of La Malinche and Cortés.

Los recuerdos is set in the period of the Cristero rebellion, from 1926 through 1928, when the country was ostensibly divided between religious and antireligious factions. The nature of this historical context is just as important in explaining the development of the Malinche paradigm as the republicanism of the author of *Xicoténcatl* or the anti-Spanish sentiments of Ancona during the postindependence period. The Cristeros organized in response to the implementation of the anticlerical articles of the Constitution of 1917.

When civil authorities in Mexico attempted to regulate the Catholic church, its response was unexpected. A strike was called and "for the first time since the arrival of the Spaniards four centuries earlier, no masses were celebrated in Mexico."[6] In relation to religious battles and cultural divisiveness, the Cristero rebellion recalls the period of the conquest and La Malinche, for she had become the symbol of Indian acceptance of Christianity, based on the chronicles' documentation of her behavior.[7] The rebellion of the Cristeros also brought about the liminal state in society that Victor Turner discusses, a time in which a reevaluation of the cultural script might take place.[8] It is within this context that Garro presents her contribution to the deconstruction of the Malinche paradigm.

The narrative is situated in the small town of Ixtepec. One of the innovative aspects of Garro's technique is her identification of the town itself as the narrative voice that addresses the reader. This nonrealistic narrator prepares the reader for other events that do not conform to verifiable reality but impart a mythic quality to the text. We read the story on one level as an example of the eternal consciousness of the Mexican people and not as a circumscribed historical rendering of a finite time. Just as the narrative perspective is mythologized, so, too, is the treatment of women. The characteristics associated with Julia, one of the major characters, and then with Isabel, the young woman who takes her place, are elements I have identified as part of the Malinche paradigm. Garro implies that because of the sociocultural conditions in Mexico, the destiny of Mexican women has been to repeat the tragic past of La Malinche. Garo also suggests, however, that a new paradigm can be developed by changing those conditions.

Julia is identified as the lover of General Francisco Rosas, the military ruler of Ixtepec, a "foreigner" who invaded the town. By this characterization he is identified with Cortés, the archetypal enemy invader of Mexico. Just as the townspeople resent Rosas/Cortés, they also hate his mistress and blame Julia for all the evil in their society. The reactions of the Moncada family are typical. When they suffer financial problems, they find themselves forced to send their sons to work in the mines out of town. Julia is blamed for their difficulty and their unhappy decision: "It's Julia's fault that the children have to go so far away and all alone in the midst of the dangers of men and the temptations of the devil."[9] This statement should surprise the reader, since the narrator has not confirmed that Julia knows the Moncada family. That it is said with such finality and without dissension presupposes that women are to be blamed for all the iniquity and imperfections in their world.

Characters from all levels of Ixtepec society single Julia out as if she were the source of all evil and an ally of the devil, or the serpent in their garden, as Marina was described in *Xicoténcatl*. The narrator comments: "In those days Julia determined the destiny of us all and we blamed her for the least of our misfortunes."[10] The idea of her culpability is repeated as a leitmotif throughout the text, just as the judgment that Marina was a "vendepatrias" (seller of her country) was repeated by Ancona. Whenever an event occurs in the community that disturbs the townspeople, Julia is immediately blamed. When five Indians are assassinated, Doña Elvira, another townswoman, assures her family that "it is Julia . . . she is to blame for all that happens to us. When will that woman's desires be satisfied?"[11] The use of the verb *saciar* in the Spanish text, which signifies more "to satiate" than "to satisfy," relates Julia to the ancient religious rites of the Aztecs, whose gods required human sacrifices in order to be satisfied with their subjects' behavior, implying that her behavior inevitably reverts to the past.[12] Yet Julia is in no way responsible for the events described but is rather a passive figure inadvertently placed in difficult situations because of her relationship with a man. The pattern could easily describe La Malinche's relationship to Cortés, for as the gift of one tribe (the Tabascans) to another (the Spaniards), La Malinche was a possession of Cortés and thereby linked to his exploits.

Just as La Malinche did not give the orders to exterminate the Indians of Cholula, Julia had no role in ordering the assassination of the five Indians; yet both women receive censure: "Julia was the true guilty party"[13] is the narrator's remark, just as Marina/Malinche was blamed for the violent actions of Cortés. It is ironic that along with the Spaniards, another Indian nation, the Tlaxcalans, were involved in the sacking and looting of their enemies, the Cholulans; similarly, the townspeople are eager to implicate Julia in order to exculpate the son of one of their friends, Rodolfo Goribar. A member of the town elite, Goribar planned the murder of the Indians because of their interest in agrarian reform. Although he had persuaded General Rosas to order the killing, the townspeople prefer to place the guilt on the outsider and a woman rather than condemn one of their own: "They found it difficult to accept that it could be Rodolfito."[14] Each time additional Indians are killed, Julia is blamed by the people, reflecting an attitudinal pattern according to which women are the root of all trouble, despite their real lack of power in patriarchal society.

Julia's role as the scapegoat is revealed in the comment, "Julia had to be the beautiful creature who would absorb our failures."[15] This statement repeats the function that La Malinche performs for the Mexicans as the one figure to blame for the conquest, despite the other crucial factors that contributed to the Spanish victory.

The reference to the positive aspect of Julia—her physical attractiveness as "the beautiful creature"—also relates her to the Malinche paradigm, because the beauty of the Malinche women is both a curse and a blessing. Because of their attractiveness, they function as destructive temptresses, as in *Xicoténcatl* or as Usigli's "marine voice, deceitful and sibilant." In this text the narrator says that Julia brings discord, antagonism, and conflict by her very being: "The scent of vanilla came forth and the invisible presence of Julia, a stranger to Damián Alvarez, settled like discord in the center of the tavern."[16]

The paradoxical nature of Julia/Malinche is indicated in the oxymoronic phrase "invisible presence" and is repeated in the love-hate relationship the townspeople feel for her. Like La Malinche, Julia is considered "the herald of misfortune"[17] because of her association with General Rosas. On the other hand, she is admired and inspires love because of her beauty. Felipe Hurtado is so moved by her attractiveness that, like Juan Jaramillo, he risks the wrath of the general to be with Julia. Nicolás Moncada, another man smitten by her beauty, admits: "For him, as for Hurtado and all of Ixtepec, Julia was the image of love."[18] Men desire her and envy her lover; women often both admire and hate her. Doña Ana Moncada, mother of Nicolás, Juan, and Isabel, also shares with her children "an unlimited admiration" because "[one] cannot deny that she has something."[19] Julia is a constant preoccupation for all the townspeople, partly because of her physical appeal but also because she is the companion of General Rosas and the repository of blame for all the problems that occur.

Julia is not the only Malinche figure in *Recuerdos*. When part 1 ends with her disappearance from Ixtepec with Felipe Hurtado (as La Malinche faded from history with Juan Jaramillo), another woman is already in place to continue the Malinche paradigm in part 2. A Malinche appears to be eternally present in Mexican society. This repetition of the signified (the symbol) with various signifiers (or visual figures) reflects Garro's presentation of temporal activity in general. Her texts presuppose the eternal reduplication of performance: "One generation follows another and each one repeats the acts of the preceding one."[20] The paradoxical titular phrase "recollections of things to come" is possible because the future will be no different from what has already taken place in the past. The re-creation of the Malinche paradigm by Isabel Moncada is proof of the repetition of the past in the present and the future.

Although her mother and brother had been attracted to Julia, it is only Isabel Moncada, as the young woman of the family, who is marked to repeat Julia's destiny, Malinche's pattern. Even before Julia leaves, Isabel is described by her brother Nicolás as "traitor" ("traidora"), marking her role in the paradigm. After Julia leaves Francisco Rosas, Isabel's actions appear to draw her into the trajectory of the Malinche pattern, as she is drawn to the man as well: "If she could, she would rush to be at Francisco Rosas's side."[21] Isabel's actions seem predetermined: "She was very far from her room, traveling a future that began to be traced in her memory."[22] She also suffers from a sense of guilt without apparent reason: "In front of [her father], Isabel lowered her eyes, she felt guilty."[23] These phrases prepare the reader for her subsequent actions, which repeat the pattern popularly attributed to La Malinche.

In the perspective of her society, Isabel causes the deaths of her brothers because of her traitorous acts. First she rejects her family: "she distanced herself from her family";[24] then she favors the enemy by becoming Julia's replacement in his bed. The betrayal of Isabel ("la traición de Isabel") that Nicolás had foreseen earlier is conceded in the same manner as Julia's culpability had been acknowledged.

Just as Julia was a paradoxical figure, Isabel, too, is portrayed with the dualities of La Malinche. Either betrayal or salvation is possible as a result of her actions, depending on whether one reads her acceptance of the conquistador in the manner of Octavio Paz or Ireneo Paz. Although most of Ixtepec are willing to brand Isabel a traitor, some look to her for their salvation: "Some thought that Nicolás's words meant that salvation would come to us from Isabel. The young woman had not entered the hotel to betray us. She was there, like the avenging goddess of justice, waiting for the appropriate moment."[25] On one level, Isabel may seem to be acting as the good goddess, giving herself to Rosas as a way of saving her brother, who had been captured by the general. Seeking the liberation of her brother associates her with the Good Mother archetype.[26] By using her body, however, she acts as a prostitute and portrays the negative paradigm. Isabel, like Julia, then, functions as the embodiment of an impossible duality, as both savior and whore, just as La Malinche is both mother of the Mexican people and traitor to the *patria*.

In response to Isabel's behavior, Rosas complains that "all women are whores," an adage underscored by the reputation of La Malinche.[27] Not only Julia and Isabel but the women who live in the hotel with the military men are "whores," women who open themselves to men. At the same time, however, Rosas and the other military men ignore their own role in the relationship, following a pattern that Sor Juana Inés de la Cruz highlighted in her famous poem "Hombres necios" (Misguided men), in which she scolds men who censure women for behavior they themselves originally provoked.[28] When Octavio Paz addressed the theme of male-female relations in *El laberinto*, he did not fix blame but stated that in order for there to be a Malinche, or La Chingada, the violated woman, there must be *chingones*, the strong ones, those who violate: "The *chingón* is the male, the one who opens. The *chingada* is the female, pure passivity."[29] According to Paz's description, Rosas is the *chingón* while Isabel and Julia play the role of *chingadas*, the violated and betrayed women.

At the same time that Garro recalls the eternal paradigm as outlined by Paz, she also deconstructs the sociocultural system and its myths of women's behavior. This subversion becomes apparent through an analysis of the women's actions in relation to Rosas's behavior. On the surface, Rosas is the foreign enemy who has come to subdue the town and all its inhabitants. His treatment of women is typical of the macho, who feels he is in control and can possess them as sexual objects. He beat Julia unmercifully because another man looked at her and she returned his glance. Julia accepted his will and behavior toward her, no matter how detrimental, until one day she abruptly changed her pattern and escaped.

This change in conditioned female behavior was so dramatic that it required the aid of another man and a magical event as well. Julia realized that for a female in Mexican society, the exercise of power would require the help of a male; Felipe Hurtado's love empowered her to escape from Rosas. (Fuentes's Malinche invoked the aid of men, too, to bring about change.) The two lovers were also helped by a miracle; time stood still so that the darkness of night hid their flight: "Time stopped dead. I don't know if it stopped or if it slipped away and sleep fell upon us."[30] According to the narrator's comment, time was altered in Ixtepec. A special, liminal period was created, signifying a rupture in the old social pattern, to allow a new model to develop. Although innovative patterns are not easily established, Julia's rebellious act succeeded in one sense. Her partial accomplishment may be inferred from Isabel's ability to alter the Malinche pattern.

When Isabel seeks out Rosas, this daughter of the bourgeoisie breaks the traditional social code for female behavior. By becoming the mistress of Rosas, she accepts the role of La Malinche as the *chingada*, as Paz described it: "a figure representing the Indian women who were fascinated, violated or seduced by the Spaniards."[31] As the new signifier for the signified, however, she does not accept unilaterally her own culpability in conforming to this role. She directs this knowledge to Rosas—"I'm not the only guilty one"[32]—giving voice to the generations of silent women before her. Rosas, however, refuses to acknowledge his share of this guilt, following the typical pattern.

In alluding to their guilt, Isabel does not refer only to the sexual act between the two of them but also to the political act of Rosas, who has ordered the execution of her brother and other family and friends. Isabel does not just give herself to Rosas; she is asking for her brother's life: "'I want Nicolás,' she demanded in a very low voice."[33] This request changes her from a passive creature to an active agent. That she is exhibiting "manly valor," as did La Malinche according to Bernal Díaz, is revealed when she becomes merged with her brother in the perception of Rosas: "'I want Nicolás,' Isabel's face repeated, more and more like the face of her brother."[34] She sheds her appearance as a submissive woman and is almost transformed into the masculine mode as she makes demands upon Rosas.

Although Isabel, following Julia, tries to change the paradigm, she fails because she cannot change it alone. Women need the cooperation of men to alter the pattern of the past and forge a new path. Isabel is able to convince Rosas to help her, but Nicolás refuses to escape: "He didn't allow himself to be freed," admits a soldier to General Rosas.[35] Faced with an unwanted prisoner who has refused to accept pardon, Rosas is forced to break his promise to Isabel. The execution of Nicolás takes place, a death that has become inextricably bound up with the sexual implications of Isabel's actions and the conflict of opposing forces of power. This death not only causes the end of the Moncada line but also terminates the relationship between Isabel and Rosas and brings about Isabel's own death together with the psychological destruction of Rosas. Just as the martyrdom of Cuauhtemoc is the gravest crime on the list of Cortés's infamies, Rosas is aware that he has brought about his own downfall with the execution of Nicolás: "Why did he have always to kill what he loved? His life was a permanent lie, he was condemned to wander all alone, deprived of good fortune."[36] The destruction of the enemy has taken place, yet Isabel, too, believes that she has been deceived and therefore beaten. Her attempt to change the future is unsuccessful in two ways, and the failures, both personal and social, are symbolized by her transformation into a stone image, as narrated at the end of the work.

Isabel/Malinche suffered for her role as a woman going against societal norms. In becoming the mistress of Rosas, she rejected the pattern of behavior expected from a Christian woman of the bourgeoisie. She was raised to be given by her father to another man. As a child she had already expressed her rebellion against this aspect of female life that converts women into merchandise: "Isabel disliked it when they established differences between herself and her brothers. She found humiliating the idea that the only future for a woman was marriage. To speak of marriage as a solution made her feel like merchandise that had to be sold at any cost."[37] By choosing Rosas, Isabel is no longer merchandise controlled by another but becomes an agent in her own right making deals for what she wants. By joining Rosas of her own will she places herself outside the institution of marriage, which controls female sexuality in patriarchal societies. Her behavior deconstructs the dominant social practices, which require passive and submissive females. Yet she still exists within an androcentric framework, and her attempt at liberation fails because she is still male-oriented. Despite all the events of betrayal, violence, death, and destruction, Isabel still believes she loves Francisco Rosas. Like the Doña Marina portrayed by such historians as Gustavo Rodríguez (discussed in chapter 5), Isabel refuses to expiate her sins and ultimately remains faithful to her love.

Her refusal to change is symbolized by her transformation into a stone statue. Gregoria, her maid, advises her to pray at the statue of the Virgin as a way of exculpating herself for the deaths of her brothers and her association with Rosas: "Let's go to the Sanctuary, child; there the Virgin will take Rosas out of your body."[38] Yet Isabel does not reunite with the Virgin, the traditional image of the Good Mother and saintly submissiveness, because she cannot return to her state of passive acceptance of the traditional female role. The text is clear about Isabel's rebellion and its consequences: "In her flight to find her lover, Isabel Moncada got lost. After looking for her for a long time, Gregoria found her lying way down the hill, transformed into a stone, and terror-stricken, she made the sign of the cross. Something told her that Miss Isabel did not want to be saved; she was very much involved with General Francisco Rosas."[39]

The final image of Isabel as a stone statue is rich in interpretive possibilities. By its juxtaposition with the statue of the Virgin, the stone Isabel suggests her polar opposition to the Good Mother in her role as a Malinche figure. Within this paradigm, Isabel represents in a narrow vein a stereotyped belief in female treachery. Like La Malinche, however, Isabel is a complex and paradoxical figure. Although the expression of her love for Rosas releases her from the pattern of submission implied by matrimony, that love is considered illicit and condemns her in the eyes of her society. In a larger sense, she is castigated for her attempt to change the traditional female pattern by means of her own will and action. This was the fate of La Malinche: on the one hand she was active in the conquest, a maker of history who undertook great sacrifices for her convictions; yet she had to perform her actions within the traditional role of concubine and so is often cast as a misguided and lovesick woman, like Isabel. Despite Garro's attempt to shake up the deeply embedded presuppositions about women, her Isabel ends up as a stone figure, frozen into a paradigm that has not been allowed to change for centuries.

Although *Recuerdos* stresses the oppression of the past, Garro appears to suggest that Mexico can create a new paradigm. In "La culpa es de los tlaxcaltecas," the writer offers a solution based on reevaluating the past to break the repetitive pattern. In her reading of this short story, Cynthia Duncan sees the expression of this theme: "Only through a mythic reevaluation of the past can the Mexican come to terms with his identity in the present and break out of the oppressive cycle of history which haunts him in the modern world."[40] The story does indeed transform the cyclical nature of the Malinche paradigm of *Recuerdos* into an open-ended textuality.

The title begins the transformation of the myth of La Malinche by broadening the concept of culpability. It is not La Malinche alone who is guilty but "the Tlaxcalans are to blame," a direct reference to one of the major Indian allies of Cortés in the conquest. Although La Malinche is not mentioned by name, following the indirection of *Recuerdos*, the female protagonist, Laura Aldama, shares key characteristics with La Malinche.

Like Julia and Isabel, Laura is linked with the theme of betrayal and guilt, but in this text it is Laura herself who makes the judgment: "'I am like them: a traitor,' said Laura dejectedly."[41] She makes this confession to Nacha, the cook, who then reveals her solidarity with Laura by agreeing to accept the same guilty state: "Yes, I also am a traitor, Señora Laurita."[42] Nacha indicates that no one person can escape being considered guilty, neither La Malinche nor the Tlaxcalans, neither the individual nor the group. Laura, however, appears transfixed by the idea of guilt and betrayal. As she begins to narrate her story and "the shame of [her] betrayal" ("la vergüenza de mi traición"), she recounts elements that recall the Malinche paradigm. She refers to a mysterious past, which connects her with the time of the conquest: "He asked me about my childhood, my father and mother. But, I, Nachita, didn't know which childhood, which mother or father he wanted to know about. So I chatted with him about the [*True History of the*] *Conquest of Mexico.*"[43] Laura's interest in the *Historia verdadera* of Bernal Díaz del Castillo, her focus on the theme of the fall of Tenochtitlan, and her conversations with her *primo marido* (her cousin-husband, as she refers to her first husband), lead the reader to believe that Laura exists on two planes, one in contemporary Mexico City and the other in the time of the conquest as a native Amerindian who witnesses the destruction of Tenochtitlan by the Spaniards in 1521. Because of her existential duality, Laura Aldama functions as the quintessential Malinche figure, an illustration of the palimpsest the sign has become.

Like La Malinche, who gained status and recognition because of her relationship with two different men, Laura changes identities depending on the man she is with. When her first husband appears, she reverts to the time of the conquest; when he recedes, she is once again expected to behave as a twentieth-century, upper-class white woman married to Pablo. Like La Malinche, Laura serves as a bridge between two cultures; she is able to exist in both time periods because as a Malinche figure she is a part of Mexico's indigenous past, which lives on in the present. Cynthia Duncan's comment is germane: "In this story, the past literally *does* live on in the present, not through some fantastic encounter with a threatening being from the past but, because within the framework of pre-Hispanic mythology, the past and present *are one.*"[44] The influence of the past on the present was seen in *Recuerdos* because temporal events were eternally repeating diachronically; in "La culpa" Garro shows a past that coexists with the present. In both cases, the effect is the same: the past, present, and future are identical.

This concept of changeless time also influences the treatment of women and the application of the Malinche paradigm to the identity of every Mexican woman. Whatever her socioeconomic status, the Mexican woman of today is labeled "Malinche," betrayer of the *patria*, whether of the Indian civilization of the past or of today's Mexico. As the popular song by Gabino Palomares clearly reiterates: "We remain with the evil curse / to offer to the foreigner / our faith, our culture / our bread, our money . . . / Today in the twentieth century! / Blondies (foreigners) continue to arrive, / and we open our houses to them; / and we call them friends. / O curse, from La Malinche, sickness of the present / when will you leave my land? / when will you free my people!"[45]

Yet just as this paradigm exists, Garro shows that it is possible for a sign or act to have more than one meaning, hence to change meanings. Laura herself offers alternative interpretations of an event when she says: "I'm a coward. Or perhaps the smoke and dust caused me to cry."[46] There are no fixed signs, just as there is no fixed chronology. The geographical loci of Mexico are also considered as signs with multiple signification. For example, when Laura gets lost in Chapultepec Park, the area is simultaneously filled with the battle of the conquest and with modern-day cars and passersby. When she describes the Zócalo, she sees in one site two scenes from widely separated times: "At nightfall we arrived in Mexico City. How it had changed, Nachita, I almost couldn't believe it! At twelve o'clock noon the warriors were still there, and now not a trace of them. Nor was there any rubble. We passed by the silent and sad Zócalo; nothing remained of that other plaza, nothing!"[47] Similarly, when the car mechanic comments, "estos indios salvajes" (these savage Indians), the signifiers have two possible signifieds, because Laura has just recalled the scene of battle from the conquest; "savage Indians" can be both a literal and a figurative reference.

The question of identity is an important one in this story, whether it be the identity of savages or civilized beings or the identity of Laura as La Malinche. Laura also calls into question the nature of men—machos—as she begins to compare her two husbands and their manner of being. Although her first husband is an "Indian," he does not seem to be "savage"; he is gentle and tender with her. On the other hand, her description of Pablo offers a critique of modern men that suggests insensitivity and cruelty: "When we were eating I noticed that Pablo didn't speak with words but with letters. And I began to count them while I looked at his thick mouth and his dead eye."[48] Although she says the two men look alike, there are negative characteristics in Pablo that her Indian husband does not share: "Pablo speaks in bursts, he gets furious about nothing and is always asking, 'What are you thinking about?'"[49] Laura's statements are both revealing and revolutionary from thematic and formal perspectives. Historically, just as in the case of La Malinche, women have not served as narrators of their own stories, yet Laura is a first-person narrator in part of the text. Rather than Pablo's perspective, we are given the thoughts and comments of the woman, here commenting critically on the behavior of the male and comparing one male to another. She attempts to position herself as subject and not object.

Laura's interpretation of events establishes the confrontation between the Indian and Pablo as a fight for her. This view is based on Pablo's reaction when the servants report that an Indian has been spying through the windows of the house. Pablo finds blood on her dress and on the window, and she inadvertently admits that an Indian had followed her from Cuitzeo to Mexico City; Pablo reacts to the suggestion of impropriety as evidenced by the blood stains and slaps his wife. He accepts her betrayal as a fact with no proof other than his own suspicions; he treats her as a Malinche. His physical violence against her may be typical of the macho but it cannot be considered civilized. Laura's comments on his cruelty are revealing for what they imply about the allegorical nature of their interaction: "'His gestures are violent and his conduct is as incoherent as his words. I'm not to blame that he accepted defeat,' said Laura with disdain."[50] By referring to defeat, she identifies the relationship between her husband and the Indian as a struggle and implies that the Indian will win the battle for her because Pablo is undeserving. Laura shows that she analyzes her husband's actions and rejects her own culpability because of the nature of his actions. She does not act passively, waiting for the men to decide her fate, but draws her own conclusions, functioning positively, as did the historical Malinche in her role as reader of signs.

Laura's phrase, "I'm not to blame that he accepted defeat," can also be read with the understanding that Laura is recalling other aspects of the Malinche subtext. Thus Laura/Malinche is refusing blame for the outcome of the conquest. Those who accept defeat are to blame, says Laura, which could refer to the historical accounts of the many omens interpreted by the Indians as signs of impending doom in the year Ce-Acatl.[51] Placed within the context of the twentieth century, Laura's comment is reversing the outcome of the conquest by suggesting that Pablo will be defeated by the Indian. This reading is another example of the many instances in the text in which multiple possibilities are presented to preclude any one-dimensional reality.

In many ways Laura redesigns the Malinche paradigm of male-female relations. She had initially interpreted her betrayal of her first husband as a rejection of the Indian context he represented. This reading is supported by Duncan: "In her former existence, Laura was a native American, but she could not stoically accept defeat and destruction at the hands of the whites as her first husband did. She fled into another time, another existence, wherein she herself has become a white woman rather than a member of the 'defeated race.'"[52] What happens to Laura, however, is that she has a second opportunity—which the historical Malinche did not—to assess the two civilizations represented by her two husbands and determine to which way of life, to which group, she will pledge her loyalty. Garro posits this cultural question in terms of an active evaluation by Laura of her husbands. Each time that Laura leaves the twentieth century to reenter the time of the conquest, she then rejects her first husband and returns to the modern period; she acts according to the pattern of Ireneo Paz's Otila, Garro's Isabel, and Bernal Díaz's Doña Marina by preferring the Hispanic husband. Yet with each reappearance Laura finds herself more critical of Pablo and his world. During each return to the past, she stays longer with the Indian, until she finally leaves Pablo for good after the third encounter; her choice is to remain with the Indian at the beginning point of Mexican civilization.

Laura's renunciation of Pablo and her statement "I'm not to blame," a phrase that echoes Isabel's "I'm not the only guilty one," are related to sexual encounters. The presupposition implied by Laura's new attitude is the subtext inherent in Magnus Mörner's conclusion that "the Spanish Conquest of the Americas was a conquest of women."[53] If the conquest is attributed to the acquiescence of Woman/Malinche, then the recuperation of that rejected civilization is being initiated by that same woman.

Laura's transfer of emotions (Otila's "change of organization") from Pablo to her Indian husband functions as a synecdoche for the change in women's perspective on the values of the Europocentrist, patriarchal culture that the women configured in the Malinche paradigm had previously expressed, in which the European was nobler, more intelligent, and especially more civilized, offering the true religion and the economic security that the primitive Indian had no way of providing.[54]

Within the context of contemporary Mexican society, Laura's rejection of Pablo also can be read as a gesture symbolic of contemporary women refusing to accept the patriarchal values that have imprisoned them in a restrictive social code. The name Pablo—Paul— offers a rich subtext in relation to the patriarchy because it recalls presuppositions concerning St. Paul and his teachings about women. It should be remembered that "St. Paul gave unprecedented emphasis to the sin of Adam and Eve . . . and that woman was at fault."[55] Garro's Pablo, as representative of the church and the patriarchy, does not value Mexico's indigenous past and rejects its vitality and significance, just as he blames the woman for any problems. Laura has learned through contact with both cultures to value the behavior patterns of the native American culture. She functions in opposition to Margarita, Pablo's mother, whose behavior marks her as an innocent, unquestioning woman who supports the patriarchy.

Garro reminds the reader through the experiences of Laura, Julia, and Isabel that contemporary Mexican women are still associated with La Malinche's betrayal, which determines how the men in society treat them. Through the experiences of her protagonists she explores the standard myth of female behavior and subverts the tradition of the submissive, passive, guilty female. She not only redistributes and reconfigures La Malinche's burden of guilt but also suggests a new pattern of behavior for Mexican women that would enable them to establish an authentic relationship with the indigenous past.

Although Laura first attempted to escape her indigenous past, she was unable to evade the reality of its existence in the present moment. Her experiences teach her, as Duncan observes, the importance of reestablishing contact "with a heritage she has long since abandoned and forgotten."[56] It appears that Mexicans must return to the moment of their culture's inception in order to move forward without the burden of guilt and misunderstanding that informs their present lives. Octavio Paz's comment is germane: "When he repudiates La Malinche . . . the Mexican breaks his ties with the past, renounces his origins, and lives in isolation and solitude."[57] Following the nineteenth-century tradition, Paz symbolizes the Mexican repudiation of the indigenous past in terms of the male's rejection of La Malinche. In an ironic reverse gesture, Garro has recast the situation of recovery as the repudiation by the female of the Hispanic, "foreign" male.

For both Paz and Garro, resolution of the Mexican dilemma is identified as a reunion with the initial object of rebuff, the indigenous culture. In addition, Garro points out that Mexicans can regain the past in a positive sense when both parties exist on a level of equality. She illustrates this point through the contrasts shown between the relationship of Pablo and Laura and that of Laura and Nacha. Pablo, as representative of the modern male, does not offer comprehension or civilization even if he is of the same social class as Laura. It is Nacha, the Indian maid, who provides Laura with compassion and wisdom. Garro suggests the possibility of female solidarity as Laura and Nacha share each other's secrets, guilt, responsibilities, and perspective. Pablo strikes Laura, while Nacha extends comfort and support: "Nacha drew near her mistress in order to increase the sudden intimacy that had been established between them."[58] When Laura abandons the Aldama household, Nacha also leaves "without even collecting her wages,"[59] for economic considerations are not as important as her loyalty to Laura and her identity with the indigenous part of Mexican culture.

The initial references to Julia, Isabel, and Laura as traitors and as women guilty of sexual betrayal prove that the past discourse of La Malinche and Cortés coexists within the present configuration of male-female relations. By first identifying Laura with the subtext of La Malinche and then subverting the presuppositions associated with the image, Garro joins the enterprise of such writers as the Fuentes of *Todos los gatos*, and Castellanos, López, and Berman, who have also attempted to deconstruct the national myths. Garro shows that it is possible to recoup the image of La Malinche and excise the negative elements.

Although Garro's narratives were ostensibly about other topics, the Malinche paradigm functioned as a subtext. Some of the plays of Emilio Carballido also include the Malinche paradigm as a key subtext for a consideration of male-female relationships and comments on national identity. As did Fuentes in *El tuerto es rey*, Carballido makes use of the name Marina. In addition, he recalls the Malinche subtext as a way of introducing the theme of *malinchismo*, as my essay "The Malinchista Syndrome in Carballido's Plays" shows in detail. He explores the presence of the pattern of behavior whereby Mexicans prefer foreign elements to the detriment of their own nation. Although the theme of *malinchismo* should not be conflated with the Malinche paradigm, since it forms only one aspect of the constellation of meanings inherent in the sign, the pattern of behavior that it labels persists as a preoccupation for contemporary Mexicans. Carballido, like Garro, shows that it is possible to reject *malinchismo* as a pattern of action. In exploring the ways some of Carballido's texts make use of the Malinche subtext, we learn again the multiple significations the sign bears.

Tiempo de ladrones: La historia de Chucho el Roto (1983; Time for thieves, the story of Poor Chucho) provides examples of both uses of the Malinche paradigm. Carballido gives the name Doña Marina to the woman caught in bed with the archbishop in the scene "El secuestro del arzobispo" (The kidnapping of the archbishop). Her name is a sign of her sexual function, which leads to her betrayal with the archbishop of his religious vows and her marriage rites. *Chucho* also includes a commentary on the *malinchismo* prevalent in Mexican society, although it has other major thematic concerns. Perhaps because the play focuses on the cultural traditions of the Mexican people and the collective memory surrounding the figure of Jesús Arriaga, Chucho el Roto, examples of *malinchismo* are included.[60]

Carballido focuses on events in the theater when he introduces the endemic negative attitude about Mexican products, a self-referential allusion that increases the audience's enjoyment of the scene. He has the Spanish impresario Guasp complain that "Mexican plays all belong to a distasteful genre. I'm not going to force the public to see them just because the government subsidizes the season."[61] In contrast to the disparaging remarks about Mexican plays made by Guasp, the Mexican artist Amelia defends the quality of Mexican work and confesses to Chucho that her goal is "a company of Mexicans with Mexican dreams and a Mexican soul, with many people trained in our Conservatory instead of so many colonial hold-overs."[62] In response to Amelia's complaint, echoed by the news reporter, that "Mexican authors complain that nobody produces their work," Guasp blames his failure to present Mexican plays on the work of the reading committee: "You know. Until now they haven't found a single work worthy of us."[63] Carballido's answer to such excuses is found in the actions of Chucho, who responds in his own appropriate "anti-*malinchista*" manner. Chucho "provides" Amelia with stolen gems that will enable her to start her own theatrical company with a thoroughly Mexican flavor: "With young people from the Conservatory and with a Mexican repertoire."[64] It is clear that support for Mexican authors is not always provided by government officials.

The episode in the theater points out the perennial problems suffered by Mexican authors, but Carballido's critique is not focused only on the theatrical world. In other scenes of this multifaceted work, he censures the behavior of Mexicans in various situations who act as *malinchistas* and betray their patrimony. The collector of antiques, Salmones, disparages Chucho's piece of Mexican art and confesses, "My tastes are closer to the European Masters."[65] Chucho's response to one who prefers to be closer to European than to Mexican artifacts is to oblige by taking away his *moneda nacional* (coin of the realm, so to speak); Chucho invariably prefers to steal from such people and transfer the booty to more grateful patriots. Like Garro's Laura, Chucho is a hero because he sets out to reverse the pattern of behavior that valorizes only the foreign elements in Mexican culture.

In *Ceremonia en el templo del tigre* (1983; Ceremony in the Temple of the Tiger), Carballido includes a young Indian named Marina as one of two main women figures. As the servant, she is identified with the Malinche paradigm by her sexual relations with the master of the house. She also serves as the interpreter and guide for Eugenio, the protagonist, in his role as newly arrived outsider. But it is the Malinche subtext conjoined with the exploration of *malinchismo* in *Ceremonia* that is of special interest for us here.

The play dramatizes the political reality of a people exploited by international forces that interfere within the country, a topic previously presented through the character Lucio in *Acapulco, los lunes* (1969; Acapulco, on Mondays).[66] Carballido is concerned with a paradigm of behavior according to which Mexicans and Latin Americans have relinquished their responsibilities and rights to a foreign power. He suggests that Mexicans will never be independent until they accept their past heritage, come to terms with its varied and syncretic characteristics, and reject the foreigner as a way of solving their internal problems. He also seems to question the inevitability of the repetition of past events by taking the traditional paradigm and showing that it can be changed.

In the final scene of *Ceremonia*, Carballido presents a dance ceremony that takes place in the Temple of the Tiger. Marina functions according to the Malinche paradigm as she serves as guide for her young master Eugenio. She explains that the dance is an ancient ritual in which only Indians used to perform but which the white elite took over. As the whites enact the ritual, they are invaded by a group of peasants who break the pattern of traditional, repetitive dance steps and rebel against the upper classes, who had assumed all the roles in the "play." Both the tourists on stage who watch the conflict and the members of the audience think at first it is still the enactment of a folkloric rite when the peasants attack. It soon becomes clear to the audience and Eugenio, however, that they are witnessing a massacre not written into the script of the "play ceremony."

It is possible that another subtext is at work in this reenactment of the bloody massacre of unsuspecting dancers that relates the rite to the conquest. A massacre of Amerindians by the Spanish, second in violence perhaps only to the incident at Cholula, occurred during Cortés's absence from the city when the Spanish troops were under the command of Pedro de Alvarado. According to the chronicles, the nobles of Tenochtitlan had received permission to hold a ceremony in honor of Huitzilopochtli in the palace of Axayacatl, which was to be attended by the conquistadors as well. The warriors were dressed in their finery and ready to show off in front of the Spaniards. Once they began to dance and shout their war cries—part of the ritual— Alvarado gave the signal to attack, and hundreds of the nobles were slaughtered. Alvarado claimed that he had been informed that the dance would be the pretext for an attack on the small band of Spaniards left to defend the city. Carballido's ceremony appears to be an inversion of this event; instead of the Indians being surprised, the white elite are the target of the massacre. By altering the pattern of events documented in the chronicles, Carballido shows that the past need not determine the future, that if *malinchismo* has been the history, it need not inform tomorrow's pattern.

Although Carballido evokes the past by his use of various motifs— the dance, the presence of Marina, the *malinchismo* theme—he does so to remind his audience that there are choices to be made. Too often Mexican writers have suggested that the past not only continues to influence the present but dictates the pattern of the future, as is implied by Garro's paradoxical title *Los recuerdos del porvenir.*[67] Carballido tries to counteract the belief in an inescapable future already inscribed in the relationship of the past. In the way Eugenio is presented with the choice of helping either the peasants or the elite, this text is a call to action, not to historical determinism. Just as Carballido creates a dramatized *rite du passage* for Eugenio in *Ceremonia*, the dramatic structure provides a message to all Mexicans and Hispanics to reject the dominant cultural pattern known as *malinchismo* and find a new strategy for exposing, escaping, and subverting the oppressive paradigm. Texts like Garro's and Carballido's draw attention less to the past than to the future in the way they critique the historical paradigm's validity for the future. The writers who use the subtext understand that the set of presuppositions inherent in their cultural myths motivates the nation to accept the presence of the repetitive patterns of behavior of the Malinche paradigm.

As the texts of writers engaged in re/visions and re/formations indicate, the Malinche sign can be stripped of its negative signifieds regarding nationalism and female subordination. In its stead, a new image of sexual equality and cultural diversity seeks its place on the palimpsest of Mexican cultural history. The palimpsest is an important archaeological image in Mexico; just as it refers to the way the Amerindian tribes built one pyramid atop another or how the Catholic church constructed its religious sites in the same places used by the indigenous tribes, it also describes the way a sociohistorical group takes advantage of the cultural meanings formed by previous groups, adding, altering, but not completely destroying the previous suppositions. In using the subtext as a way of deconstructing the set of presuppositions that still cling to Mexican cultural myths, writers such as Fuentes, Castellanos, López, Berman, and Carballido question the belief inherited from the Aztecs that posits cyclical patterns for human behavior and for social acts. Despite the texts that offer a picture of culture as a set of sacred repetitions excluding historical renovation, my study of La Malinche in different historical periods has shown that changes in fact occurred, depending on the ideological context within which the individual author was rooted. The elements of the paradigm continue to evolve depending on the author's ideological agenda rather than on eternal social structures.

As the Chicana poets and feminist writers have shown, male hegemony and women's subordination are not the only patterns of behavior on the personal level, nor is cultural imperialism the preferred pattern for the encounter of cultures. The writers who critique the

Malinche myth recognize that myths and metaphors—the whole of symbolic activity—do more than merely express reality: they also structure experience. Since the creation of presentational symbols actively structures experience, one way to change behaviors is through the creation of a different symbolic system. I suggest that it will be fruitful to investigate in further studies the effect of the Malinche figure on other cultures in order to evaluate how different sociopolitical influences affect the representations of the paradigm.

Notes

1. La Malinche as Palimpsest

1. La Malinche is the "first mother of Mexican nationality," as Alfonso León de Garay expressed it in *Una aproximación a la psicología del mexicano*, p. 36. Although tangential to this study, it is important to remember nevertheless that the shipwrecked Spanish sailor Gonzalo Guerrero, a native of Palos, had taken a Mayan wife and had become so assimilated to Indian culture that he refused to be "liberated" when Cortés's expedition found him and Father Jerónimo de Aguilar. Bernal Díaz mentions Guerrero's experiences, relating that he "was married and had three children, that he was tattooed, and that his ears and lower lip were pierced" (*Conquest*, p. 65). Based on this chronology, the births of his children precede the arrival of La Malinche's child with Cortés. A study of the historical and literary treatment of Guerrero in comparison with that of La Malinche would offer many important insights into aspects of Mexican culture, especially attitudes regarding patriarchy and indigenism. I want to thank Gonzalo Santos for reminding me of Guerrero's story.

2. The development of the figure of Boadicea as a legendary character is delineated by Antonia Fraser in *The Warrior Queens*.

3. Discussions of Malinal/Malinche's name abound in the historical and critical texts, while the literary narratives usually settle on one particular form according to the author's ideological perspective. Further discussion of her name will be found in chapter 3.

4. As part of his investigations in *The Aztec Image in Western Thought*, Benjamin Keen traces a multitude of versions of the conquest theme found in literary texts from many countries and different time periods. La Malinche figures in a number of non-Mexican and non-Spanish works. Examples from the twentieth century include Antonin Artaud's dramatic sketch "La Conquête du Mexique," an example of his Theater of Cruelty. Archibald MacLeish composed an epic poem on the topic, "Conquistador" (1932), which won him the Pulitzer Prize and established his reputation. José Sánchez notes the presence of La Malinche and other figures of the conquest in Spanish and world literatures in *Hispanic Heroes of Discovery and Conquest of Spanish America in European Drama*. Further investigation of the

nature of the presentation of La Malinche in these non-Mexican works merits a separate study.

5. Juana Armanda Alegría, *Psicología de las mexicanas*, p. 69: "Lo que se sabe a ciencia cierta es que Malinche fue le única mujer importante durante la conquista de México, y como tal, merece ser reconsiderada. . . . La historia no ha sido justa con doña Marina." (This and all subsequent translations from the Spanish are mine, unless otherwise noted.)

6. In "Looking for a Logic of Culture," p. 15, Umberto Eco describes these units as "the *expression plane*, which is correlated (by a code) to units of a *content plane*, in which another system of oppositions has made pertinent certain (semantic) units through which a given culture 'thinks' and communicates the undifferentiated continuum which is the world. The sign, therefore, is the correlation, the function which unites two 'functives,' expression and content. But the 'functives' can enter into different correlations; correlations are mobile, and a given object can stand for many other objects, which is how one can explain the ambiguity, the semantic richness of the various types of language and the creation, the modification, the overlapping of different codes."

7. Jonathan Culler, "Presupposition and Intertextuality," p. 1382.

8. Ibid., p. 1388.

9. See Edward L. Keenan, "Two Types of Presuppositions in Natural Language," p. 45.

10. Culler, "Presuppositions," p. 1389.

11. Ibid., p. 1391.

12. R. Patai, *Myth and Modern Man*.

13. María del Carmen Elu de Leñero, in *¿Hacia dónde va la mujer mexicana?*, refers to Mexico as a society in change with regard to the image of women and their role in society. The possibility for change is also noted by John A. Booth and Mitchell A. Seligson, "The Political Culture of Authoritarianism in Mexico: A Reexamination."

14. Luis Leal, "Female Archetypes in Mexican Literature."

15. Alfredo Mirandé and Evangelina Enríquez, *La Chicana: The Mexican American Woman*, p. 28.

16. "Once Again Sor Juana," in *A Rosario Castellanos Reader*, ed. and trans. Maureen Ahern, p. 222; in Spanish, from "Otra vez Sor Juana," reprinted in *El uso de la palabra*, p. 21: "Hay tres figuras en la historia de México en las que encarnan, hasta sus últimos extremos, diversas posibilidades de la femineidad. Cada una de ellas representa un símbolo, ejerce una vasta y profunda influencia en sectores amplios de la nación y suscita reacciones apasionadas. Estas figuras son la Virgen de Guadalupe, La Malinche y Sor Juana."

It is noteworthy that in his study of the formation of Mexican national consciousness, *Quetzalcoatl and Guadalupe*, tr. Benjamin Keen, Jacques Lafaye equates the Virgin of Guadalupe with Sor Juana: "a woman of genius reputed superhuman, I see her as a human replica of the image of Tepeyac [the Virgin of Guadalupe]" (p. 70). It is also interesting that Lafaye does not develop the figure of La Malinche; Castellanos thus presents the more complete analysis of female images when she includes La Malinche.

17. See the work of Leal in "Female Achetypes" as examplary of the literary critics; for the sociological perspective, see Mirandé and Enríquez, *La Chicana*; for that of the historian, see Jacques Lafaye, *Quetzalcoatl and Guadalupe*. See also Ann Pescatello, "Modernization of Female Status in Mexico: The Image of Women's Magazines," pp. 246–257.

18. Castellanos, "Otra vez," p. 22: "Traidora la llaman unos, fundadora de la nacionalidad, otros, según la perspectiva desde la cual se coloquen para juzgarla."

19. Shirlene A. Soto, "Tres modelos culturales: La Virgen de Guadalupe, la Malinche y la Llorona," p. 16.

20. Consult Agogino, Stevens, and Carlotta, "Doña Marina and the Legend of La Llorona," for a review of the various versions of the legend of La Llorona and possible reasons for the identification of Doña Marina with La Llorona: "Doña Marina played an instrumental role in Cortéz's conquest of the high civilizations of Indian Mexico. Herein may be the basis of the 'woman who weeps.' The reasons for her remorse were the destruction of her people or their subjugation to the pale-faced invader. Her 'children' in this instance are the countless millions of Indians who fell under the rule of the Spanish" (p. 28).

21. Turner, *Dramas, Fields, and Metaphors*, p. 154.

22. Ibid., p. 98.

23. Ibid., p. 99.

24. See Elu de Leñero, *¿Hacia dónde va la mujer mexicana?*, especially pp. 22–23, where she describes the traditional view of the Mexican woman as "un objeto de conquista" (an object of conquest). Other researchers in the field of Mexican psychohistory have observed that the Malinche paradigm affects the psychology of mestizo males as well. Salvador Reyes Nevares says that the contemporary Mexican mestizo identifies himself with the violated element of the conquest, the indigenous element represented by La Malinche, and is ashamed ("El machismo mexicano," p. 16).

25. One investigator whose work should be consulted is Inés Hernández, who is active in the popular dance movement that takes La Malinche as one of the roles. See "Cascadas de estrellas: La espiritualidad de la chicana (mexicana) indígena."

26. See the study of this tradition as it relates to some of the chronicles in *Women in Colonial Spanish American Literature* by Julie Greer Johnson.

27. See José Sánchez, *Hispanic Heroes of Discovery and Conquest of Spanish America in European Drama*; he discusses the theme of the conquest in European texts and notes that its absence is striking, given the importance of the historical event.

28. See Turner's discussion of the liminal period of independence in *Drama*. The Mexican historian Edmundo O'Gorman refers to the metahistorical reasons that gave rise to the scapegoat theory of Mexican historiography; see his introduction in Justo Sierra, *The Political Evolution of the Mexican People*, especially p. xvi.

29. Leal presents one of the more enlightening analyses of the style and possible authorship of the novel in *"Jicoténcal,* primera novela histórica en castellano."

30. Nicholson, *The X in Mexico: Growth within Tradition,* p. 103.

31. For a review of literary works that reflect the Tlatelolco Massacre of 1968, see Dolly J. Young, "Mexican Literary Reactions to Tlatelolco 1968."

32. Kevin Brownlee, in a special issue of *Yale French Studies,* refers to Walter Benjamin's comments on the motivation for historical writing: "To recall the past is a political act: a *recherche* that involves us with images of a peculiar power, images that may constrain us to identify with them" (p. 1).

33. Adelaida Del Castillo, "Malintzin Tenépal: A Preliminary Look into a New Perspective," p. 141.

2. Aztec Society before the Conquest

1. I acknowledge that, although it is a popular convenience, it is technically incorrect nevertheless to use the term *Aztec* to refer either to the people who were the rulers of the Valley of Mexico when the Spaniards entered Tenochtitlan, their island capital, or to all the indigenous peoples of the area known today as Mexico. *Mexica* was the designation for the Nahuatl-speaking tribute empire of central Mexico. *Aztec* is used in this study because of its wide acceptance, to refer to the Mexica and other groups of related culture within their empire. The following discussion clarifies that there were rivalries and differences among the various groups in Mesoamerica.

2. Compare Todorov's comment that the documents are "sources of information about a reality of which they do not constitute a part" (*The Conquest of America,* tr. Richard Howard, p. 53).

3. Miguel León-Portilla, *The Broken Spears: The Aztec Account of the Conquest of the Mexican Empire,* p. viii. In "Recent Writing on the Spanish Conquest," Benjamin Keen points out that attitudes toward the conquest and its protagonists have often varied from generation to generation because of ideological bias and faulty methodology.

4. For a discussion of Sahagún, see the essays in J. Jorge Klor de Alva, H. B. Nicholson, and Eloise Quiñones Keber, eds., *The Work of Bernardino de Sahagún: Pioneer Ethnographer of Sixteenth Century Mexico.*

5. León-Portilla, *Broken Spears,* p. xv.

6. In reference to Spain, consult John H. Elliot, *Imperial Spain, 1469–1716,* and Trevor R. Davies, *The Golden Century of Spain, 1502–1621.*

7. In addition to the sources provided on Spain, consult Charles Gibson, *The Aztecs under Spanish Rule: A History of the Indians of the Valley of Mexico 1519–1810,* and Rudolph van Zantwijk, *The Aztec Arrangement.*

8. Cortés arrived in Mexico when the Aztec or Mexica empire was ruled by Moctezuma, whose Nahuatl name in a phoneticized form was most likely Motecuçoma, popularized in Spanish as Montezuma. I have chosen the most commonly used modern forms for all Amerindian names, hence

Moctezuma, Cuauhtemoc, etc. In Spanish, the Nahuatl names are given an accent mark to conform with stress patterns, hence Cuauhtémoc, Quetzalcóatl, and so forth.

9. María J. Rodríguez, *La mujer azteca*, p. 62.

10. Ibid., pp. 62–68.

11. Huitzilopochtli was born of Coatlicue, as was another powerful deity, the goddess Cihuacoatl, "wife of the Serpent." Cihuacoatl has the additional sobriquet Tonantzin, equivalent in meaning to "our Lady" as a designation for the Virgin Mary. Cihuacoatl is identified with Tonantzin by Father Sahagún in his *Historia general*, where he devotes several chapters to the goddesses of Mexican society.

12. León-Portilla, *Broken Spears*, p. xxv.

13. John Manchip White, *Cortés and the Downfall of the Aztec Empire: A Study in a Conflict of Cultures*, p. 121.

14. Professor Sisson's comments were conveyed to me as part of his helpful review of this chapter, an assistance for which I repeat my thanks. Sisson is preparing an article on the intertribal Flowery Wars that will explore the complex reasons for these military exploits occurring before the Spanish encounter.

15. Obviously the act of rewriting the past to conform to the needs of the present is not a twentieth-century invention. This information verifies that we cannot expect to know the "truth" of past actions; we can learn only what a people thought about themselves in the way they fashioned their past.

16. León-Portilla, *Broken Spears*, p. xx.

17. Ibid., p. xxi.

18. Ibid., p. xxii.

19. For the Aztecs it was a convenient way to maintain a steady stream of victims for Huitzilopochtli and to test their warriors.

20. León-Portilla, *Broken Spears*, p. xxvi.

21. Charles E. Dibble, *The Conquest through Aztec Eyes*, p. 12. For a discussion of the omens and portents that were associated with the conquest, consult Bernardino de Sahagún, *Florentine Codex: General History of the Things of New Spain*, ed. and trans. Arthur J. O. Anderson and Charles E. Dibble, book 12.

22. Ibid., p. 11.

23. Ibid., p. 11.

24. Todorov, *Conquest*, p. 5.

25. See Stephanie Merrim's review of Todorov's book in *Modern Language Studies* 14.3 (1984).

26. Todorov, *Conquest*, p. 64.

27. Ibid., p. 66.

28. David Carrasco, *Quetzalcoatl and the Irony of Empire*.

29. Jacques Lafaye, *Quetzalcoatl and Guadalupe: The Formation of Mexican National Consciousness 1531–1813*, tr. Benjamin Keen, p. 150.

30. Alfred Crosby, *The Columbian Exchange: Biological and Cultural*

Consequences of 1492, and *The Columbian Voyages: Ecological Imperialism: The Biological Expansion of Europe 900–1900* (see note 36 for references to the revision of demographic data).

31. William H. McNeill, *Plagues and People,* p. 2.

32. Ibid., p. 207.

33. Justo Sierra, *Evolución política del pueblo mexicano,* p. 60.

34. Teja Zabre, *Historia de México:* "Cortés parece dirigido en la conquista de México, por una mano que lo salva y lo conduce por los mejores caminos" (p. 131).

35. Eligio Ancona, *Los mártires del Anáhuac,* p. 593.

36. The revision of demographic statistics began with the work of Sherburne F. Cook, "The Extent and Significance of Disease among the Indians of Baja California." See also his "La despoblación del México central en siglo XVI" and "The Conquest and Population: A Demographic Approach to Mexican History"; Sherburne F. Cook and Woodrow Borah, *The Indian Population of Central Mexico, 1531–1610* and *The Aboriginal Population of Central Mexico on the Eve of the Spanish Conquest;* Nicolás Sánchez Albornoz, *The Population of Latin America,* pp. 54–56. Compare T. R. Fehrenback, *Fire and Blood: A History of Mexico:* "Smallpox had become endemic once it had been brought in by Cortés' men; it recurred about every seven years. New Spain was never free of it. . . . The destruction . . . by disease was a slow, steady process that soon cast a terrible pall of suffering and death over all central Mexico. Death, and the constant consciousness of death, were embedded indelibly in the native mind. . . . Disaster heightened religious fears and feelings at the same time it completed the demoralization of the old culture" (p. 221).

37. Ancona, *Los mártires,* p. 444: "los dioses protegen a los extranjeros."

38. In Aztec society polygyny was permitted, with males in noble families taking several secondary wives and concubines, but only the children of the principal marriage were legitimate (Mirandé and Enríquez, *La Chicana,* p. 103).

39. Rodríguez, *La mujer azteca,* p. 56. Unless otherwise noted, my discussion of the role of Aztec women is based on Rodríguez.

40. Meyer and Sherman, *The Course of Mexican History,* p. 78.

41. Rascón, *Imagen y realidad de la mujer,* p. 150. Rascón quotes Adelina Zendejas (*La mujer en la intervención francesa,* p. 150) to prove that there was little discrimination among the Aztecs: "their opinion and functions were respected and as important as the men's; that is, there was no discrimination" ("su opinión y funciones eran respetadas y tan importantes como las de los hombres; es decir no había discriminación"). Other texts, such as Rodríguez's *La mujer azteca,* add an opposing perspective to the debate regarding the position of women in the Amerindian world.

42. Alfredo López Austin, *The Human Body and Ideology: Concepts of the Ancient Nahuas,* tr. Thelma Ortiz de Montellano and Bernardo Ortiz de Montellano, p. 291.

43. Rodríguez, *La mujer azteca,* p. 65.

44. Mirandé and Enríquez, *La Chicana: The Mexican-American Woman*, pp. 21, 23.

45. Ibid., p. 21.

3. The Creation of Doña Marina in the Colonial Period

1. The quotation comes from *Hernán Cortés: Letters from Mexico*, trans. A. R. Pagden, p. 73; in Spanish: "la lengua que yo tengo, que es una india desta tierra" (Cortés, *Cartas de relación*). I will use Pagden's translation for all quotations from Cortés's letters in text.

2. Ibid., p. 376; in Spanish: "para que creyese ser verdad, que se informase de aquella lengua que con él hablaba, que es Marina, la que yo siempre llevaba conmigo."

3. It is informative to review the following comment on the significance of the Cholula massacre found in Alfonso Teja Zabre's *Historia de México: Una moderna interpretación*, a textbook for Mexican students: "La matanza de Cholula y después otros grandes asesinatos en masa, fueron causa poderosa para que la mezcla de las culturas no se realizara por medios pacíficos y se abriera entre las dos razas un foso de rencores que durante siglos no se pudo borrar" (p. 134).

With regard to the Black Legend, see William S. Maltby, *Black Legend in England*, together with the revisionist perspective offered by Roberto Fernández Retamar, "Against the Black Legend," whose bibliographic references are also helpful.

4. Bernal Díaz del Castillo, *The Conquest of New Spain*, trans. J. M. Cohen, p. 172. All quotations in English are taken from this edition unless otherwise noted.

5. Todorov, *The Conquest of America*, trans. Richard Howard, p. 101.

6. Julie Greer Johnson, *Women in Colonial Spanish American Literature*, p. 15.

7. Bernal Díaz, *Conquest*, p. 80.

8. Johnson, *Women*, p. 20.

9. Bernal Díaz, *Conquest*, p. 153.

10. As noted in chapter 2, among the Indian groups it was a common practice to solidify political unions by the exchange of women, not unlike European customs at the time. The Indian chieftains continued this tradition throughout the period of the conquest, giving women to the Spaniards "as a sign of peace, friendship, alliance, or as a way of signalling the end of hostilities" (Angel Palerm Vich, "Sobre las relaciones poligámicas entre indígenas y españoles durante la conquista de México, y sobre algunos de sus antecedentes en España," p. 242). According to Palerm Vich, union with Indian women and polygamy among the Spaniards were ways of "contraer amistades y vínculos familiares, creando así lazos más sólidos entre indios y españoles que los de conquistadores y conquistados" (p. 235).

11. Bernal Díaz, p. 82.

12. Ibid., p. 52.

13. Johnson, *Women*, p. 16.

14. Ibid., p. 17.

15. Bernal Díaz, *Conquest*, p. 86.

16. Prescott, *History of the Conquest of Mexico and History of the Conquest of Peru 1843–1847*, p. 651 n. 23: "Y todo esto que digo se lo oí muy certificadamente, y lo juro amen." It should be remembered that Bernal Díaz was motivated to compose his own version of the events of the conquest after reading Gómara's and finding it full of errors and misconceptions. He often repeats the phrase, "This is what happened, and not the way it was told by Gomara," to emphasize his disagreements with the account put forth by the secretary to Cortés. See the comments of Lesley Byrd Simpson, translator of Gómara's *Historia de la conquista de México*, in the introduction to *Cortés*, especially pp. xv–xix.

17. Bernal Díaz, *Conquest*, p. 87.

18. Gómara, *Cortés: The Life of the Conqueror by His Secretary*, trans. Lesley Byrd Simpson, p. 56.

19. Ibid., p. 57.

20. Gómara's work was discredited because of his close association with Cortés, not only by Bernal Díaz and Bartolomé de Las Casas but by later historians as well. Las Casas, in his *Historia de las Indias*, claims that Gómara's account is "nothing but what Cortés himself told him to write" and that he "fabricated many stories in Cortés' favor which are manifestly false" (vol. 3, p. 529), especially since Gómara himself had never been to the New World. For a discussion of the polemic regarding the biases of Gómara's text, see the introduction to the translation by Simpson.

21. Gómara, *Cortés*, p. 346.

22. Somonte, *Doña Marina*, p. 78: "lo incorporó a la historia."

23. Gómara, *Cortés*, p. 408.

24. See Pagden's translation of Cortés's *Letters* (p. 464, n. 26) for a brief summary of the various points of contention regarding the name of Doña Marina. Compare also the comments of Don Joaquín García Icazbalceta as quoted by Fernández de Velasco: "The origin of the name 'Malinche' by which she was and is known and which the Mexicans also used to refer to Cortés, is attributed to the fact that the alphabet of the Mexican language lacks *r* so that the Indians substituted an *l*, as the closest sound, and 'Marina' was converted into 'Malina,' to which they added the ending 'tzin,' which denotes affection or respect, resulting in 'Malintzin,' which the Spaniards mispronounced, leading to Malinche. But others, evidently with more accurate information, believe that the change in names followed the opposite path; the name of Marina was imposed during her baptism, perhaps by analogy with the name she previously used; from that one and not the new name, and without the need to substitute letters, 'Malintzin' was derived, with the addition of the suffix that denotes reverence to the root form. 'Malinali' is the name or symbol of one of the 20 days in the Mexican calendar and is interpreted as 'twisting action.' It is known that the Mexicans gave to their children the name of the day on which they were born and then

would add another, without omitting the original one. Therefore, the name of Marina came afterward, that is, during her baptism, since her own pedigree, or rather her pagan name, was Malintzin Tenepal. The Malintzin or Malinalli was the original name, taken from the day of birth and the Tenepal was taken or added afterward according to the prevailing custom, described by Father Motolinía" ("La importancia de doña Marina en la conquista de México," pp. 149–50, translated from the original Spanish: "El origen del nombre 'Malinche' con que fue y es conocida, y que los mexicanos aplicaron también a Cortés, se atribuye a que por carecer de la letra r el alfabeto de la lengua mexicana, los indios la sustituyeron con la l, como la más análoga, y 'Marina' se convirtieron en 'Malina', a cuyo nombre agregaron la terminación 'tzin', que denota cariño o respeto, resultando 'Malintzin', y corrompido por los españoles vino a quedar Malinche. Pero otros, al parecer mejor fundados, creen que el cambio de nombre siguió camino inverso; y que el nombre de Marina se le impuso en el bautismo, tal vez por analogía con el que antes llevaba; de este y no del nuevo salió directamente sin sustitución de letras el de 'Malintzin' con solo poner el reverencial tzin en el cambio de la terminación, según lo pide el genio de la lengua. 'Malinali' es el nombre o símbolo de uno de los veinte días mexicanos y se interpreta por 'retorcedura'. Es sabido que los mexicanos daban a los niños el nombre del día en que nacían y más adelante les añadían otro, sin quitarles el que ya tenían. Por lo tanto el nombre de Marina vino después, esto es en el bautismo, ya que su propia alcurnia, o sea el nombre gentil, era Malintzin Tenepal. El Malintzin o Malinalli, sería nombre primitivo, tomado del día de nacimiento, y el Tenepal el que tomó o agregó después según la costumbre general, referida por el padre Motolinía." Gustavo Rodríguez adds that according to the Nahuatl philologist Don Mariano Rojas, *Tenepal* is derived from the root *tene*, which means in a figurative sense one who has a facility with words, a person who speaks with animation, which describes Marina's role (*Doña Marina*, p. 8).

25. Gómara, *Cortés*, p. 124.

26. Ibid., p. 127: a nobleman's wife "either moved by pity, or because she liked the looks of the bearded men, told Marina to stay with her, for she would be much afflicted if Marina should be killed along with her masters. Marina dissembled her feeings at this bad news, and got out of her who the plotters were and what they aimed to do. Then she ran to find Jerónimo de Aguilar and the two of them informed Cortés of this matter."

27. Bernal Díaz, *Conquest*, p. 194. Compare Todorov's comment: "On the one hand, she performs a sort of cultural conversion, interpreting for Cortés not only the Indians' words but also their actions; on the other hand, she can take the initiative when necessary, and addresses appropriate words to Montezuma (notably in the episode of his arrest) without Cortés's having spoken them previously" (*Conquest*, p. 100).

28. Ibid., p. 197.

29. In the case of the massacre of Cholula, Bernal Díaz writes as one of the participants when he attempts to justify their harsh reprisals against the

Indians by reminding his readers that the Cholulans had planned, after all, to massacre the Spaniards and had been foiled only because of the aid and advice of Doña Marina, who had been informed of the ambush unwittingly by the older Cholulan woman.

30. I wish to thank Dianne Bono for sharing her insights about the Lienzo de Tlaxcala during a personal interview that took place after she had presented her paper on the subject at the 1990 Kentucky Foreign Language Conference.

31. Cortés had left for Veracruz to head off an attack against him by forces under the direction of Pánfilo Narváez; the troops had been sent by Diego de Velázquez, governor of Cuba. Although the governor had first sent Cortés to Mexico, he soon regarded him as a rebel for exceeding explicit orders. Cortés left Pedro Alvarado in charge. Alvarado was considered a hothead, and he proved his volatility by his actions. He became nervous when the Aztec warriors were dancing at the feast of Toxcatl in their full regalia; perhaps recalling the massacre of Cholula, he believed they were preparing to attack the small number of Spaniards left to guard the capital. Alvarado and his troops rushed at the warriors, who were unprepared for the battle, and many died. (See Carballido's play *Ceremonia en el templo del tigre*, discussed in chapter 9, which appears to be a modern re/vision of this event.) As a result of the unexpected Spanish aggression, soon after Cortés returned he was attacked by the Aztecs. One version of the events reported in the chronicles states that Moctezuma came to the rooftop to ask his soldiers to desist in fighting and was accidentally hit by rocks used in the attack against the Spanish. The Aztec chieftain died a few days later.

32. Bernal Díaz, *Conquest*, p. 302.

33. Bernal Díaz also relates the reactions of the chief of the Tlaxcalans, whom he calls Mase Escasi (and who will be addressed as Maxixcatzin in *Xicoténcatl* and *Amor y suplicio*, both nineteenth-century novels, which will be analyzed in chapters 4 and 5): "How they rejoiced and how happy they seemed when they saw that Doña Luisa y Doña Marina were safe! And how sorrowfully they wept for the others who were absent and dead, especially Mae Escasi, who bewailed his daughter Doña Elvira and the death of Joan Velázquez de León, to whom he had given her" (*Conquest*, p. 307).

34. Todorov, *Conquest*, p. 101.

35. T. R. Fehrenback, *Fire and Blood: A History of Mexico*, p. 192.

36. Ibid., p. 19.

37. Todorov, *Conquest*, p. 101.

38. José Sánchez, *Hispanic Heroes of Discovery and Conquest of Spanish America in European Drama*, p. 14.

39. Ibid., pp. 17–18.

40. Several European countries succeeded in purveying an unfavorable impression of the two leading conquistadors in the civilized world, a concept not likely to be incorporated into the drama of Spanish writers. See Maltby, *Black Legend in England*, and Fernández Retamar, "Against the Black Legend," for bibliography on the formation of the Black Legend.

41. Octavio Paz calls the work "tiresome" but gives Terrazas credit as the first creole poet on the basis of the sonnets he wrote (*Trampas de la fe*, p. 72).

42. Ibid., p. 65.

43. Paz, in Lafaye, *Quetzalcoatl and Guadalupe*, p. xvii.

44. Ibid., p. xxi.

4. Eve and the Serpent: The Nationalists' View

1. As quoted by Aínsa, *Identidad cultural de Iberoamérica en su narrativa*, p. 116: "Ya los brazos de España no nos oprimen, pero sus tradiciones nos abruman."

2. See chapter 5, in which the discussion points out that Ireneo Paz employs similar metaphors to show that Mexico should reconsider its attitude toward Spain: "Tell Mexico that Spain is not her step-mother, but her worthy mother" (*Amor y suplicio*, p. 157).

3. See the valuable insights of Michel Foucault in *History and Sexuality, Vol. 1: An Introduction*, tr. Robert Hurley, regarding *patria potestas*.

4. José Joaquín Blanco, *Crónica de la poesía mexicana*, pp. 19–25.

5. In *Sensational Designs* Jane Tompkins makes these observations concerning the novels of the nineteenth-century United States, but they also apply to Mexico. For a reinterpretation of nineteenth-century Latin American texts in the light of contemporary critical theory, see John Brushwood, *Genteel Barbarism: Experiments in Analysis of Nineteenth-Century Spanish American Novels*; Hernán Vidal, *Literatura hispanoamericana e ideología liberal: Surgimiento y crisis*; Helena Araújo, *La scherezada criolla: Ensayos sobre escritura femenina latinoamericana*; and Sharon Magnarelli, *The Lost Rib: Female Characters in the Spanish American Novel*. I refer to these nineteenth-century writers as "he" since they are all men.

6. Charles C. Griffin, "The Enlightenment and Latin American Independence," p. 139.

7. D. W. McPheeters calls the author "un ardiente republicano y un amante de la libertad ("an ardent republican and a lover of liberty") in "*Xicoténcatl*, símbolo republicano y romántico," p. 406. See also Luis Leal, "*Jicoténcal*, primera novela histórica en castellano," p. 27. My citations of the text come from the version published by Antonio Castro Leal in *La novela del México colonial*, vol. 1. He uses the spelling "Xicoténcatl," as do others, although the anonymous author used "Jicoténcal." In this and subsequent cases, I use the standard form for general discussion and follow the spelling variants selected by the author in direct citations from the text.

In my use of "author" and "narrator," I follow the distinctions in these terms as defined by Wayne Booth in *The Rhetoric of Fiction*: "author" stands for the implied author or the official scribe of the narrative who appears as a variant of the real author (p. 71). The narrator refers to "the speaker in the work who is after all only one of the elements created by the implied author and who may be separated from him by large ironies" (p. 73).

8. See Edmundo O'Gorman, "Introducción," in Justo Sierra, *Evolución política del pueblo mexicano.* In his view, the Mexican historian resorted to a scapegoat in order to justify the disorder, economic ruin, and administrative chaos of the postindependence period because the Mexicans had expected political independence to be followed by progress and improved economic status, the pattern of the United States.

9. Castro Leal, *La novela,* p. 16. In contrast to Castro Leal, Ralph Warner refers to Eligio Ancona's *Los mártires del Anáhuac* as the first of the Mexican novels to deal with the conquest (*Historia de la novela mexicana en el siglo XIX,* p. 28).

10. Leal, "*Jicoténcal.*" Like Leal, McPheeters believes that the author could not have been Mexican, although he proves that the work did have an influence in Mexico ("*Xicoténcatl,*" pp. 406–409).

11. Wogan, "The Indian in Mexican Dramatic Poetry," p. 164; McPheeters also supports Wogan ("*Xicoténcatl,*" p. 404–408).

12. According to Wogan, Mangino's play, the best of the three with regard to its dramatization of the theme, offers an interesting treatment of Doña Marina. She is presented as the victim of a faithless lover: "Marina is not tormented by the thought that she has betrayed her country for the love of the Spanish captain: the conflict in her soul is human and personal; she hates Cortés, not because he is a Spaniard, but because he loves Teutila" ("The Indian," p. 165).

13. Leal notes that *Jicoténcal* and *Teutila* can be located in the British Museum: *Xicohténcatl* in the Biblioteca Nacional of Mexico; *Xicoténcatl* in the New York Public Library and at Yale ("*Jicoténcal,*" p. 12).

14. Leal refers to the influence of the French Enlightenment on the philosophical and religious ideas of the author of *Xicoténcatl* ("*Jicoténcal,*" p. 28), a judgment I find further substantiation for in considering the positive attitude of the author toward American Indians. As Arthur P. Whitaker notes, the American Indians were "the object of a major cult of the Enlightenment"; see "The Dual Role of Latin America in the Enlightenment," p. 11.

15. Hayden White, *Metahistory: The Historical Imagination in Nineteenth Century Europe,* pp. 34–36.

16. See chapter 2 above for a discussion of the historical relationship between the Aztecs and the Tlaxcalans.

17. According to the chronicle of Bernal Díaz, Xicotenga the Younger, as he calls him, was intent on rebelling against the Spaniards although the other Tlaxcalan chiefs remained loyal (see *The Conquest of New Spain,* p. 342). According to Gómara, Xicotencatl, captain-general of Tlaxcala, had been punished by Maxixca, the chieftain, for having advised the people to slay the Spaniards and appease the Mexicans (*Cortés,* pp. 226–227). This report of a rivalry between the two factions is re-created in *Xicoténcatl.*

18. In his *Evolución política del pueblo mexicano,* Sierra comments that as for the enterprise of conquest, "lo que en él tuvo importancia suprema fue la alianza con Tlaxcala, que, en odio a Tenochtitlán, se reconoció vasallo de España" (p. 51; "what was of supreme importance was the alliance with

Tlaxcala, who, because of hatred for Tenochtitlan, became vassals of Spain"|.
But the Tlaxcalans should not be held solely responsible, for Sierra adds that
all the tribes were divided: "las divisiones y las luchas intestinas ayudaron a
los españoles más que sus arcabuces y sus caballos y sus perros" ("the divisions and intestine battles helped the Spaniards more than their guns and
horses and dogs"| (p. 64|.

19. Irene Nicholson reminds us that "feelings rose against Cortés during
the independence struggle" (*The X in Mexico*, p. 45|.

20. According to Bernal Díaz, Diego de Ordaz was loyal at first to Governor Diego Velázquez of Cuba in his conflict with Cortés. Although he was
later won over to the side of Cortés, this initial difference may have led the
author of *Xicoténcatl* to cast Ordaz in the role of antagonist to Cortés.

21. As noted in previous chapters, women as objects of exchange between Indian groups has been documented by anthropologists and feminists
working in a number of fields. For references see Ann M. Pescatello, *Power
and Pawn: The Female in Iberian Families, Societies and Cultures*: it "was
a social courtesy among several Mexican tribes for families to present their
daughters to guests or allies as a token of friendship" (p. 126|, and "presenta-
tion of women as gifts or tokens of friendship was considered an important
procedural part of Indian foreign relations" (p. 134|. My discussions with re-
gard to Ireneo Paz's treatment of women elaborate upon this idea.

22. "Mi nación ha deseado siempre la alianza con los tlaxcaltecas, porque
casi nos son insoportables las exacciones y tributos con que nos grave el
gobierno de Moctezuma, y enteramente insufribles el orgullo y violencia de
sus agentes" (pp. 89–90|.

23. "Esta Doña Marina era una americana, natural de Guazacoalco, que
después de varios accidentes de fortuna, vino a ser esclava del cacique de
Tabasco. Este la pasó al dominio de Hernán Cortés, después de la sumisión
de su país. . . . Los buenos talentos y las gracias de esta esclava llamaron
la atención de su amo, el que, después de haberla hecho bautizar con el
nombre de Marina, puso en ella su amor y su confianza, de manera que en
pocos días pasó de esclava a su concubina y confidenta. Este último oficio lo
desempeñó con grandes ventajas para Hernán Cortés, pues no sospechando
en ella los naturales las artes . . . de los europeos, supo emplear con mas
efecto la corrupción y la intriga" (p. 99|.

24. The reference to Eden is an acknowledgment of an established Mexican tradition of relating Mexico to Eden or paradise. For example, as Jacques
Lafaye points out in *Quetzalcoatl and Guadalupe*, Sor Juana uses images in
her poetry that suggest Mexico is Eden (pp. 70–71|.

25. "'Bravo, bravo, Señor virtuoso,' dijo interrumpiéndole Doña Marina,
'le sienta a usted bien hacer el modesto en una sala y venir a otra a seducir
indignamente a una esclava. Salga usted de aquí'" (p. 101|.

26. The use of the serpent to represent evil derives from the Judaeo-
Christian tradition and was brought to Mexico by the Spaniards. In Amerindian mythology, in contrast, the serpent in the form of the "plumed serpent" functions as the positive symbol of Quetzalcoatl. It is ironic that the

American narrator of *Xicoténcatl* unconsciously supports the European ideology he wants to reject.

27. *Xicoténcatl*, p. 106: "Hay casos en que toda la prudencia de un hombre honrado no puede impedir que lo arrastre el torrente de la fatalidad."

28. Ibid., p. 106: "El cuarto era tan pequeño y sin luz; se tenían que hablar tan de cerca para no ser oídos; Ordaz era joven; Doña Marina era hermosa y amable, y . . . Un tardo desengaño vino a sacar al honrado Ordaz de su letargo para cubrirlo de vergüenza. '¡Intrigante y seductora mujer!' le dijo. 'Al fin has abusado de la honradez de Diego de Ordaz. Abrame la puerta, que prefiero exponer a mil peligros mi vida a la vergonzosa situación a que me has arrastrado.'"

29. Ibid., p. 118: "Felizmente para Ordaz todo esto no era más que sospechas que quedaron desvanecidas a la época del parto de Doña Marina, y entonces conoció que esta intriganta llevaba en su seno el fruto de sus amores con Hernán Cortés la noche de su galante aventura."

30. See note 14 above, which refers to the Enlightenment. The narrator's ideas, reflective of the Enlightenment, are attributed in the novel to Ordaz with regard to education and elsewhere with regard to politics. See the peroration directed to Father Bartolomé de Olmedo in the novel, pp. 108–109.

31. Ibid., p. 11: "'¿Eres,' le dijo él, 'todavía americana? ¿Arde aún en tu pecho la llama del amor patrio? ¿O bien te han corrompido y contaminado las artes mágicas de esos hombres que transtornan todas las ideas de lo justo y de lo injusto, de lo bueno y de lo malo?'"

32. Ibid., p. 114: "ser útil a los míos, y expiar con mi conducta posterior las apariencias criminales que hoy tiene mi vida."

33. Ibid., p. 118: "sin apoyo, sin defensores, sin amigos, sin parientes, sola y abandonada de todo el mundo."

34. Ibid., p. 116: "está muy querida entre los extranjeros, lo que en verdad no es la mejor recomendación."

35. Ibid., p. 116: "el bravo tlaxcalteca cayó poco a poco en las redes de su astuta y hábil compatriota. . . . Sin dejar de amar a su Teutila se enamoró de las gracias con que Doña Marina se había embellecido en su trato con los europeos."

36. Ibid., p. 116: "pues ella puede muy bien ser una mujer virtuosa que sepa sacar partido de su desgracia."

37. Ibid., p. 117: "¿Es posible tanta perfidia, y tanta doblez, y tanta falsedad, y tanto arte, y tanta infamia? Esa americana indigna, hija espúrea de estas sencillas regiones, mil veces más detestable que sus corruptores, ha abusado indignamente de la franqueza de mi corazón."

38. Ibid., p. 117: "[en su] seno lleva el fruto de su amor criminal."

39. Ibid., p. 117: "indigna prostituida"; p. 137: "una serpiente tan venenosa."

40. Ibid., p. 118: "La perfidia unida a la franqueza, el vicio a la virtud, el envilecimiento a la nobleza."

41. Ibid., p. 119: "su fiel Marina luchando en la cama con los dolores que le causa el fruto de su amor, vela sobre sus intereses cuando quizá él busca otras nuevas rivales con quien repartir sus caricias."

42. Ibid., p. 134: "las artes de la corrupción europea."

43. Ibid., p. 139: "esta americana hubiera podido ser una mujer apreciable sin la corrupción a que se la adiestró desde que se reunió a los españoles."

44. Xicotencatl the Elder is made to worry about the health of his nation, calling the traitorous acts of Magiscatzin "the first symptom that threatened the health of his nation" ("vio en el crimen de Magiscatzin el primer síntoma que amenazaba a la salud de su patria" (p. 111). The traitorous crime of Magiscatzin is also called "patricide" (p. 111), and for his corruption he is made to fall sick and die.

45. Ann M. Pescatello mentions that official church doctrine required that an Indian woman become a Christian before having sexual intercourse with a Spaniard (*Power and Pawn*, p. 135).

46. *Xicoténcatl*, p. 127: "Pueblos! Si amáis vuestra libertad, reunid vuestros intereses y vuestras fuerzas y aprended de una vez que, si no hay poder que no se estrelle cuando choca contra la inmensa fuerza de vuestra unión, tampoco hay enemigo tan débil que no os venza y esclavice cuando os falta aquélla. Tlaxcala es un ejemplo palpable de esta verdad."

47. Ibid., p. 127: "El gobierno de uno solo no me parece soportable. . . . Este gobierno tiene para mí el grande inconveniente de la natural propensión del hombre a abusar del poder, y, cuando el poder de uno solo domina, no hay más leyes que su voluntad. ¡Desgraciado el pueblo cuya dicha depende de las virtudes de un hombre solo!"

48. Nicholson, *The X*, p. 104.

49. Ibid., p. 103.

50. Hugh Harter, *Gertrudis Gómez de Avellaneda*, p. 173.

51. Ibid., pp. 150–151.

52. Gertrudis Gómez de Avellaneda, *Guatimozín*, p. 442: "yo no soy más que eso: una mujer loca de amor por ti."

53. My discussion of historical events is based on readings from a number of sources, in particular from Meyer and Sherman's *The Course of Mexican History* and Fehrenback's *Fire and Blood*. For his role as a moderating force in the invasion, General Prim was remembered kindly by Ireneo Paz, as noted in chapter 5 (see especially n. 4). For further information on the French presence, see Jack Dabbs, *The French Army in Mexico City, 1861–1867*.

54. Ralph E. Warner, *Historia de la novela mexicana en el siglo XIX*, p. 104: "Añádase a todo ello la terminación de una intervención extranjera con el éxito de las armas mexicanas y la reafirmación del espíritu nacional como resultado de la cooperación necesaria para echar las tropas de Napoleón, y no sorprenderá a nadie que surjan estos novelistas de asuntos mexicanos."

55. Ibid., pp. 29–30.

56. *Los mártires*, p. 514: "Su sistema era el terror"; p. 515: "aquel envilecido monarca."

57. Castro Leal, *La novela*, p. 13.

58. *Xicoténcatl*, p. 99: "una americana . . . que después de varios accidentes de fortuna, vino a ser esclava del cacique de Tabasco."

59. *Los mártires*, p. 413: "Cuando esa niña llegue a la adolescencia amará al mayor enemigo de nuestra raza. Este amor la arrastrará a renegar de los dioses, a vender a sus hermanos y a entregar su patria al extranjero."

60. Gutierre Tibón, *Historia*, pp. 537–538: "No creo que alguien haya observado hasta ahora que la Malinal Xochitl mitológica es llamada también Malintzin. . . . Ella es hermana de los hombres-estrellas y única hembra entre los astros . . . llamada en forma abreviada y reverencial Malintzin (como la Malinche, única hembra entre los conquistadores." ("I don't believe that anyone has noticed until now that the mythological Malinal Xochitl is also called Malintzin. . . . She is the sister of the men-stars and the only female among the stars, called in a shortened but reverential form Malintzin, like La Malinche, the only woman among the conquistadors.")

61. María Rodríguez, *La mujer azteca*, pp. 62–68.

62. *Los mártires*, p. 416: "ha de amar a un enemigo de nuestro pueblo y vender por ese amor a sus hermanos y a su patria."

63. Ibid., p. 475: "Era que la joven azteca había creído escuchar al mismo tiempo otra voz que se levantaba del fondo de su consciencia y le decía: 'Y el Anáhuac te maldecirá [sic] eternamente por la traición con que acabas de mancharte.'"

64. Ibid., p. 476: "Y en efecto, se había obrado un milagro en Marina no por el Dios de los cristianos, que probablemente no miraría con muy buenos ojos aquella cruzada de terror y destrucción, sino por ese dios niño que la mitología griega representaba con los ojos vendados y a que se da el nombre de amor."

65. Ibid., p. 443: "Los guerreros que navegan en esas grandes piraguas son los que han de someter el Anáhuac por medio de las armas y destruir el culto de los dioses. . . . Cuando los sacerdotes de esos hombres promulguen el baño sagrado, tú serás la primera que lo reciba, y la que arrastrará en pos de sí a todos los aztecas."

66. Ibid., p. 509: "Si no fuera sobrenatural el poder que ejercen sobre nosotros los hombres blancos del Oriente, ¿cómo hubieran podido conducir preso, en medio de su pueblo, al señor de tan vastos dominios?"

67. Ibid., p. 540: "El extranjero era el hijo predilecto de los dioses y ellos sin duda habían hecho emigrar el narcótico al vaso de la infeliz azteca."

68. Ibid., p. 467: "'Desgraciado Anáhuac,' prorrumpió Tizoc con acento profético, 'si la valerosa república de Tlaxcala tiende los brazos al enemigo común de nuestra raza.'"

69. Ibid., p. 503: "A pesar del color de tu semblante, más pareces compatriota de los hombres blancos del Oriente que de los cobrizos aztecas. Ayudas a los extranjeros en sus iniquidades . . . y aún se asegura que tú has tenido la culpa de la sangre azteca que se ha derramado en Cholula. Has adoptado una patria que no es la tuya y has renegado del Anáhuac, que te vio nacer."

70. Ibid., p. 554: "aquellos hombres que eran absueltos por un sacerdote cristiano habían saqueado pocos meses antes los tesoros de Motecuzoma, habían violado a las vírgenes del Anáhuac y habían manchado sus manos con la sangre de las víctimas indefensas de Cholula."

5. Doña Marina Recast:
From the Postintervention Period to 1950

1. For further information relating to the Juárez years and the nineteenth century in general, see Walter Scholes, *Mexican Politics during the Juárez Regime.* See also Robert J. Knowlton, "Recent Historical Works on Nineteenth-Century Mexico," and Stephen R. Niblo and Laurens B. Perry, "Recent Additions to Nineteenth-Century Mexican Historiography."

2. Paz states his purpose explicitly in the foreword to his first novel to deal with the conquest, *Amor y suplicio:* "When [the author] made a study of the history of Mexico, he reunited the episodes of the conquest that seemed to be of most interest to him" and would enable his countrymen to "shed a tear for their ancestors." Elsewhere in the text he also refers to his objectives in some of his direct addresses to his readers. (The original Spanish of *Amor y suplicio* will be preceded by *AS* in the notes.)

3. Keen's discussion in *The Aztec Image*, pp. 416–419, is valuable in the way it describes the spectrum of attitudes among the Porfiristas (supporters of Porfirio Díaz during his dictatorship from 1876–1910). Although the policies of the Porfirista government were decidedly *malinchista*, that is, favoring foreign interests against the Indians, some scholars were able to turn their attention to the Indians of the pre-Hispanic period.

4. *AS*, pp. 157–158: "resucitar rencores que ya están extinguidos desde que el ilustre general Prim vino a decir a México que España no era su madrastra sino su digna madre." See chapter 4 for other uses of familial metaphors as well as references to the foreign intervention in which General Prim (1814–1870) played a role. A military and political leader, he was a powerful figure in mid-nineteenth-century Spanish politics, especially in the Revolution of 1868 that resulted in the dethronement of Isabel II. Prim made himself popular in Mexico at the time he was in command of the joint Spanish, English, and French expedition of 1861 by appearing to respond to Mexican concerns.

5. *AS*, p. 157: "Y si tenemos una palabra de perdón y de olvido para los españoles de hace tres siglos que vinieron a martirizar a nuestros abuelos, ¿cómo no la hemos de tener fraternidad para los republicanos de ahora que nos instruyen con sus obras, que nos electrizan con su palabra y que se colocan a la cabeza de la civilización europea?"

6. Lafaye, *Quetzalcoatl and Guadalupe*, trans. Benjamin Keen, p. 9.

7. Otila may be a name invented by Paz. In other texts, for example, J. Jesús Figueroa Torres's biography *Doña Marina: Una india ejemplar*, the daughter of Maxixcatzin is referred to by the Spanish name Doña Elvira.

8. *AS*, p. 99: "¡qué mal haces con proteger así a un enemigo! Aborreces a los que han nacido a tu lado, a los que han respirado una misma brisa. . . . Odias a tus hermanos ¡y amas a un extranjero!"

9. *AS*, pp. 123–124: "para ti abandonaría padre, pariente, patria, deberes y cuánto hay demás santo en este suelo." The explanation given by the author for this unnatural state, in which a woman is willing to abandon her homeland for another and which causes her tribe to go mad with jealousy, is

based on the egotism of love: "Love makes the heart more egotistical than it naturally is. A person controlled by passion acts crazy" (p. 103: "El amor hace al corazón egoísta más de lo que lo es naturalmente. Una persona presa de las pasiones es igual a un loco"). The narrator also calls Xicotencatl mad with love, which implies that it may affect both men and women. Guatimozin is also called "loco."

10. *AS*, p. 130: "¿Cómo, pues, había Otila de vacilar entre un compatriota y un amante? No la juzguemos con severidad, amaba y amaba con toda la fuerza de sus diez y ocho años."

11. *AS*, p. 106: "Estar enamorado de Otila era tanto como querer lo imposible. Los odios que existían entre los dos pueblos eran irreconciliables, y primero se prestaría Maxixcatzín a matar a su hija que a entregarla al guerrero mexicano."

12. *AS*, pp. 57–58: "Así es, hijo querido, que mientras vivas no permitas jamás que un solo hombre usurpe el poder de todo tu pueblo, y menos permitas una dominación extranjera."

13. *AS*, p. 106: "la alianza que le había ofrecido Guatimozín, asunto de tanta importancia para ambas naciones y que sólo podría llevarse a cabo por el enlace de su hija con el mexicano, pendía sólo de éste, y si perecía, todas sus esperanzas de paz y de progreso para su patria quedaban destruidas."

14. *AS*, p. 127: "'No olvides,' continuó el anciano, 'que tenemos hecho un pacto de alianza que debemos cumplir cuando tengamos posibilidad de hacerlo.'

'No solo no lo olvido, sino que no me ocuparé de otra cosa desde que llegue a mi patria; pero tú no olvides tampoco que amo a tu hija y que ella debe anudar más la amistad entre nosotros. Es el precio de nuestra alianza!'"

15. *AS*, p. 169: "sois dueño de una rica joya."

16. *AS*, p. 193: "Creo que no habrá ningún conquistador con mejor fortuna."

17. *AS*, p. 202: "para más afianzar nuestra alianza, quisiera que nos proporcionarais algunas mujeres. Ya sabéis que los vencidos tienen el deber de poner sus mujeres a las ordenes del vencedor." (Paz's Cortés sounds like a cultural anthropologist in this discourse.)

18. Pescatello, *Power and Pawn*, pp. 126, 134.

19. *AS*, p. 171: "más que un hombre me ha parecido un dios. ¿No es verdad que es hermoso?"

20. When Paz describes the Indians' first encounter with the Spaniards, he says they appeared to them as "celestial visions" (*AS*, p. 156: "visiones celestes").

21. *AS*, p. 184: "Vámonos a mi Castilla / Donde cristianos seremos"; *AS*, p. 185: "religioso extasis . . . en el idioma de los dioses." The religious theme is also developed in other ways. Guatimozin expresses doubts about the efficacy of his own gods and foreshadows the teachings of the Christians in his comments: "¿Quién sabe si los dioses no serán más sabios que nosotros para explicar esos misterios? Tal vez un Dios más grande que gobierna a los que conocemos, oculta aún de ellos mismos la causa del

orden inmutable que se observa en esa creación maravillosa" (*AS*, p. 116).

22. *AS*, p. 194: "tez cobriza . . . trajes de pluma . . . más bello y más noble porque era descendiente de reyes."

23. *AS*, p. 182: "[el] blanco que . . . me ha quitado el sueño"; *AS*, p. 194: "Velázquez se presentó luego a su vista y quedó deslumbrada. Entonces sus ensueños venían a ser realizados con más perfección."

24. Count Gobineau (1816–1882) produced a four-volume *Sur l'inégalité des races humaines* (1853–1855), translated by Adrian Collins as *Inequality of Human Races*, in which he not only proclaimed the superiority of the white over the "colored" races but associated civilization and "godlike" reason with the white race. He influenced many others, as documented by Keen in his discussion of the influence of Gobineau's ideas on the study of the Aztec world; see *The Aztec Image*, pp. 437–438. Count Gobineau, it should be noted, lived in Brazil for a while when he was French envoy in Rio de Janeiro, and his racist ideas traveled with him to the New World.

25. Earlier, Maxixcatzin had likened the love relation between his daughter and Guatimozin to a political pact that would bring peace and progress to his nation: "La alianza que le había ofrecido Guatimozín, asunto de tanta importancia para ambas naciones y que sólo podría llevarse a cabo por el enlace de su hija con el mexicano, pendía sólo de éste, y si perecía, todas sus esperanzas de paz y de progreso para su patria quedaban destruidas" (*AS*, p. 106).

26. *AS*, p. 197: "Guatimozín no volverá a verme nunca, se dijo, hay entre los dos un abismo que ni él ni yo podemos salvar. Su nación y la mía se aborrecen. En México hay princesas hermosas y él será más feliz casándose con una mexicana. . . . Es una locura este amor entre ambos. Pero ¿debo amar a este extranjero? ¿Me ama él a mí? Yo lo preguntaré a los augures. . . . los dioses serán los que dispongan del porvenir de la hija de Maxixcatzín."

27. "I have seen our huts burned by your warriors . . . our fields covered with cadavers and thousands of widows mourning the death of their husbands. I have heard the cries of vengeance that our unhappy orphans have sworn against your people." (*AS*, pp. 124–125: "He visto nuestras chozas encendidas por tus guerreros, porque he visto nuestros campos cubiertos de cadáveres y a millares de viudas llorando la muerte de sus esposos, he oído los juramentos de venganza que han pronunciado los infelices huérfanos contra tu pueblo.")

28. *AS*, p. 128: "Quizás alguna vez será tu reino grande y floreciente; pero es necesario para esto que concluya la tiránica opresión con que domina a todos los pueblos que se te ame y no los que se te tema. Gobierna con dulzura y dispondrás de un poderoso imperio."

29. *Doña Marina*, vol. 1, p. 25: "¡Parece una diosa! ¡Esta no es una hermosura de la tierra, sino que es un encanto sobrenatural!" (Hereafter all references to this novel will use *DM1* for the first volume and *DM2* for the second volume.)

30. It is interesting that by calling her a goddess, Paz echoes some of the references in the chronicles as well as the Indian belief in the goddess Ma-

linal Xochitl, with whom La Malinche shares a name. Prescott notes that the Indians considered her as "beautiful as a goddess," and that the Spanish playwright Moratín in *Las naves de Cortés* is also favorable to Doña Marina (*History of the Conquest of Mexico*, p. 163, n.4). For a full discussion of the relationships between La Malinche and other Mexican figures, see Tibón's *Historia del nombre y de la fundación de México*, pp. 541–550. Tibón's text reminds us that in the early years of the conquest, "La Malinche was not considered a simple mortal but a goddess" (p. 541: "la Malinche no fue considerada una simple mortal, sino una diosa").

31. *DMI*, p. 26: "el artista que la formó fue el autor de toda la naturaleza."

32. The humanity of the Indians was a grave point of contention, conditioned by economic interests as much as by theological considerations. The missionaries championed the "humanity" of the Indians while the conquistadors often sought to identify them as nonhuman monsters, all the better to exploit their labor. See the summary of the debate in Lafaye, *Quetzalcoatl and Guadalupe*, pp. 38–40.

33. *DMI*, pp. 26–27: "Cuando Marina se proponía luchar, luchaba hasta el fin sin temor a nada ni a nadie, hasta vencer o ser vencida; pero ella jamás dejaba solamente comenzadas sus femeniles y a veces varoniles empresas." The attribution of manly valor to Marina echoes one of the characteristics attributed to the Aztec goddess Malinal Xochitl, who is described as "manly" ("varonil"), according to Tibón (*Historia del nombre y de la fundación de México*, pp. 541–550).

34. Although Paz appears to follow Bernal Díaz in referring to La Malinche's "manly valor," this aspect of the paradigm seems not to have been continued into the modern period. For example, as I note in chapter 8, Adelaida Del Castillo believes that Doña Marina was never associated with manly attributes.

35. *DMI*, p. 27: "Marina, como si no hubiera tenido que soportar las mismas fatigas y privaciones, se ocupaba de curar a los enfermos, de dar de comer a los que tenían hambre, de reanimar el espíritu a los que daban muestras de estar desalentados. Su buen corazón estaba dispuesto a interceder una gracia por el que había merecido algún castigo, lo mismo que a interponer todos los recursos imaginables para salvar la vida de los prisioneros."

36. *DMI*, p. 252: "Por más feroz que fuera Cortés, se había humanizado hasta donde le era posible humanizarse, ante las lágrimas y el empeño de doña Marina." Doña Isabel also expresses the idea that, although Cortés is considered "stubborn" (p. 253: "testarudo"), he will "do whatever Marina asks of him" (p. 253: "hace cuanto le dice Marina"). Cortés had planned to cut off the right hand of Pedro Gallego and the leg of José de Jaramillo, but Marina pleads for leniency for both. Marina considers it a miracle that the punishment has been averted and offers prayers of thanksgiving to the Virgin. She is told by one of the soldiers: "'It has been a true miracle, because the governor was furious with them when he gave me the order, and only because of your intercession could he have revoked it'" (p. 252: "'Ha sido un verdadero milagro, porque el gobernador estaba furioso contra ellos cuando

me dio la orden, y sólo por la intercesión vuestra puede haberla revocado'").
The narrator explains Cortés's change of heart as a direct result of the efforts
of Doña Marina.

37. *DMI*, p. 27: "Este don sirvió mucho a Marina en su papel de intérprete, en multitud de ocasiones, aun tratándose de lenguas que no conocía.
Bastaba que viera ciertas líneas de la fisonomía, los movimentos de la boca,
la expresión de los ojos, para que en el acto se pudiera en posesión de todo
el asunto. Su mirada nunca dejaba de abarcar en un segundo todo los por-
menores de las escenas que se presentaran a su vista."

38. Marina is shown to be personally responsible for thwarting the plan
to assassinate Cortés. It is she who takes the dagger out of the hand of the
royal treasurer Julián de Aldarete as he hides behind a curtain ready to
plunge it into Cortés (*DMI*, pp. 325–326).

39. *DMI*, p. 247: "el hombre que la había sacado de la esclavitud para ele-
varla casi hasta su altura."

40. *DMI*, p. 247: "Más feliz soy siendo la sierva de don Hernando que si
fuera la reina de España."

41. *DMI*, pp. 281–282: "Ah exclamó ella dando un ligero grito luego que
entró el conquistador, y procurando cubrirse. Cortés vio bien la desnudez de
su amada por más que ella hubiera andado presurosa en cubrirse, así es que
sin poder contener su impetuosidad, se approximó a ella y la cubrió de besos
en el cuello y en los brazos."

42. *DMI*, p. 282:

"¿Querrías acaso echarme?"

"Si eres mi dueño, señor, y puedes hacer lo que gustes . . ."

"Gracias. . . . Si no se ofende tu pudor, puedes continuar vistiéndose
delante de mí . . . entretanto hablaremos de negocios."

"Pero hemos de hablar de negocios cuando no dejas de besarme."

"Hace tanto tiempo que no nos vemos, que estoy sediente de tus
caricias."

"Está bien, siéntate allí; pero has de estar juicioso. . . . me lo
prometes?"

"Te lo prometo."

43. *DMI*, p. 282: "¿no recuerdas ya que soy mujer de campaña?"

44. *DMI*, pp. 282–283: "No olvido nunca que antes y después de los
combates, cuando hemos tenido que andar toda una noche o que huir por
entre las montañas, tú siempre te nos has presentado aseada en tu traje, con
tu semblante reluciente . . . con tus dientes brillantes como el marfil y esto
ha llenado de grande admiración a todos."

45. The *soldaderas* were more than camp followers, for they not only
provided feminine companionship but actually served in the ranks as well
as being nurses, cooks, food preparers, etc. See Castellanos's re-creation of
the famous Adelita in *El eterno femenino*, as well as the comments of Jesusa
Palancares in *Hasta no verte Jesús mío* by Elena Poniatowska. For a discussion of the corridos, see Merle E. Simmons, *The Mexican Corrido as a
Source of Interpretive Study of Modern Mexico 1870–1950*. María Herrera-

Sobek, *The Mexican Corrido: A Feminist Analysis* (pp. 84–116) offers many useful insights regarding the *soldadera*'s origin, although she does not refer to La Malinche in this regard.

46. *DMI*, p. 283: "Tú perteneces a una raza muy distinta de la de las mexicas."

47. *DMI*, p. 283: "Yo soy discreta y sabia contigo, porque te amo; tú me encuentras graciosa y llena de encantos, porque me amas. . . . ¿Qué milagros no hace el amor?"

48. Rodríguez, *Doña Marina*, p. 50. Paz anticipates this idea, for he has Doña Marina show her unswerving love for Cortés long after she has been married to Jaramillo. Her confession occurs when she hears that Cortés has remarried in Spain, at the very end of the novel.

49. Figueroa Torres, *Doña Marina*, p. 93. Paz appears to have based his narrative on the historical fact that Tecuichpuic was married at one time to a Don Pedro Gallejo.

50. *DMI*, p. 228: "construiremos una cabaña y formaremos nuestro reino."

51. *DMI*, p. 229: 'Llevo un hijo del Malinche en las entrañas.'"

52. *DMI*, p. 380: "aún sin ser amado de Marina, había pensado ya mil veces en hundir su arma más constante en el seno de su aborrecido rival."

53. *DMI*, p. 391: "concluyendo de esta triste suerte, con el último varon de aquella raza, el alto linaje de los emperadores mexicanos." Paz takes advantage of the assassination of Cuautlizin to make a connection between the events of the conquest and those of his own period. He makes use of it to rail against the "barbarie" and political assassinations that have taken place in the narrator's own lifetime (*DMI*, p. 379). In commenting that with the death of Cuauhtlizin the line of noble Aztecs dies, the narrator/Paz seems to equate the fictional Cuauhtlizin with the historical Cuauhtemoc, the last emperor of the Aztecs. Cuauhtemoc, under the name Guatimozin, had already appeared in fictional form in *Amor y suplicio*.

54. *DMI*, p. 383: "'¿Qué diantres tendrá Marina, que es una mujer tan peligrosa?' 'Yo no sé pero el caso es que tiene atractivos para todos los hombres.'"

55. Her part in the massacre of Indians at Cholula was clearly for Marina a controversial role that has been interpreted in different ways. Paz does not include any reference to the incident, but Marina's actions with regard to Cuautlizin in contrast to her support of Jaramillo show her distance from the Indian cause.

56. *DMI*, p. 385: "entonces es claro que D. Hernando está celoso de un príncipe aturdido e ignorante."

57. *DMI*, p. 223: "Yo, como tú sabes, no soy libre, pertenezco a un español, pero ni así quiero que se derrame la sangre de mis hermanos, ni así quiero que haya entre los españoles quien toque un pelo de tu cabeza. No podré ser tuya porque soy de otro, pero te lo juro, príncipe, si no amara a Hernán Cortés, no amaría a otro hombre más que a ti en el mundo."

58. *DMI*, p. 386: "¡Ah! no, jamás ni por compasión amaría más a Cuauhtli-

zín que a Jaramillo, ni a Jaramillo más que a Cortés. ¡Si este hombre es mi Dios!"

59. *DM1*, p. 230: "Aunque nunca he pedido gracia ninguna para los españoles, sino siempre para los de mi raza, por tratarse de ti, voy a hablar a don Hernando."

60. *DM1*, p. 247: "al revés de los demás españoles, [Jaramillo] la trataba siempre con finura y con distinción."

61. Jaramillo explains that he had been loyal to Cortés but had joined the rebels because of his love for La Malinche: "'Por vos, Marina, yo que he sido y podría seguir siendo el más humilde vasallo de Cortés, me he unido con sus enemigos que querían matarlo'" (*DM1*, p. 258).

62. See the review of the various opinions/controversies surrounding the marriage of Marina to Jaramillo that Somonte offers (*Doña Marina,* pp. 75–83).

63. Somonte, p. 69 and passim; compare Pescatello's observation that "it was customary among Aztec aristocracy for the emperor to bequeath his concubines as wives to his loyal captains and chieftains" (*Power and Pawn,* p. 126).

64. *DM1*, p. 260: "Al escuchar ese nombre, se puso horriblemente pálida y dijo con voz débil: 'Don Hernando nunca ha querido confesarme eso pero lo he sabido.' 'Cortés la ha llamado?' 'Cortés ha dado orden secretamente a todos los oficiales que tengan en España, o en las islas españolas, para que las traigan, dando él, primero que nadie, el ejemplo. A la vez ha mandado que se flete una embarcación por su cuenta para que traiga a todas las mujeres europeas que quieran venirse a formar la colonia.'" The information that Cortés has secretly sent for his wife contradicts Bernal Díaz, who reports that the leader was not pleased to see her and considered her arrival in Mexico a surprise (*Historia verdadera*, ch. 160, p. 413; see also Johnson, *Women in Colonial Spanish American Literature*, p. 19).

65. *DM1*, p. 247: "yo no soy de otro, ni puedo ser de otros más que de Hernán Cortés. Es mi vida, es la mitad de mi alma, es mi adoración."

66. There is much controversy surrounding Cortés's attitude toward his wife Doña Catalina Juárez. Even Las Casas, no apologist for Cortés, says that they had lived happily for a time (*Historia*, p. 134), yet Bernal Díaz states that her coming to Mexico was not pleasing to Cortés (*Historia verdadera*, chap. 160). Her death within three months of arrival provoked a scandal; Paz makes it appear even more suspicious by placing it even closer to her arrival. Prescott tries to be impartial and notes that most Spanish sources do not give credence to the accusation that Cortés caused her death, although Mexicans show their dislike of Cortés by keeping the accusations a current topic even in the nineteenth century (pp. 668–669, n.2). The longevity of the charges is evidenced by Fuentes's inclusion of these references in *Todos los gatos son pardos.*

67. *DM1*, p. 397: "Necesito arreglar cuanto antes mi casamiento con ese joven que tiene un nombre limpio con que cubrir el del hijo de Hernán Cortés. Mejor que sea éste su padre y no un asesino . . .'"

68. See chapter 3, which summarizes the narratives of Bernal Díaz and Gómara. Gómara's introduction of Doña Marina states that she was born of wealthy parents (verifying her nobility) but she had been stolen during a war and sold into slavery. Prescott prefers to follow the story of Bernal Díaz, as do most Mexican historians, mentioning that her "infamous mother sold her to some foreign traders . . . in order to secure her inheritance for a younger brother" (p. 651).

69. *DM2*, p. 452: "Mi madre debió haberse resistido mucho a cometer acción tan villana, porque casi todas las mañanas la veía yo con los ojos llorosos."

70. *DM2*, p. 455.

71. *DM2*, p. 455: "una mujer honesta que sólo ha delinquido llevada por la fatalidad."

72. *DM1*, pp. 246–247: "Y luego cuando se ponía a hacer comparaciones entre los dos hombres que le habían declarado su pasión, entre Cuauhtlizín y José de Jaramillo, encontraba siempre a éste más hermoso, más noble, más inteligente, más varonil, y sobre todo, más civilizado. Cuauhtlizín no podía ofrecerle otra cosa que un amor salvaje; para amarlo a él, necesitaba despojarse de sus galas que le había traído la poca ilustración aprendida, y volver a tomar la corteza de la barbarie; necesitaba huir de los españoles quienes eran una parte de su vida y cuyas costumbres eran ya las suyas; necesitaba abandonar la religión del verdadero Dios que era en su corazón una creencia arraigada; necesitaba, por último, remontarse a los montes como las fieras y desterrarse para siempre de todo lo que ahora formaba sus gustos y sus necesidades. José Jaramillo halagaba más sus aspiraciones. Poderse presentar de igual a igual enfrente de los españoles, salir de su condición de fiera, para ser la ama de su casa como mujer libre, estar en aptitud de conocer las costas europeas viajando por ellas a lado de su marido . . . todo esto formaba para ella un ideal en sus horas de recogimiento."

73. The Porfirista positivists considered the abundance of Indian blood in Mexico a matter of concern, particularly under the impact of European racist ideas as conceived by Count Gobineau as well as by Vacher de Lapouge, Houston Chamberlain, and others. For specific observations on Mexico, see Martin B. Stabb, "Indigenism and Racism in Mexican Thought, 1857–1911." Also important is the work of Magnus Mörner, "Historical Research on Race Relations in Latin America during the National Period," *Race and Class in Latin America* (pp. 199–230), as well as his own book, *Race Mixture in the History of Latin America.*

74. *DM2*, p. 452: "la índole de una obra de esta naturaleza."

75. According to most accounts of the period, turbulence and political chaos marked the nineteenth century. Meyer and Sherman comment: "In 1876 Díaz inherited an empty treasury, a long list of foreign debts, and a huge bureaucratic corps whose salaries were in arrears. Mexico's credit rating abroad was abominable, and her politics had become somewhat of a joke in Europe" (p. 432). Just as Díaz attempted to make Mexico an acceptable political and economic entity in the eyes of the world market, novelists

such as Ireneo Paz also attempted to civilize the Indian aspect of Mexico and render the culture socially acceptable according to European standards.

76. The idea of woman as a metaphor for land can be considered a cliché today; texts that use this metaphor are legion, as Doris Sommer points out in her perceptive article on nineteenth-century texts, "Not Just Any Narrative: How Romance Can Love Us to Death."

77. Consult Keen, *The Aztec Image*, chs. 14 and 15, for references to other figures of the conquest in the literary texts of the early twentieth century.

78. Although these texts are favorable toward Doña Marina, they censure the actions of Cortés, especially with regard to his amorous entanglements. For example, in contrast to Ireneo Paz's narrative, which has Doña Isabel, Moctezuma's daughter, fall in love at first sight with Pedro Gallego, Figueroa Torres claims that her first Spanish lover was Cortés, with whom she had a child (*Doña Marina*, p. 93). He attributes Cortés's torture and assassination of Cuauhtemoc to the conquistador's interest in Cuauhtemoc's betrothed: "so in love was Cortés with Doña Isabel—whose father had betrothed her to Cuauhtemoc—that the conqueror, under the pretext of an Indian uprising, ordered the hanging of his rival in love, [an act that demonstrated] a most horrible crime of passion" (p. 82: "pues tan el enamoramiento que mostraba Cortés por doña Isabel de Moctezuma—que su padre había comprometido en matrimonio con el joven Cuauhtémoc—que el conquistador, pretextando una sublevación de los indios, mandó ahorcar a su rival en amores en el más horrendo crimen pasional").

79. As noted in earlier chapters, the facts of La Malinche's birth, birthplace, and death are in dispute. Gómez de Orozco declares that it is impossible to be certain (pp. 181–182, n.9), while Rodríguez places her birth in 1505 (p. 20).

80. Rodríguez, *Doña Marina*, p. 21: "¡No! La amó toda su vida como lo demostraremos más tarde, y fue correspondido por ella con tremendo y sincero amor."

81. Ibid., p. 42. Ireneo Paz had already anticipated this idea, for he has Doña Marina express her unswerving love for Cortés long after she has been married to Jaramillo. Her confession of loyal devotion is prompted by the knowledge that he has remarried in Spain and is narrated at the very end of the novel.

82. Ibid., p. 29: "por el amor que entonces se profesaban ambos."

83. Ibid., p. 29: "lleno de contento Cortés y los soldados"; Bernal Díaz: "how glad we were to see our Doña Marina" (*Conquest*, p. 302).

84. Ibid., p. 30.

85. Fernández de Velasco, "La importancia," p. 147: "Hablar dignamente de doña Marina y de lo que significa para nosotros, es empresa difícil y arriesgada. . . . Parece imposible que tratándose de un personaje tan importante en la conquista de México, casi nada se sepa de doña Marina."

86. Fernández de Velasco comments on the novelistic aspect of her life ("lo novelesco de su vida") and suggests that her life offers a human docu-

ment and a historical element of a superior category ("documento humano y elemento histórico de orden superior") (ibid., p. 148).

87. The image of La Malinche found in the discourse of popular culture merits further analysis and is an undertaking I have begun as a result of this study.

88. Keen, *The Aztec Image*, p. 528.

89. Ibid., p. 531.

90. Kemp's translation of this together with some of Paz's later essays is now reprinted in *The Labyrinth of Solitude*. My discussion of Paz's ideas is based on the Spanish text of "Los hijos de la Malinche," but I will use Kemp's translations. The reader should be warned, however, that *hijos* can be translated as "children" as well as "sons." Kemp uses the masculine term because, in accordance with Paz's perspective in the essay, his focus of concern is the males, not the women of Mexico; the latter are objects, the "other," and not thinking subjects. See Del Castillo, "Malintzin Tenépal," for a feminist critique of Paz's essay, esp. pp. 143–146.

91. *Labyrinth*, p. 78; from the Spanish edition: "Para el mexicano, la vida es una posibilidad de chingar o de ser chingado" (p. 71).

92. *Labyrinth*, p. 82; "Es imposible no advertir la semejanza que guarda la figura del 'macho' con la del conquistador español. Ese es el modelo—más mítico que real—que rige las representaciones que el pueblo mexicano se ha hecho de los poderosos: caciques, señores feudales, hacendados, políticos, generales, capitanes de industria. Todos ellos son 'machos' 'chingones'" (p. 74). In Constance Sullivan's informative overview, "*Macho* and *Machismo* as Loan Words to American English," she notes that "Latin American culture, most importantly Mexican culture, has for years explicitly articulated the values and attitudes of the macho and has a heightened and active awareness of what a macho is" (p. 48).

93. While Paz considers La Malinche to be a more receptive—and therefore more passive—figure than the Virgin, one may disagree with his choice of who is the more passive figure. Indeed, one may agree with Del Castillo that Paz's description of female images emphasizes their vulnerability to the detriment of their possible equality with male images ("Malintzin Tenépal," pp. 143–146).

94. *Labyrinth*, p. 87; "La extraña permanencia de Cortés y de La Malinche en la imaginación y en la sensibilidad de los mexicanos actuales revela que son algo más que figuras históricas: son símbolos de un conflicto secreto, que aún no hemos resuelto" (p. 78).

95. *Labyrinth*, p. 86; "El símbolo de la entrega es doña Malinche, la amante de Cortés. . . . Doña Marina se ha convertido en una figura que representa a las indias, fascinadas, violadas o seducidas por los españoles" (pp. 77–78).

96. *Labyrinth*, p. 86; "Es verdad que ella se da voluntariamente al conquistador" (p. 77).

97. Refer to the discussion of slavery in the Aztec world in chapter 2. Likewise compare the kind of excuse she provides for herself in Salvador Novo's play, discussed in chapter 6, whose text, for all his negative attitudes

toward La Malinche, does acknowledge the importance of her being a slave ("I was banished to Tabasco as a slave and as a slave the Tabascans delivered me to the Spaniards. What else can I do but serve as a slave?").

98. *Labyrinth*, p. 86; "Cuauhtémoc y doña Marina son así dos símbolos antagónicos y complementarios. Y si no es sorprendente el culto que todos profesamos al joven emperador . . . tampoco es extraña la maldición que pesa sobre la Malinche. De ahí el éxito del adjetivo despectivo 'malinchista', recientemente puesto en circulación por los periódicos para denunciar a todos los contagiados por tendencias extranjerizantes. Los malinchistas son los partidarios de que México se abra al exterior: los verdaderos hijos de la Malinche, que es la Chingada en persona" (p. 78).

99. *Labyrinth*, p. 87; "Al repudiar a la Malinche . . . el mexicano rompe sus ligas con el pasado, reniega de su origen y se adentra sólo en la vida histórica" (p. 78). Compare the comment of Salvador Reyes Nevares, who notes also that the contemporary mestizo of Mexico "identifies with the violated element of the conquest, with the indigenous element, but at the same time feels the shame of it" ("se identifica con el elemento violado de la Conquista, con el elemento indígena representado por la Malinche, pero a la vez se averigüenza de él") ("El machismo mexicano," p. 16).

100. I believe it is important to point out that in one tradition, the more popular and more promulgated, La Malinche and Cortés are the figures who comprise the founding couple: Another tradition, which is gaining adherents, considers the founding couple of the mestizo to be Gonzalo Guerrero and his Mayan wife, as I observed in chapter 1. By rejecting reunion with his Spanish company and choosing instead to identify with Amerindian culture, Guerrero represents the polar paradigm to that of La Malinche in popular culture.

6. La Malinche on Stage

1. Frank Dauster, "La generación de 1924: El dilema del realismo," p. 18: "tantas veces vilipendiados por su supuesto antinacionalismo." For a discussion of the Ulises Group in the theater, see Dauster's *Xavier Villaurrutia*.

2. Usigli's *Corona de sombra* (written 1943, produced 1947; Crown of shadows) deals with the presence and meaning of the Maximilian and Carlota monarchy in Mexico, the stimulus for Mexican political independence according to his interpretation. *Corona de luz* (1963; Crown of light) offers Usigli's version of the miracle of the appearance of the Virgin of Guadalupe, which for him initiated Mexico's spiritual independence. *Corona de fuego* (1960; Crown of fire) then describes the beginning of Mexican nationhood and its relationship to its Spanish roots.

3. Dauster, "La generación," p. 21: "para Usigli lo principal no es la verdad del detalle histórico sino su importancia en el desarrollo del concepto de la nacionalidad, verdadero asunto de la trilogía."

4. Hayden White, *Tropics of Discourse*, p. 34.

5. Both his use of historical details and his metaliterary devices have been discussed by Ramón Layera, "Mecanismos de fabulación y mitificación

de la historia en las 'comedias impolíticas' y las *Coronas* de Rodolfo Usigli," and by Denise Di Puccio, "Metatheatrical Histories in *Corona de luz.*"

6. Usigli, "Advertencias" (Notice to the reader) in *Corona de sombra,* p. xv: "[no] el esclavo sino el intérprete del acontecimiento histórico." As an example of his creative use of historical detail, Usigli justifies his inclusion of Father Bartolomé de Las Casas as one of the ecclesiastics in act 2 of *Corona de luz* even though he may not have actually been in Mexico during the time of the action: "I consider Las Casas to be an incomparable theatrical character, so decisive against the conquest and the conquistadors and in support of Mexico" ("Considero a Las Casas un personaje teatral incomparable, tan afirmativo en contra de la Conquista y los conquistadores y en pro de México") (*Corona de sombra. Corona de fuego. Corona de luz,* p. 172). This comment anticipates Usigli's negative judgment of the conquistadors' treatment of the Indians, an idea he makes a dramatic part of his play through the anachronistic presence of Las Casas.

7. Usigli, *Corona,* p. 137: According to Lomelí, this *Corona* "synthesizes the chaos of the moment between the two opposing forces (the Spanish and the indigenous) at the same time it projects his vision toward the future, in an attempt to create a country that still does not exist" ("sintetiza el caos del momento entre las dos fuerzas opuestas (la española y la indígena) a la medida que proyecta su visión hacia el futuro en busca de crear un país que todavía no existe") ("Los mitos de la mexicanidad en la trilogía de Rodolfo Usigli," p. 471).

8. Lomelí, "Los mitos," p. 471.

9. Todorov, *The Conquest,* p. 57.

10. Usigli, *Corona,* p. 125: "la misma sangre nos liga y nos enciende." Although Usigli writes in verse form, my translation renders the content only and does not attempt to duplicate meter or rhyme.

11. Ibid., pp. 124–125: "voz impura, voz traidora . . . mancha de aceite de tu raza / que más y más se ensancha cada día."

12. Eugene Nicole, as quoted by Susan D. Cohen, "An Onomastic Double Bind: Colette's *Gigi* and the Politics of Naming," p. 793.

13. Cuauhtemoc calls her Malitzin; Usigli's rendering often omits the *n* usually found in the Indian form of her name.

14. Sapir, "The Anatomy of Metaphor," p. 16.

15. The Mexican chorus's introduction of her connects her active role in events with negative labels: ". . . truchimán La Malintzin / la princesa de espaldas a su raza / cuya voz fue la voz de la denuncia / la voz de la matanza de Cholula . . ." (p. 112). By identifying her as the "voice of the massacre of Cholula," the chorus associates La Malinche with one of the great massacres that anticipated the Spaniards' harsh treatment of all the Indians. The chronicles relate that La Malinche played an important role in the incident at Cholula, where she acted decisively and in favor of the Spaniards. By including a reference to Cholula here, Usigli's Mexican chorus marks her actions in Cholula as a synecdoche for the totality of her conduct in the conquest, associated here with "voice."

16. Usigli, *Corona*, p. 112: "Voz marina engañosa y sibilante / que cambiaste el sonido del idioma / de los tuyos para alterar su pensamiento."

17. Cirlot, *Dictionary*, p. 284.

18. Usigli, *Corona*, p. 112: "pues tus hijos y los que creen / son ecos de esa voz y a la vez son astillas del ahuehuete que amenaza el rayo / y que para hacer cruces raja el hacha española."

19. Ibid., p. 125: "Yo sé lo que es fundir dos mundos en mi sexo / Y saberlo me basta y me exculpa y me salva. / Mi traducción es fiel y declaré verdad."

20. Ibid., p. 131: "una mujer en quien conquista y guerra / fecundaron un vientre endémico y longevo." Malintzin announces to Cuauhtemoc that the children of the women will belong to the one who rules:

... Señor rey,
Yo solo sé que los días son siempre nuevos
como los niños en los vientres longevos,
y que Malinche es hoy quien da la ley. (p. 113)

This comment is a response to Cuauhtemoc's remark that he hopes the "bad dream" of conquest will go away. In the context of that idea, her reply, then, designates the children as belonging to the conqueror.

21. Ibid., p. 129: "increíble, claro mundo nuevo"; p. 125: "mundo que aún no llega."

22. Ibid., p. 129: "Y yo, que pierdo todas las batallas, / sé que habrá de surgir en el futuro / la nación mexicana por que muero."

23. Ibid., p. 129: "Ojalá que en el fruto de tu prole / el mexicano venza al español / y el sentido de México perdure."

24. As noted earlier, Novo wrote a dialogue entitled "Malinche y Carlota," which reiterates the negative attitudes toward La Malinche. Although she is a major persona in the playlet, unlike in *Cuauhtémoc*, Novo does not add any significant nuances to the figure but accentuates, rather, her faithfulness to Cortés. I shall return, however, to his addition of a contemporary political context in relation to my discussion of *Malinche Show* by Willebaldo López in chapter 7.

25. Novo, *Cuauhtémoc*, p. 278:

Malinche: El Capitán me ha encargado que hable contigo. No va a hacerte daño. Su dios es bueno, ¿sabes? Yo ya me he bautizado—y voy a misa, y comulgo, todos los días. . . . ¿Por qué me vuelves la espalda, señor?

Cuauhtémoc: No entiendo tu lengua, Malinche.

Malinche: ¿Hablo mal la lengua de Anáhuac?

Cuauhtémoc: Hablas un lenguaje—que yo no sabré nunca.

26. The varying attributions regarding La Malinche's birthplace and native language originated in the chronicles and have continued through later texts. Bernal Díaz says she was from Painala, but Gómara places her in "Viluta" near Jalisco. Ancona's text labels her Aztec, but here Novo implies that she was not a native speaker of Nahuatl.

27. Novo, *Cuauhtémoc*, p. 282: "Todos a su turno depositan sus más-

caras en el suelo, como si las enterraran y volvieran a surgir, libres de ellas y transformados."

28. Ibid., p. 282: "Y Cuauhtémoc no ha muerto. Sé que está en mí; que vivirá siempre; en mí y en mis hijos—y en todos los que vengan después—a nacer en la tierra de México—formados con los huesos de nuestros muertos—nutridos como el sol con la sangre de nuestros corazones." This speech recalls the last dialogue of the Youth (who calls himself Cuauhtemoc) in Novo's *Cuauhtémoc y Eulalia* (1970). The Eulalia of the title refers to the anthropologist Eulalia Guzmán, well known as an enthusiastic supporter of the Aztec contribution to the Mexican nationality (see Keen, *The Aztec Image*, pp. 468–469).

29. Novo repeats some of the imagery and philosophy regarding the importance of Cuauhtemoc in *Cuauhtémoc y Eulalia*. Eulalia Guzmán referred to Cuitlahuac and Cuauhtemoc as "the seeds of our Mexican nationality" (Keen, *The Aztec Image*, p. 481).

30. Magaña Esquivel, quoted in *Teatro mexicano*, p. 319: "el fuego que todavía arde en torno a la cuestión del llamado 'malinchismo' y del fenómeno de la conquista, donde Cuauhtémoc de un lado, Cortés del otro lado, y la Malinche entre los dos, siguen siendo banderas ideológicas de algunos obcecados."

31. In Novo's play, Ixtolinque informs Cuauhtemoc of the planned torment: "¿Esa hoguera, ves? Hasta aquí llega el humo y el resplandor. Es para ti, Cuauhtémoc. Te van a dar tormento en el fuego hasta que confieses" (*Cuauhtémoc*, p. 280).

32. Salvador Novo shows the similarities between the couples when he pairs La Malinche and Carlota in his dialogue *Malinche y Carlota*. His portrayal of La Malinche as a woman whose passion for Cortés led her to betray her country conforms to the popular version.

33. Nigro, "Rhetoric and History in Three Mexican Plays," p. 67.

34. Figueroa Torres, *Doña Marina*, p. 75: "fue la primera ciudadana, la primera cristiana y la primera mexicana que habló el español, la primera en mezclar su sangre con el conquistador para dar a luz un hijo, elementos que forjaron una patria y una nueva raza."

35. Gorostiza, *La Malinche*, p. 23: "cacica e hija de caciques, y en verdad gran señora, los indios le dicen Malintzin o Malinche en señal de respeto. Nosotros la hemos bautizado con el nombre de doña Marina."

36. Nigro, "Rhetoric," p. 66.

37. Gorostiza, *La Malinche*, p. 340: "¡Mi dios! ¡Mi dios blanco!"; p. 345: "el ángel guardián que Dios me ha dado en esta empresa."

38. Ibid., p. 339:

Cortés: Tu carne apretada y morena que hace temblar a esta carne blanca mía con el mismo deseo y el mismo miedo con que lo hace temblar el misterio de esta tierra que no sé si me reserva el goce o la muerte . . . pero hacia la que yo voy alucinado sin poder hacer nada para impedirlo.

Malinche: Ni tú ni yo podemos impedirlo. Así lo han dispuesto los dioses.

Cortés: ¿Los dioses?

Malinche: Sí. . . . También los míos. Este momento . . . ellos lo anunciaron desde el principio de los siglos. . . . Somos un juguete en sus manos. . . .

39. See chapter 4 regarding the idea of using woman as a metaphor for land; see also Doris Sommer's perceptive article, "Not Just Any Narrative: How Romance Can Love Us to Death." It is interesting to compare the comments of Ernesto Giménez Caballero in *Las mujeres de América;* a Spaniard, he elaborates on the metaphor that America is "mujer" (p. 11) and describes the women of America as "mujer hecha tierra" (p. 15).

40. Gorostiza, *La Malinche,* p. 355: "¡Dios está con nosotros! ¡El nos señala el camino que hemos de seguir en esta tierra tan pródiga y generosa, que ella misma abre su seno y nos brinda los medios para conquistarla!"

41. Ibid., p. 332: "¿Hay algún mal en que una mujer siga a un hombre?"

42. Ibid., p. 363: "si ellas están dispuestas a regresar."

43. Ibid., pp. 371–372: "Sólo tres quisieron regresar. (Con humor.) Así son las mujeres. Lo que hace una, enseguida lo quieren hacer las otras. Ahora todas desean tener un hijo blanco."

44. Sapir, "The Anatomy of Metaphor," p. 14.

45. Gorostiza, *La Malinche,* p. 332: "fui relegada a los de Tabasco en calidad de esclava y en calidad de esclava me han regalado los de Tabasco a los españoles. ¿Qué otra cosa puedo hacer, sino servir como esclava?"

46. Ibid., p. 333: "un militar al servicio de Moctezuma."

47. Ibid., p. 332:

Joven: (irónico) ¿Y por liberarte de tu propia raza, vas a permitir que unos extraños la esclavicen?

Malinche: ¡Ah! ¿Pero depende de mí? No lo sabía. ¿Y los otros? ¿Los de Cempoala que vienen a pedirle a Cortés que los ampare contra Moctezuma y a ofrecerse de intermediarios para una alianza con los de Tlaxcala? Por el mismo cacique de Cempoala, sé que hasta los parientes más cercanos de Moctezuma disputan entre sí, se denigran unos a otros y tratan de obtener ventajas amenazando aliarse con los españoles. (Divertida) Y ahora resulta que va a depender de mí que los españoles esclavicen a los mexicanos.

48. Ibid., p. 356: "Me duele ver morir a la gente de mi raza y pensar que todo eso sucede por mi culpa." The Cholula incident is often blamed on La Malinche, even in the text of her supporter, Figueroa Torres: "En Cholula, un total de seis mil indios muertos entre cholultecas y mexicanos, los que se hacen pesar sobre la conciencia de doña Marina" (*Doña Marina,* p. 175).

49. Ibid., p. 332. It is interesting to note that Gorostiza expects a great deal from the secondary code, since when Cuauhtemoc identifies himself, he and Cortés are described as exchanging a telling look, one that acknowledges that they will face each other as adversaries (ibid., p. 333).

50. Ibid., p. 332: ". . . los jóvenes estamos trabajando por cambiar las cosas, por lograr que los mexicanos nos estimemos y nos respetemos unos a otros. Cuando eso se consiga, que no es muy difícil, se establecerá la unidad entre todos, y seremos una gran nación fuerte y feliz."

51. Ibid., p. 358: "En mis entrañas empieza a moverse un ser que no tiene ya tu sangre ni la mía. Tampoco la de Cortés. Es un ser nuevo que quiere vivir y que da con la suya un nuevo sentido a mi vida . . . a él no puedo traicionarlo. ¡Por él viviré y lucharé contra todo y contra todos, a pesar de todas las amenazas, de todos los castigos, de todos los sufrimientos, hasta el martirio . . . hasta la muerte!" It is not possible to determine if La Malinche refers to the child she carries as "he" because of her idea that it must be a male child or if the use of the masculine forms is merely the result of Spanish grammatical usage, in which the referents to "un ser" have to agree with the substantive's masculine grammatical gender. In other texts, too, references to the child have always been masculine—due to knowledge of the historical Martín Cortés, one assumes.

52. Ibid., p. 376: "un hombre nuevo y con el que empieza una raza nueva en un mundo nuevo."

53. Ibid., p. 377: "Son los padres los que engendran a los hijos, pero que son los hijos los que, a la medida de su propia estatura, honran y engrandecen a sus padres. Algún día ellos nos harán grandes a nosotros."

54. Ibid., p. 361:

Malinche: (. . . alarmada) ¿Su esposa? ¿Ha dicho que viene hacia aquí su esposa?

Cuauhtémoc: (disimulando) No estaba prestando atención . . .

Malinche: ¡Sí! Dijo que ha llegado a Texcoco y viene hacia Coyoacán. ¿Por qué no me dijo nada? ¿Por qué esta traición y este engaño?

Cuauhtémoc: (tratando de calmarla) Nunca oí decir que fuera casado. . . . (conciliador) El mismo podrá explicártelo. Tal vez has oído mal. En todo caso, él trendrá razones que darte.

55. I mention religion as one of the differences between Cuauhtemoc on one side and Cortés-Malinche on the other because prior to the jealous outburst of La Malinche, she had discredited the old gods that Cuauhtemoc still defended (Gorostiza, *La Malinche*, p. 361). While Cuauhtemoc supports the religion of his ancestors, La Malinche speaks as a Christian, affirming the religious discourse of Cortés.

56. Gyurko, "Myth and Mythification," p. 109. See also Malva Filer, "Los mitos indígenas en Carlos Fuentes," and Luis Leal, "History and Myth in the Narrative of Carlos Fuentes."

57. Fuentes, "Remember the Future," p. 320. He comments that "we must also remember the past if we are to have a future which shall be more than an ever-receding illusion . . ." (p. 338).

58. Fuentes, *Tiempo mexicano*, p. 140: "genera la traición y la corrupción en la mujer."

59. Gyurko, "The Vindication of La Malinche," p. 234.

60. Fuentes, *Todos los gatos son pardos*, pp. 13–14: "Malintzin, Malintzin, Malintzin, Marina, Marina, Marina . . . Malinche, Malinche, Malinche. . . . Tres fueron tus nombres, mujer: el que te dieron tus padres, el que te dio tu amante y el que te dio tu pueblo. Diosa, amante o madre, yo viví esta historia y puedo contarla. . . . Malintzin, Marina, Malinche: yo fui la partera de esta historia porque primero fui la diosa que la imaginó, luego la

amante que recibió su semilla y finalmente la madre que la parió. Diosa, Malintzin; puta, Marina; madre, Malinche." In preparing my translation, I consulted the fragment of the play translated in Antonia Castañeda Shular et al., *Literatura chicana: Texto y contexto*, pp. 305–306.

61. Gyurko, "Vindication," p. 235.

62. Fuentes, *Gatos*, p. 67: "Eres plebeyo y mortal; serás, por mi boca, dios e inmortal."

63. In relation to women, Fuentes has often portrayed them within the paradigm of the patriarchy in the manner of Gorostiza, that is, at times with sympathy but often without regard to the constraints within which tradition has placed them. See Sharon Magnarelli's *The Lost Rib*, pp. 80–101.

64. Fuentes, *Gatos*, p. 100: "no asesines el bien de mi pueblo, señor, . . . trata de entendernos, danos una oportunidad, no borres nuestros sueños de la tierra con tu espada, no destruyas nuestro frágil identidad; toma lo que está contruido aquí y contruye al lado de nosotros; déjanos aprender de tu mundo, aprende tú del nuestro."

65. Forster, "Carlos Fuentes as Dramatist," p. 186.

66. Fuentes, *Gatos*, p. 101: "Nos has bañado en sangre. . . . Has traído el terror y la esclavitud"; p. 152: "Has impuesto tu tiranía en vez de la de Moctezuma."

67. Ibid., p. 107: "Los imperios no han hecho más que pasar de unas manos a otras, desde Alejandro hasta Carlos"; p. 129: "Los imperios no han hecho más que pasar de unas manos a otras."

68. Ibid., p. 105: "un hijo de nuestras dos sangres."

69. Ibid., p. 114: "Sal, hijo de la traición . . . sal, hijo de puta . . . sal, hijo de la chingada . . . adorado hijo mío, sal ya . . . cae sobre la tierra que ya no es mía ni de tu padre, sino tuya . . . sal, hijo de las dos sangres enemigas . . . sal a recobrar tu tierra maldita."

70. Ibid., p. 116: "tú mismo, mi hijito de la chingada; tú deberás ser la serpiente emplumada, la tierra con alas, el ave de barro, el cabrón y encabronado hijo de México y España: tú eres mi única herencia, la herencia de Malintzin, la diosa, de Marina, la puta, de Malinche, la madre."

71. See Gyurko, "Fuentes's *Aura*," p. 106.

7. Re/visions of the Cultural Metaphor

1. Perhaps, too, Fuentes's seriousness in *Gatos* stems from the 1968 tragedy of Tlatelolco, which, as we have just seen, provides a contemporary historical subtext for his play on the conquest.

2. Joseph Sommers, "Interpreting Tomás Rivera," p. 100.

3. Arthur Miller, "The Family in Modern Drama," p. 232.

4. Literary theorists note that writers often include fantastic and otherwise incredible elements within a realistic frame in order to provide credibility; see Wolfgang Kayser, *Interpretación y análisis de la obra literaria*, p. 264.

5. Turner, *Dramas*, p. 99. See also the discussion of liminal periods in chapter 1.

6. Castellanos, *El eterno femenino*, p. 24. All translations derive from Maureen Ahern, *A Rosario Castellanos Reader*, pp. 273–367.

7. Ahern, *Castellanos Reader*, p. 277; Castellanos, *El eterno femenino*, p. 31: "Se trata de una ocasión muy especial: viene hoy a peinarse para su boda."

8. Castellanos, p. 278; "¿Qué me reserva el porvenir?" p. 31.

9. Ibid., p. 277; p. 32: "una máquina, una computadora, un cerebro electrónico. Lo que no se puede equivocarse nunca."

10. Ibid., p. 296; p. 69: "una horrible pesadilla."

11. All the women mentioned are historical figures, even Adelita, who is identified with the *soldadera* Adela Maldonado. See Shirlene A. Soto, *The Mexican Woman: A Study of Her Participation in the Revolution, 1910–1940*, p. 27.

12. Castellanos, p. 304; p. 87: "como lo que creemos que fuimos."

13. The essay was first published in October 1963, reprinted in *Juicios sumarios* (1966) and in *El uso de la palabra* in 1974 after her untimely death. For Castellanos, "there are three figures in Mexican history that embody the most extreme and diverse possibilities of femininity. Each one of them represents a symbol, exercises a vast and profound influence on very wide sectors of the nation and arouses passionate reactions. These figures are the Virgin of Guadalupe, Malinche and Sor Juana" (*A Rosario Castellanos Reader*, p. 222).

14. Castellanos, p. 305; pp. 88–89:

Cortés: ¡Ay, cuánto diera yo por tener en mis manos un momento, nada más un momento, al marinero que se puso a fumar en la bodega del barco y se quedó dormido! . . . No quedó ni rastro de ninguna de las naves.

Malinche: . . . ¿Por qué no aprovechas esta circunstancia para hacer correr el rumor de que tú, *tú*, quemaste las naves?

Cortés: ¿Yo? ¿Para qué?

Malinche: Para cortar la retirada a Cuba. Hay en tu ejército muchos cobardes y uno que otro traidor que querían volver. Ahora no pueden hacerlo y no les queda más remedio que enfrentarse a los hechos.

15. Ibid., p. 305; p. 89:

Cortés: ¡Cómo te atreves a decir que no. Eres mi esclava, mi propiedad, mi cosa!

Malinche: Soy tu instrumento, de acuerdo. Pero, al menos aprende usarme en tu beneficio.

16. Ibid., p. 305; p. 89:

Malinche: Si te despojas de ella los indios verían lo que he visto y me callo: que eres un hombre como cualquier otro. Quizá mas débil que algunos. Armado te semejas a un dios.

Cortés (halagado): Dame un espejo. (Se contempla y se aprueba.) Es verdad. Y este papel de dios me viene pintiparado.

17. Sierra, *Evolución política del pueblo mexicano*, p. 60.

18. Simpson, "Prologue," Gómara, *Cortés: The Life of the Conqueror by His Secretary*, trans. Lesley Byrd Simpson, p. xv.

19. Castellanos, p. 315; p. 208: "No es siquiera diversión; es, si acaso, una mera versión."

20. Foucault, *The History of Sexuality*, p. 100.

21. Castellanos, p. 321–322; p. 121: "... 'redimir a los mexicanos, reconciliarlos y unirlos, civilizarlos' ... 'Exactamente lo mismo que decían los ideólogos de Hernán Cortés.'"

22. Ibid., p. 329; p. 136: "Pero los libros de historia dicen que la Revolución triunfó."

23. Ibid., p. 329; p. 137: "Si hubiera triunfado ¿estaría esta muchacha [Lupita] aquí? ¿Existirían aún muchachas como ella, con padres como los de ella, con novios como el de ella, con vida como la de ella?"

24. Willebaldo López, *Malinche Show*, p. 56: "otro mundo ajeno al suyo."

25. Ibid., p. 30: "prestan su nombre y meten inversionistas clandestinas a nuestro país." López's Malinche refers to a practice by which Mexicans themselves evade their country's laws, which forbid foreign ownership of national companies.

26. Ibid., p. 15: "la puerta del país a las peores intenciones que vienen del extrajero ... la madre de las fuerzas inversionistas del país."

27. Mirandé and Enríquez, *La Chicana*, pp. 27–28. Gabino Palomares's popular recording of the song is available.

28. Quoted in Mirandé and Enríquez: "Se nos quedó el maleficio / de brindar al extranjero / nuestra fe, nuestra cultura, / nuestro pan, nuestro dinero ... / ¡Hoy en pleno siglo veinte! / nos siguen llegando rubios / y les abrimos la casa / y los llamamos amigos ... / ¡Oh! ¡Maldición, de Malinche! / enfermedad del presente, / ¿cuándo dejarás mi tierra? / ¡cuándo harás libre a mi gente!"

29. In "The Malinchista Syndrome in Carballido's Plays," I refer to uses of *malinchismo* in Carballido's plays and in specific contemporary essays, such as Cervantes Ayala's "Existe en el medio teatral de México malinchismo para el autor nacional."

30. López, *Malinche Show*, p. 30: "llevar nuestras riquezas, dejando a la gran mayoría de los mexicanos en la miseria. (Al Público) ¿o no?"

31. See chap. 6, n.4; for Novo, the complaint centers more on the lack of passion evinced by the new conquerors, the North Americans, whereas López is more concerned with the economic aspects of imperialism.

32. Berman, *Aguila o sol*, p. 225: "Se fundamenta en las crónicas indígenas de los sucesos recopilados por el maestro León Portilla en *La visión de los vencidos*. Así, es el punto de vista de los conquistados el que se expresa."

33. As brought out in chapter 2, the importance of the Tlaxcalan military and economic support (supplying food and provisions and so forth) to the Spanish conquistadors has been treated by many historians of all nationalities. Like Garro in "La culpa es de los tlaxcaltecas," Berman shows that no one person is culpable.

34. Berman, *Aguila*, pp. 240–241:
Cómico 2: Siga contando. ¿Qué hicieron los tlaxcaltecas del pueblo?
Cómico 1: P's todos tuvieron que ir a agacharse también frente a los blancos. Fue como se dice, un mitin de a huevo y de apoyo.

Cómico 2: Ujule, ¿mitin de a huevo y de apoyo?

Cómico 1: Es que cada tlaxcalteca tuvo que llevarle a los güeros un huevo y un pollo; tortillas blancas, huevitos, pollitos, gallinitas; les juntaron un montonsote de provisiones.

Cómico 2: ¡Huevos! Los que les hicieron falta a esos jijos de . . .

35. M. M. Bakhtin, *The Dialogic Imagination,* trans. Caryl Emerson and Michael Holquist, p. 23.

36. Ibid., p. 24.

37. Berman, *Aguila,* p. 234: "¿Gato por libre, sucios negros trajinantes? Mas cus-cus ¿io? nieve de orozuz."

38. See Fanon's *The Wretched of the Earth.*

39. Berman, *Aguila,* p. 237: "Quiere medirlos. Mañana se hará en la playa un torneo. Se guerreará por parejas: hombre blanco contra hombre indio."

40. Ibid., p. 255:

Moctezuma: Ven y descansa; toma posesión de tus casas reales: da refrigerio a tu cuerpo. ¡Pásenle a su casa señores nuestros!

Cortés: Calmantes montes alicantes pintos pájaros volantes.

Malinche: Dice: tenga confianza señor Moctezuma. No tema nada.

Cortés: ¡Cuore mío! ¡Oh, cuore mío!

Malinche: En verdad le amamos; intensamente le amamos.

Cortés: ¿Pokarito? Paso. ¿Blof yo? Ve: cinco ases, digo cuatro: chécame las mangas.

Malinche: Dice: Ya estando en su casa podrán hablar en calma. Tenga fe.

41. Ibid., p. 248: "Mucho han chupado los aztecas a los otros pueblos, mucho han crecido de aplastar a otros."

42. One of the earliest definitions of *malinchismo* in a literary work appears in *El laberinto de la soledad* by Octavio Paz (p. 78).

43. Berman, *Aguila,* p. 262: "Moctezuma: Mexicanos, tenochcas, tlatelolcas: pues no somos competentes para igualar a los forasteros, que no luchen los mexicanos."

44. Fanon, *Wretched,* pp. 217–218.

45. Ibid., p. 232.

8. Re/formation of the Tradition by Chicana Writers

1. The English translation is by Maureen Ahern, *A Rosario Castellanos Reader,* pp. 96–97; the Spanish appears in *Poesía no eres tú,* pp. 285–287:

Desde el sillón de mando mi madre dijo: "Ha muerto."

Y se dejó caer, como abatida,
en los brazos del otro, usurpador, padrastro
que la sostuvo no con el respeto
que el siervo da a la majestad de reina
sino con ese abajamiento mutuo
en que se humillan ambos, los amantes, los cómplices.

Desde la Plaza de los Intercambios
mi madre anunció: "Ha muerto."

La balanza
se sostuvo un instante sin moverse
y el grano de cacao quedó quieto en la arca
y el sol permanecía en la mitad del cielo
como aguardando un signo
que fue, cuando partió como una flecha,
el ay agudo de las plañideras.

"Se deshojó la flor de muchos pétalos,
se evaporó el perfume
se consumó la llama de la antorcha.

Una niña regresa, escarbando, al lugar
en el que la partera depositó su ombligo.

Regresa al Sitio de los que Vivieron.

Reconoce a su padre asesinado.
ay, ay, ay, con veneno, con puñal,
con trampa ante sus pies, con lazo de horca.

Se toman de la mano y caminan, caminan
perdiéndose en la niebla."

Tal era el llanto y las lamentaciones
sobre algún cuerpo anónimo; un cadáver
que no era el mío porque yo, vendida
a mercaderes, iba como esclava, como nadie, al destierro.

Arrojada, expulsada
del reino, del palacio y de la entraña tibia
de la que me dio a luz en tálamo legítimo
y que me aborreció porque yo era su igual
en figura y en rango
y se contempló en mí y odió su imagen
y destrozó el espejo contra el suelo.

Yo avanzo hacia el destino entre cadenas
y dejo atrás lo que todavía escucho:
los fúnebres rumores con los que se me encierra.

Y la voz de mi madre con lágrimas ¡con lágrimas!
que decreta mi muerte.

2. Yvonne Yarbro-Bejarano, "Chicana Literature from a Chicana Feminist Perspective," p. 141. I want to thank Yarbro-Bejarano for sending me material on the Chicana writers.

3. Ibid., p. 142.

4. See the article by George A. Agogino, Dominique E. Stevens, and Lynda Carlotta, "Doña Marina and the Legend of La Llorona," *Anthropological Journal of Canada* 11. 1 (1973): 27–29.

5. In addition to some of the patriarchal women in *El eterno femenino,* in the character Zoraida of *Balún-Canán* Castellanos portrayed the image of the patriarchal woman who attempts to foist on her daughter the traditional inferior role of women (see Cypess, *"Balún-Canán"*). In an essay titled "Femenismo y liberación," Adelaida Foppa remarks about women that "las víctimas son al mismo tiempo cómplices, y las dominadas se vuelven también terribles dominadoras (por un mecanismo de compensación) de los hijos, de los sirvientes, y, a veces, de los mismo maridos" (p. 94) ("the victims are at the same time accomplices, and the dominated women also become terrible oppressors [by a compensation mechanism] of their children, servants, and, at times, of their very husbands").

6. Cherríe Moraga, "A Long Line of Vendidas," from *Loving in the War Years,* p. 100.

7. Adelaida Del Castillo, "Malintzín Tenépal: A Preliminary Look into a New Perspective," In *Essays on La Mujer.* After completing this chapter, I read another valuable article that should also be consulted for the revisionist view: Norma Alarcón, "Chicana's Feminist Literature: A Re-vision through Malintzin/or Malintzin: Putting Flesh Back on the Object."

8. Del Castillo, "Malintzín," p. 142; the Chicana critic offers differing interpretations for a number of events in the life of La Malinche. While we have seen that her marriage to Jaramillo was considered by Ireneo Paz as a positive and welcome event, Del Castillo considers it but another of the ignominies suffered by Marina, who complains that after "spending most of her youth on the road alongside Hernán Cortés, [he] married her off to the Spaniard ingrate Don Juan Jaramillo" (p. 143). She goes on to list other mean acts, such as her children being tortured and robbed of their rightful inheritance. The reader is advised that in the absence of verifying documents, much of what is said about La Malinche, even by Del Castillo, is based on the suppositions of the writer and reflects ideological biases.

9. Fuentes, quoted by Del Castillo, "Malintzín," p. 140.

10. Elizabeth Ordóñez, "The Concept of Cultural Identity in Chicana Poetry," p. 175.

11. "Pinche, cómo duele ser Malinche," from Sosa Riddell's poem "Cómo duele." Notice that the Spanish phrase rhymes the curse "pinche" with "Malinche."

12. Corpi, *Fireflight,* p. 43. I want to thank Becky Boling for sending me a copy of the *Marina* poems.

13. I am led to this consideration by a note associated with the poems in the anthology *Fireflight;* "her Indian name, Malinche, has become a syno-

nym in Mexico for treachery. These poems were written by way of vindication" (p. 61).

14. Corpi, in *Contemporary Chicana Poetry*, ed. Marta E. Sánchez, p. 184: "con la sangre de un cordero tierno / su nombre escribieron los viejos / en la corteza de ese árbol / tan viejo como ellos." The English translations are by Corpi's friend Catherine Rodríguez-Nieto. I use Sánchez's text for the English translations although I formulated my own readings of Corpi's poems before I was informed of Sánchez's interpretations.

15. Ibid., p. 185: ". . . fue vendida . . . / de mano en mano, noche a noche, / negada y desecrada, esperando el alba."

16. Ibid., p. 184: "Tú no la querías ya y él la negaba / Y aquél que cuando niño ¡mama! le gritaba / cuando creció le puso por nombre 'la chingada.'" For these lines I do not follow Rodríguez-Nieto, who translates "y él la negaba" as "the elders denied her"—which avoids the ambiguity of the Spanish and gives a concrete albeit nonpersonalized face to "él" as "the elders," presumably an indigenous group.

17. Alfonso León de Garay, *Una aproximación a la psicología del mexicano*, p. 36.

18. Corpi, p. 185: ". . . Y arropaba / su cuerpo con una manta gruesa y nítida / para que no supieras que su piel / morena estaba maldita."

19. Ibid., p. 185–186: "Alguna vez, te detuviste a pensar / en dónde estaba su alma escondida. / No sabías que la había sembrado / en las entrañas de la tierra / que sus manos cultivaban— / la tierra negra y húmeda de tu vida."

20. Mirandé and Enríquez, *La Chicana*, p. 28; see also Leal, "Female Archetypes in Mexican Literature."

21. Corpi, pp. 186:
Cuando murió, el trueno se reventó en el norte,
y junto al altar de piedra la noche entera
el copal ardió. Su mística pulsación para
siempre calló. Cayó hecho pedazos el ídolo
de barro sucio y viejo, y su nombre se lo llevó
el viento con un solo murmullo ronco:
su nombre tan parecido a la profundidad
salina del mar. Poco quedó. Sólo una semilla
a medio germinar.

22. Ibid., pp. 186–187.
Ella. Una flor quizá, un remanso fresco . . .
una noche tibia, tropical,
o una criatura triste, en una prisión
encerrada; de barro húmedo y suave;
en la sombra enlutada de un recuerdo
ancestral que vendrá por la mañana
cruzando el puente con manos llenas—
llenas de sol y de tierra.

9. The Malinche Paradigm as Subtext

1. In *Quetzalcoatl and Guadalupe: The Formation of Mexican National Consciousness 1531–1813,* Jacques Lafaye explores the way historical memory and myth-making processes were woven together to make Quetzalcoatl a symbol for political and social legitimacy. He shows how both Quetzalcoatl and the Virgin of Guadalupe have continued to be relevant in the modern Mexican imagination (p. 62); this observation is also applicable to the image of La Malinche.

2. It is not consistent with the purpose of this study to repeat the various analyses of *La muerte de Artemio Cruz,* which can be found in abundance. See such compilations as Robert Brody and Charles Rossman, eds., *Carlos Fuentes: A Critical View;* and *World Literature Today: Carlos Fuentes Issue* 57.4 (1983).

3. Merlin Forster, "Carlos Fuentes as Dramatist," p. 189.

4. Fuentes, *El tuerto,* p. 176: "La memoria será un presagio."

5. Garro, *Los recuerdos del porvenir,* p. 63: "el porvenir era la repetición del pasado." Garro's novel has been translated as *Recollections of Things to Come* by Ruth L. C. Simms. The English translations used in this chapter are based on my own work in consultation with the Simms version.

6. Meyer and Sherman, *The Course of Mexican History,* p. 587. See also Ramón Jrade's "Inquiries into the Cristero Insurrection against the Mexican Revolution."

7. As was noted in chapter 8, the contemporary Chicana critic Adelaida Del Castillo firmly believes in the acceptance of Christianity as one of the motivating forces behind La Malinche's behavior during the conquest: "Apparently, she favored Christianity and was willing to help convert other indios to this faith" ("Malintzín Tenépal: A Preliminary Look into a New Perspective," p. 134).

8. Turner, *Dramas, Fields and Metaphors,* p. 99.

9. Garro, *Recuerdos,* p. 24: "Julia tiene la culpa de que los niños se vayan tan lejos y solos en medio de los peligros de los hombres y las tentaciones del demonio."

10. Ibid., p. 24: "En aquellos días Julia determinaba el destino de todos nosotros y la culpábamos de la menor de nuestras desdichas."

11. Ibid., p. 81: "Es Julia . . . [quien] tiene la culpa de todo lo que nos pasa. ¿Hasta cuándo se saciará esta mujer?"

12. Compare the comments on human sacrifice among the Aztecs made by Octavio Paz in *Posdata,* pp. 118–120.

13. Garro, *Recuerdos,* p. 88: "Julia era la verdadera culpable."

14. Ibid., p. 88: "Les costaba aceptar que fuera Rodolfito."

15. Ibid., p. 90: "Julia tenía que ser la criatura preciosa que absorbiera nuestras culpas."

16. Ibid., p. 122: "Llegó un perfume de vainilla y la invisible presencia de Julia . . . se instaló como la discordia en el centro de la cantina."

17. Ibid., p. 132: "el heraldo de la desdicha."

18. Ibid., p. 95: "Para él, como para Hurtado y para todo Ixtepec, Julia era la imagen del amor."

19. Ibid., p. 95: "una admiración sin reservas . . . no se puede negar que tiene algo."

20. Ibid., p. 249: "Una generación sucede a la otra, y cada una repite los actos de la anterior."

21. Ibid., p. 161: "Si pudiera daría el salto para colocarse al lado de Francisco Rosas."

22. Ibid., p. 161: "Andaba muy lejos de su cuarto caminando un porvenir que empezaba a dibujarse en su memoria."

23. Ibid., p. 162: "Delante de [su padre] Isabel bajó los ojos, se sintió culpable."

24. Ibid., p. 286: "se separó de los suyos."

25. Ibid., p. 268: "Algunos creyeron leer en las palabras de Nicolás que la salvación vendría de Isabel. La joven no había entrado al hotel a traicionarnos. Estaba allí, como la diosa vengadora de la justicia, esperando el momento propicio."

26. Luis Leal, "Female Archetypes in Mexican Literature," p. 232.

27. Garro, *Recuerdos*, p. 248: "todas las mujeres son unas putas." Rosas uses the term "putas," which recalls a popular joke that includes a reference to La Malinche as "la puta." A teacher asks his students," ¿Cuál era la ruta que tomó Cortés?" (What was the route that Cortés took?), and a student responds, "La Malinche." Realizing the reason for the incongruous answer, the teacher gives the punchline: "Dije 'ruta,' no 'puta'" (I said "route" [ruta], not "whore" [puta]), a play on the similarity in sound between the Spanish words.

28. For translations of Sor Juana's works, consult *Sor Juana Inés de la Cruz: Poems*, translated by Margaret Sayers Peden.

29. Paz, *The Labyrinth of Solitude*, p. 78; *El laberinto*, p. 70: "El chingón es el macho, el que abre. La chingada, la hembra, la pasividad pura."

30. Garro, *Recuerdos*, p. 144: "El tiempo se detuvo en seco. No sé si se detuvo o si se fue y sólo cayó el sueño."

31. Paz, *Labyrinth*, p. 86; *El laberinto*, pp. 77–78: "Una figura que representa a las indias, fascinadas, violadas o seducidas por los españoles."

32. Garro, *Recuerdos*, p. 273: "Yo no soy la única culpable."

33. Ibid., p. 273: "'Quiero a Nicolás,' ordenó en voz muy baja."

34. Ibid., p. 273: "'Quiero a Nicolás,' repitió la cara de Isabel cada vez más parecida a la cara de su hermano."

35. Ibid., p. 289: "No se dejó conducir, mi general."

36. Ibid., p. 289: "¿Por qué había que matar siempre a lo que amaba? Su vida era un engaño permanente; estaba condenado a vagar solo dejado de la suerte." The destiny of Rosas to wander alone recalls the prophesy of Cuauhtemoc concerning Cortés in Usigli's *Corona de fuego* (p. 129).

tú llorarás más de una Noche Triste;
. . . Dios te priva
del don de la palabra, y tus acciones
quedarán en la historia de otro modo

que soñaste, de otro, y tu figura
sobre el mapa de México será sólo una sombra.

37. Garro, *Recuerdos*, p. 22: "A Isabel le disgustaba que establecieran diferencias entre ella y sus hermanos. Le humillaba la idea de que el único futuro para las mujeres fuera el matrimonio. Hablar del matrimonio como de una solución le dejaba reducida a una mercancía a la que había que dar salida a cualquier precio."

38. Ibid., p. 291: "Vamos al Santuario, niña; allí la virgen le sacará del cuerpo a Rosas."

39. Ibid., p. 294: "En su carrera para encontrar a su amante, Isabel Moncada se perdió. Después de mucho buscarla, Gregoria la halló tirada muy abajo, convertida en una piedra, y aterrada se santiguó. Algo le decía que la niña Isabel no quería salvarse; era muy sembrada en el general Francisco Rosas."

40. Cynthia Duncan, "La culpa," p. 120.

41. Garro, "La culpa es de los tlaxcaltecas," p. 10: " 'Yo soy como ellos: traidora,' dijo Laura con melancolía."

42. Ibid., p. 10: "Sí, yo también soy traicionera, señora Laurita."

43. Ibid., p. 28: "Me preguntaba por mi infancia, por mi padre y por mi madre. Pero, yo, Nachita, no sabía de cuál infancia ni de cuál padre, ni de cuál madre quería saber. Por eso le platicaba de la *Conquista de México.*"

44. Duncan, " 'La culpa,' " p. 119.

45. See chapter 7, note 27.

46. Garro, "La culpa," p. 13: "Soy cobarde. O tal vez el humo y el polvo me sacaron lágrimas."

47. Ibid., p. 15: "Al anochecer llegamos a la ciudad de México. ¡Cómo había cambiado, Nachita, casi no pude creerlo! A las doce del día todavía estaban los guerreros y ahora ya ni huella de su paso. Tampoco quedaban escombros. Pasamos por el Zócalo silencioso y triste; de la otra plaza, no quedaba ¡nada!"

48. Ibid., p. 17: "Cuando estábamos cenando me fijé en que Pablo no hablaba con palabras sino con letras. Y me puse a contarlas mientras le miraba la boca gruesa y el ojo muerto."

49. Ibid., p. 17: "Pablo habla a saltitos, se enfurece por nada y pregunta a cada instante: '¿En qué piensas?' "

50. Ibid., p. 19: " 'Sus gestos son feroces y su conducta es tan incoherente como sus palabras. Yo no tengo la culpa de que aceptara la derrota,' dijo Laura con desdén."

51. Consult the discussion in chapter 2 regarding the omens and portents. Book 12 of Sahagún's *Florentine Codex: General History of the Things of New Spain*, called *The History of the Conquest of Mexico*, is a useful source of information.

52. Duncan, " 'La culpa,' " p. 117.

53. Magnus Mörner, *Race Mixture in the History of Latin America*, p. 22.

54. In Ireneo Paz's *Doña Marina* (vol. 1, pp. 246–247), Marina expresses the Europocentrist position most clearly:

Y luego cuando se ponía a hacer comparaciones entre los dos hombres que le habían declarado su pasión, entre Cuauhtlizín y José de Jaramillo, encontraba siempre a éste más hermoso, más noble, más inteligente, más varonil, y sobre todo, más civilizado. Cuauhtlizín no podía ofrecerle otra cosa que un amor salvaje; para amarlo a él, necesitaba despojarse de sus galas que le había traído la poca ilustración aprendida, y volver a tomar la corteza de la barbarie; necesitaba huir de los españoles quienes eran una parte de su vida y cuyas costumbres eran ya las suyas; necesitaba abandonar la religión del verdadero Dios que era en su corazón una creencia arraigada; necesitaba, por último, remontarse a los montes como las fieras y desterrarse para siempre de todo lo que ahora formaba sus gustos y sus necesidades. José Jaramillo halagaba más sus aspiraciones. Poderse presentar de igual a igual enfrente de los españoles, salir de su condición de fiera, para ser la ama de su casa como mujer libre, estar en aptitud de conocer las costas europeas viajando por ellas a lado de su marido . . . todo esto formaba para ella un ideal en sus horas de recogimiento. See page 89 for English translation.

55. Vern L. Bullough, *The Subordinate Sex*, p. 103.

56. Duncan, "'La culpa,'" p. 119.

57. Paz, *Labyrinth*, p. 87; *El laberinto*, p. 78: "Al repudiar a la Malinche . . . el mexicano rompe sus ligas con el pasado, reniega de su origen y se adentra solo en la vida histórica."

58. Garro, "La culpa," p. 33: "Nacha se aproximó a su patrona para estrechar la intimidad súbita que había establecida entre ellas."

59. Ibid., p. 33: "hasta sin cobrar su sueldo."

60. In *Tiempo de ladrones: La historia de Chucho el Roto*, Carballido uses the term "memoria colectiva" (p. 252) to explain the persistence of the figure of Chucho el Roto in the Mexican folkloric tradition.

61. Carballido, Ibid., p. 51: "Las obras mexicanas pertenecen todas al género detestable. No voy a forzar al público a verlas, sólo porque el gobierno subsidie la temporada."

62. Ibid., p. 53: "una compañía de mexicanos, con ilusiones y alma de mexicanos, con mucha gente salida del Conservatorio, en vez de tantas reliquias coloniales."

63. Ibid., p. 53: "se quejan los autores mexicanos que nadie los estrene"; p. 54: "Saben. Hasta ahora no han encontrado una sola obra digna de nosotros."

64. Ibid., p. 57: "Con jóvenes del Conservatorio y repertorio mexicano."

65. Ibid., p. 115: "Mis gustos están cerca de los maestros europeos."

66. For a detailed discussion of this play and its theme of *malinchismo*, see Cypess, "The Malinchista Syndrome in Carballido's Plays."

67. Although the title of Garro's novel does suggest that "the future was the repetition of the past" ("el porvenir era la repetición del pasado") (*Los recuerdos del porvenir*, p. 63), I have shown above that she does believe with Carballido that the sociocultural conditions must be changed to allow for new patterns of behavior to develop.

Bibliography

Primary Sources

Ancona, Eligio. *Los mártires del Anáhuac.* In *La novela del México colonial,* vol. 1, ed. Antonio Castro Leal, pp. 75–177. Mexico City: Aguilar, 1964.

Berman, Sabina. *Aguila o sol.* In *Teatro de Sabina Berman,* pp. 225–265. Mexico City: Editores Mexicanos Unidos, 1985.

Carballido, Emilio. *Acapulco, los lunes.* In *Tres obras,* pp. 163–254. Mexico City: Extemporáneos, 1978.

———. *Ceremonia en el templo del tigre; La rosa de dos aromas; Un pequeño día de ira.* Mexico City: Editores Mexicanos Unidos, 1986.

———. *Tiempo de ladrones: La historia de Chicho el Roto.* Mexico City: Editorial Grijalbo, 1983.

Castellanos, Rosario. *El eterno femenino.* Mexico City: Fondo de Cultura Económica, 1975. Translated as *The Eternal Feminine* by Diane Marting and Betty Tyree Osiek. In *A Rosario Castellanos Reader,* ed. Maureen Ahern, pp. 273–367. Austin: University of Texas Press, 1988.

———. *Juicios sumarios.* Xalapa: Universidad Veracruzana, 1966.

———. *Poesía no eres tú: Obra poética, 1948–1971.* Mexico City: Fondo de Cultura Económica, 1972.

———. *El uso de la palabra.* Prol. José Emilio Pacheco. Mexico City: Ediciones de Excélsior-Crónicas, 1974.

Corpi, Lucha. *Palabras de mediodía/Noon Words.* Berkeley: Fuego de Aztlán, 1980.

Cortés, Hernán. *Cartas de relación.* Mexico City: Editorial Porrúa, 1970.

———. *Hernán Cortés: Letters from Mexico.* Trans. A. R. Pagden. New York: Grossman Publishers, 1971.

Díaz del Castillo, Bernal. *The Conquest of New Spain.* Trans. J. M. Cohen. Middlesex, England: Penguin Books, 1963. Rpt. 1978.

———. *Historia verdadera de la conquista de la Nueva España.* Prol. Carlos Pereya. 6th ed. Madrid: Espasa-Calpe, 1984.

Fuentes, Carlos. *The Death of Artemio Cruz.* Trans. Sam Hileman. New York: Farrar, Straus and Giroux, 1964.

————. *La muerte de Artemio Cruz.* Mexico City: Fondo de Cultura Económica, 1970.

————. *Todos los gatos son pardos.* Mexico City: Siglo Veintiuno, 1970.

————. *El tuerto es rey: Todos los gatos son pardos.* Barcelona: Barral, 1971.

Garro, Elena. "La culpa es de los tlaxcaltecas." In *La semana de colores,* pp. 9–33. Xalapa: Universidad Veracruzana, 1964.

————. *Recollections of Things to Come.* Trans. Ruth L. C. Simms. Austin: University of Texas Press, 1969.

————. *Los recuerdos del porvenir.* Mexico City: Joaquín Mortiz, 1963.

Gómara, Francisco López de. *Historia de la conquista de México.* Translated as *Cortés: The Life of the Conqueror by His Secretary* by Lesley Byrd Simpson. Berkeley: University of California Press, 1964.

Gómez de Avellaneda, Gertrudis. *Guatimozín.* Ed. Mary Cruz. Havana: Editorial Letras Cubanas, 1979.

Gorostiza, Celestino. *La Malinche o La leña está verde.* In *Teatro mexicano del siglo XX,* vol. 4, ed. Antonio Magaña Esquivel, pp. 441–511. Mexico City: Fondo de Cultura Económica, 1970.

López, Willebaldo. *Malinche Show.* Mexico City: Ediciones del Sindicato de Trabajadores del INFONAVIT, 1980.

Moraga, Cherríe. "A Long Line of Vendidas." In *Loving in the War Years,* pp. 90–144. Boston: South End Press, 1983.

Novo, Salvador. *Cuauhtémoc.* In *Teatro mexicano del siglo XX,* vol. 4, ed. Antonio Magaña Esquivel, pp. 256–282. Mexico City: Fondo de Cultura Económica, 1970.

————. "Cuauhtémoc y Eulalia." In *Diálogos: Teatro breve,* pp. 70–77. Mexico City: Editores Mexicanos Unidos, 1987.

————. "Malinche y Cortés." In *Diálogos: Teatro breve,* pp. 49–58. Mexico City: Editores Mexicanos Unidos, 1987.

Palomares, Gabino. "La maldición de Malinche." Popular song, 1975.

Paz, Ireneo. *Amor y suplicio.* Mexico City: Rivera Hijo, 1873.

————. *Doña Marina.* Mexico City: Imp. y litografía de I. Paz, 1883.

Paz, Octavio. *El laberinto de la soledad.* 1950. Mexico City: Fondo de Cultura Económica, 1959.

————. *The Labyrinth of Solitude, The Other Mexico City, and Other Essays.* Trans. Lysander Kemp. New York: Grove Press, 1985.

Sosa Riddell, Adaljiza. "¡Como duele!" *El grito* 7.1 (1973): 61. Also in *Journal of Ethnic Studies* 2.2 (1974): 59–60.

Tafolla, Carmen. "La Malinche." *Tejidos* 4.4 (1977): 1–2.

Usigli, Rodolfo. *Corona de fuego.* In *Corona de sombra. Corona de fuego. Corona de luz,* pp. 87–133. Mexico City: Porrúa, 1983.

————. *Corona de sombra.* Ed. Rex E. Ballinger. New York: Appleton, Century, Crofts, 1961.

Xicoténcatl. In *La novela del México colonial,* vol. 1, ed. Antonio Castro Leal, pp. 401–616. Mexico City: Aguilar, 1964.

Works Consulted

Adorno, Roleno. "Discourses on Colonialism: Bernal Díaz, Las Casas, and the Twentieth-Century Reader." *Modern Language Notes* 103.2 (1988): 239–258.

Agogino, George A., Dominique E. Stevens, and Lynda Carlotta. "Doña Marina and the Legend of La Llorona." *Anthropological Journal of Canada* 11.1 (1973): 27–29.

Ahern, Maureen, ed. and trans. *A Rosario Castellanos Reader.* Austin: University of Texas Press, 1988.

Aínsa, Fernando. *Identidad cultural de Iberoamérica en su narrativa.* Madrid: Editorial Gredos, 1986.

Alarcón, Norma. "Chicana's Feminist Literature: A Re-vision through Malintzin/or Malintzin: Putting Flesh Back on the Object." In *This Bridge Called My Back,* ed. Cherríe Moraga and Gloria Anzaldúa, pp. 182–190. New York: Kitchen Table Press, 1983.

Alegría, Juana Armanda. *Psicología de las mexicanas.* Mexico City: Samo, 1975.

Araújo, Helena. *La scherezada criolla: Ensayos sobre escritura femenina latinoamericana.* Bogotá: Universidad Nacional de Colombia, 1989.

Ayala, Cervantes. "Existe en el medio teatral de México malinchismo para el autor nacional." *Excélsior,* 23 Junio 1984, 8 D.

Bakhtin, M. M. *The Dialogic Imagination: Four Essays.* Ed. Michael Holquist. Trans. Caryl Emerson and Michael Holquist. Austin: University of Texas Press, 1987.

Benítez, Fernando. *In the Footsteps of Cortés.* New York: Pantheon, 1952.

Bidney, Martin. "Uizen and Orc, Cortés, and Guatimozin: Mexican History and *The Four Zoas* VII." *Blake/ Illustrated Quarterly* 23.4 (1990): 195–198.

Blanco, Iris. "Participación de las mujeres en la sociedad prehispánica." In *Essays on La Mujer,* ed. Rosaura Sanchez and Rosa Martínez Cruz, pp. 48–81. Los Angeles: Chicano Studies Center, 1977.

Blanco, José Joaquín. *Crónica de la poesía mexicana.* 3d ed. Mexico City: Katún, 1981.

Bonilla Garcia, Luis. *La mujer a través de los siglos.* Madrid: Aguilar, 1959.

Booth, John A., and Mitchell A. Seligson. "The Political Culture of Authoritarianism in Mexico: A Reexamination." *Latin American Research Review* 19.1 (1984): 106–124.

Booth, Wayne C. *The Rhetoric of Fiction.* Chicago: University of Chicago Press, 1961.

Borah, Woodrow. "America as Model: The Demographic Impact of European Expansion upon the Non-European World." *Actas y Memorias del XXXV Congreso International de Americanistas* 3 (1964): 379–387.

Brownlee, Kevin. "Editor's Preface." *Yale French Studies* 70 (1986).

Brushwood, John. *Genteel Barbarism: Experiments in Analysis of Nineteenth Century Spanish American Novels.* Lincoln: University of Nebraska Press, 1981.

————. *Mexico in Its Novel.* Austin: University of Texas Press, 1966.

Buchanan, William. "How Others See Us." *Annals of the American Academy of Political and Social Science* 295 (1954): 1–11.

Bullough, Vern L. *The Subordinate Sex.* Urbana: University of Illinois Press, 1973.

Candelaria, Cordelia. "La Malinche, Feminist Prototype." *Frontiers* 5 (1980): 1–6.

Carrasco, David. *Quetzalcoatl and the Irony of Empire.* Chicago and London: University of Chicago Press, 1982.

Castagnaro, R. Anthony. *The Early Spanish American Novel.* New York: Las Américas, 1971.

Castañeda Shular, Antonia, et al. *Literatura chicana: Texto y contexto.* Englewood Cliffs, N.J.: Prentice-Hall, 1972.

Cirlot, Juan. *Dictionary of Symbols.* New York: Philosophical Library, 1962.

Cohen, Susan D. "An Onomastic Double Bind: Colette's *Gigi* and the Politics of Naming." *MLA* 100.5 (1985): 793–809.

Cook, Sherburne F. "The Conquest and Population: A Demographic Approach to Mexican History." *Proceedings of the American Philosophical Society* 113.2 (1969): 177–183.

————. "La despoblación del México central en siglo XVI." *Historia Mexicana* 12 (1962): 1–12.

Cook, Sherburne F., and Woodrow Borah. *The Aboriginal Population of Central Mexico on the Eve of the Spanish Conquest.* Berkeley: University of California Press, 1963.

————. *The Indian Population of Central Mexico, 1531–1610.* Berkeley: University of California Press, 1960.

Crocker, J. Christopher. "The Social Functions of Rhetorical Forms." In *The Social Use of Metaphor,* ed. J. David Sapir and J. Christopher Crocker, pp. 33–66. Philadelphia: University of Pennsylvania Press, 1977.

Crosby, Alfred. *The Columbian Exchange: Biological and Cultural Consequences of 1492.* Westport, Conn.: Greenwood Publishing Co., 1972.

————. *The Columbian Voyages: Ecological Imperialism: The Biological Expansion of Europe 900–1900.* New York: Cambridge University Press, 1986.

Cruz, Sor Juana Inés de la. *Sor Juana Inés de la Cruz: Poems.* Trans. Margaret Sayers Peden. Binghamton: Bilingual Review Press, 1985.

Culler, Jonathan. "Presupposition and Intertextuality." *MLN* 91 (1976): 1380–1396.

Cypess, Sandra Mesinger. "*Balún-Canán*: A Model Demonstration of Discourse as Power." *Revista de Estudios Hispánicos* 19.1 (1985): 1–15.

————. "The Figure of La Malinche in the Texts of Elena Garro." In *A Different Reality: Studies in the Works of Elena Garro,* ed. Anita Stoll, pp. 117–135. Lewisburg, Penn.: Bucknell University Press, 1989.

————. "The Malinchista Syndrome in Carballido's Plays." Paper presented at the 1988 Kentucky Foreign Language Conference.

———. "¿Quién ha oído hablar de ellas? Una revisión de las dramaturgas mexicanas." *Texto Crítico* 10 (1978): 55–64.

Dabbs, Jack. *The French Army in Mexico City, 1861–1867*. The Hague: Mouton, 1962.

Dauster, Frank. "La generación de 1924: El dilema del realismo." *Latin American Theatre Review* 18.2 (1985): 13–22.

———. *Xavier Villaurrutia*. New York: Twayne, 1971.

Davies, Nigel. *The Aztecs*. Norman: University Oklahoma Press, 1973.

———. *The Toltec Heritage: From the Fall of Tula to the Rise of Tenochtitlan*. Norman: University of Oklahoma Press, 1980.

Davies, Trevor R. *The Golden Century of Spain, 1502–1621*. New York: Harper and Row, 1961.

Del Castillo, Adelaida R. "Malintzín Tenépal: A Preliminary Look into a New Perspective." In *Essays on La Mujer*, ed. Rosaura Sanchez and Rosa Martinez Cruz, pp. 124–149. Los Angeles: Chicano Studies Center, 1977.

Dibble, Charles E. *The Conquest through Aztec Eyes*. Salt Lake City: University of Utah Press, 1978.

Di Puccio, Denise. "Metatheatrical Histories in *Corona de luz*," *Latin American Theatre Review* 20.1 (1986): 29–36.

Duncan, Cynthia. "'La culpa es de los tlaxcaltecas': A Reevaluation of Mexico's Past through Myth." *Crítica Hispánica* 7.2 (1985): 107–120.

Eco, Umberto. "Looking for a Logic of Culture." In *The Tell-Tale Sign: A Survey of Semiotics*, ed. Thomas Sebeok, pp. 9–17. Lisse, Netherlands: Peter de Riddle Press, 1975.

Elliot, John H. *Imperial Spain, 1469–1716*. New York: St. Martin's Press, 1962.

Elu de Leñero, María del Carmen. *¿Hacia dónde va la mujer mexicana?* Mexico City: Instituto Mexicano de Estudios Sociales, 1969.

Fehrenback, T. R. *Fire and Blood: A History of Mexico*. New York: Macmillan, 1973.

Fernández de Velasco, Guadalupe. "La importancia de doña Marina en la conquista de México." In *Cortés ante la juventud*, ed. Rafael García Granados, pp. 145–164. Publicaciones de la sociedad de estudios cortesianos, no. 3. Mexico City: Editorial Jus, 1949.

Fernández Retamar, Roberto. "Against the Black Legend." *Ideologies and Literature* 2.10 (1979): 116–135.

Figueroa Torres, J. Jesús. *Doña Marina: Una india ejemplar*. Mexico City: Costa-Amic, 1957.

Filer, Malva. "Los mitos indígenas en Carlos Fuentes." *Revista Iberoamericana* 50.127 (1984): 475–489.

Foppa, Adelaida. "Femenismo y liberación." In *Imagen y realidad de la mujer*, ed. Elena Urrutia, pp. 80–101. Mexico City: SepSetentas, 1975.

Forster, Merlin. "Carlos Fuentes as Dramatist." In *Carlos Fuentes: A Critical View*, ed. Robert Brody and Charles Rossman, 184–192. Austin: University of Texas Press, 1982.

Foucault, Michel. *The History of Sexuality*. Vol. 1. *An Introduction*. Trans. Robert Hurley. New York: Pantheon, 1978.

Franco, Jean. *Plotting Women*. New York: Columbia University Press, 1989.

Fraser, Antonia. *The Warrior Queens*. New York: Knopf, 1989.

Fuentes, Carlos. "Remember the Future." *Salmagundi* 68–69 (1986): 333–352.

———. *Tiempo mexicano*. Mexico City: Joaquín Mortiz, 1971.

Gibson, Charles. *The Aztecs under Spanish Rule: A History of the Indians of the Valley of Mexico, 1519–1810*. Stanford: Stanford University Press, 1964.

Gilman, Sander L. *Difference and Pathology: Stereotypes of Sexuality, Race, and Madness*. Ithaca: Cornell University Press, 1985.

Giménez Caballero, Ernesto. *Las mujeres de América*. Madrid: Editora Nacional, 1971.

Glantz, Margo. "Lengua y conquista." *Revista de la Universidad de México*, no. 405 (1989): 45–48.

Gobineau, Count Joseph-Arthur. *Essai sur l'inégalité des race humaines*. 1915. Translated as *Inequality of Human Races* by Adrian Collins, New York: H. Fertig, 1967.

Gómez de Orozco, Federico. *Doña Marina, la dama de la conquista*. Mexico City: Ediciones Xochitl, 1942.

Griffin, Charles C. "The Enlightenment and Latin American Independence." In *Latin America and the Enlightenment*. 2d ed., ed. Arthur P. Whitaker, pp. 119–143. Ithaca: Cornell University Press, 1961.

Gyurko, Lanin. "Myth and Mythification in Fuentes' *Aura* and Wilder's *Sunset Boulevard*." *Hispanic Journal* 7.1 (1985): 91–113.

———. "Two Visions of Moctezuma: Monterde y Fuentes." *Hispanic Journal* 4.2 (1983): 111–134.

———. "The Vindication of La Malinche in Fuentes' 'Todos los gatos son pardos.'" *Ibero-Americanisches Archiv* 3.iii (1977): 233–266.

Harter, Hugh. *Gertrudis Gómez de Avellaneda*. Boston: Twayne, 1981.

Hernández, Inés. "Cascadas de estrellas: La espiritualidad de la chicana/mexicana/indígena." In *Esta puente, mi espalda: Voces de mujeres tercemundistas en los Estados Unidos*, ed. Cherríe Moraga and Ana Castillo, pp. 256–266. San Franciso: Ism Press, 1988.

Herrera-Sobek, María. *The Mexican Corrido: A Feminist Analysis*. Bloomington and Indianapolis: Indiana University Press, 1990.

Johnson, Julie Greer. "Bernal Díaz and the Women of the Conquest." *Hispanófila* 82 (1984): 67–77.

———. *Women in Colonial Spanish American Literature*. Westport, Conn.: Greenwood Press, 1983.

Jrade, Ramón, "Inquiries into the Cristero Insurrection against the Mexican Revolution." *Latin American Research Review* 20.2 (1985): 53–70.

Kayser, Wolfgang. *Interpretación y análisis de la literaria*. Spanish version by María Mouton y V. García-Yebra. 4th ed. rev. Madrid: Editorial Gredos, 1970.

Keen, Benjamin. *The Aztec Image in Western Thought*. New Brunswick: Rutgers University Press, 1971.

————. "Recent Writing on the Spanish Conquest." *Latin American Research Review* 20.2 (1985): 161–171.

Keenen, Edward L. "Two Types of Presuppositions in Natural Language." In *Studies in Linguistic Semantics*, ed. Charles Fillmore and D. Terrence Langendoen, pp. 45–54. New York: Holt, Rinehart & Winston, 1971.

Klor de Alva, J. Jorge, H. B. Nicholson, and Eloise Quiñones Keber, eds. *The Work of Bernardino de Sahagún: Pioneer Ethnographer of Sixteenth Century Mexico*. Albany: Institute of Mesoamerican Studies, 1988.

Knowlton, Robert J. "Recent Historical Works on Nineteenth-Century Mexico." *Latin American Research Review* 20.1 (1985): 222–231.

Kolodny, Annette. *The Lay of the Land: Metaphor as Experience and History in American Life and Letters*. Chapel Hill: University of North Carolina Press, 1975.

Lafaye, Jacques. *Quetzalcoatl and Guadalupe: The Formation of Mexican National Consciousness, 1531–1813*. Trans. Benjamin Keen. Chicago: University of Chicago Press, 1976.

Las Casas, Bartolomé de. *Historia de las Indias*. 3 vols. Mexico City: Fondo de Cultura Económica, 1951.

————. *History of the Indies*. Trans. and ed. André Collard. New York: Harper and Row, 1971.

Layera, Ramón. "Mecanismos de fabulación y mitificación de la historia en las 'comedias impolíticas' y las *Coronas* de Rodolfo Usigli." *Latin American Theatre Review* 18.2 (1985): 49–55.

Leal, Luis. "Female Archetypes in Mexican Literature." In *Women in Hispanic Literature: Icons and Fallen Idols*, ed. Beth Miller, pp. 227–242. Berkeley: University of California Press, 1983.

————. "History and Myth in the Narrative of Carlos Fuentes." In *Carlos Fuentes: A Critical View*, ed. Robert Brody and Charles Rossman, pp. 3–17. Austin: University Texas Press, 1982.

————. "*Jicoténcal*, primera novela histórica en castellano." *Revista Iberoamericana* 25.49 (1960): 9–31.

León de Garay, Alfonso. *Una aproximación a la psicología del mexicano*. Mexico City: Editora Ibero-Mexicana, 1956.

León-Portilla, Miguel, ed. *The Broken Spears: The Aztec Account of the Conquest of the Mexican Empire*. Boston: Beacon Press, 1962.

————. *Visión de los vencidos*. Mexico City: Universidad Nacional Autónoma de México, 1959.

Lomelí, Francisco A. "Los mitos de la mexicanidad en la trilogía de Rodolfo Usigli." *Cuadernos Hispanoamericanos* 333 (1978): 466–477.

López Austin, Alfredo. *The Human Body and Ideology: Concepts of the Ancient Nahuas*. Trans. Thelma Ortiz de Montellano and Bernardo Ortiz de Montellano. Salt Lake City: University of Utah Press, 1988.

McNeill, William H. *Plagues and Peoples*. New York: Doubleday, 1976.

McPheeters, D. W. "*Xicoténcatl*, símbolo republicano y romántico." *Nueva Revista de Filología Hispánica* 10 (1956): 403–411.

Madariaga, Salvador. *Hernán Cortés, Conquerer of Mexico City*. 1942. Garden City, N.Y.: Doubleday, 1969.

Magnarelli, Sharon. *The Lost Rib: Female Characters in the Spanish American Novel.* Lewisburg, Penn.: Bucknell University Press, 1985.

Maltby, William S. *Black Legend in England.* Durham: Duke University Press, 1971.

Merrim, Stephanie. "Review of Todorov's *La Conquête de l'Amérique.*" *Modern Language Studies* 14.3 (1984): 93–96.

Meyer, Michael C., and William L. Sherman. *The Course of Mexican History.* New York: Oxford University Press, 1979.

Miller, Arthur. "The Family in Modern Drama." In *Modern Drama Essays in Modern Criticism,* ed. Travis Bogard and William I. Oliver, pp. 219–233. New York: Oxford University Press, 1965.

Miller, Beth. *Mujeres en la literatura.* Mexico City: Fleischer, 1978.

Mirandé, Alfredo, and Evangelina Enríquez. *La Chicana: The Mexican-American Woman.* Chicago: University of Chicago Press, 1979.

Monterde, Francisco. "Juárez, Maximiliano y Carlota en las obras de los dramaturgos mexicanos." *Cuadernos Americanos* 136 (1964): 231–240.

Mörner, Magnus. "Historical Research on Race Relations in Latin America during the National Period." In *Race and Class in Latin America,* ed. Magnus Mörner, pp. 199–230. New York and London: Columbia University Press, 1970.

———. *Race Mixture in the History of Latin America.* Boston: Little, Brown, 1967.

Motolinía (Fray Toribio de Benavente). *Historia de los indios de Nueva España.* Translated as *Motolinía's History of the Indians of New Spain* by Elizabeth Andros Foster. 1950. Westport, Conn.: Greenwood Press, 1973.

Niblo, Stephen R., and Laurens B. Perry. "Recent Additions to Nineteenth-Century Mexican Historiography." *Latin American Research Review* 13.2 (1978): 3–45.

Nicholson, Irene. *The X in Mexico: Growth within Tradition.* New York: Doubleday, 1966.

Nigro, Kirsten. "Rhetoric and History in Three Mexican Plays." *Latin American Theatre Review* 21.2 (1987): 65–73.

Ordóñez, Elizabeth. "The Concept of Cultural Identity in Chicana Poetry." *Third Woman,* 2.1 (1984): 75–82.

Orozco y Berra, Manuel. *Historia antigua y de la conquista de México.* 4 vols. Mexico City: Porrúa, 1960.

Palerm Vich, Angel. "Sobre las relaciones poligámicas entre indígenas y españoles durante la conquista de México, y sobre algunos de sus antecedentes en España." In *Cortés ante la juventud,* ed. Rafael García Granados, pp. 231–278. Publicaciones de la sociedad de estudios cortesianos, no. 3. Mexico City: Editorial Jus, 1949.

Patai, R. *Myth and Modern Man.* Englewood Cliffs, N.J.: Prentice-Hall, 1972.

Paz, Octavio. *Posdata.* Mexico City: Siglo Veintiuno, 1974.

———. *Sor Juana Inés de la Cruz o Las trampas de la fe.* Barcelona: Seix Barral, 1982. Translated as *Sor Juana: Or, The Traps of Faith* by Margaret Sayers Peden. Cambridge, Mass.: Harvard University Press, 1988.

Pescatello, Ann. "Modernization of Female Status in Mexico: The Image of Women's Magazines." In *Female and Male in Latin America*, ed. Ann Pescatello, pp. 246–257. Pittsburgh: University of Pittsburgh Press, 1973.

———. *Power and Pawn: The Female in Iberian Families, Societies, and Cultures*. Westport, Conn.: Greenwood Press, 1976.

Phillips, Rachel. "Marina/Malinche: Masks and Shadows." In *Women in Hispanic Literature: Icons and Fallen Idols*, ed. Beth Miller, pp. 97–114. Berkeley: University of California Press, 1983.

Poniatowska, Elena. *Hasta no verte Jesús mío*. Mexico City: Biblioteca Era, 1969.

Prescott, William H. *History of the Conquest of Mexico and History of the Conquest of Peru, 1843–1847*. New York: Modern Library, 1936.

Pupo-Walker, Enrique. *La vocación literaria del pensamiento histórico en América*. Madrid: Gredos, 1982.

Rascón, María Antonieta. "La mujer y la lucha social." In *Imagen y realidad de la mujer*, ed. Elena Urrutia, pp. 139–174. Mexico City: SepSetentas, 1975.

Reyes Nevares, Salvador. "El machismo mexicano." *Mundo Nuevo* 46 (1970): 14–19.

Rodríguez, Gustavo A. *Doña Marina*. Mexico City: Imprenta de la Secretaría de Relaciones Exteriores, 1935.

Rodríguez-Nieto, Catherine, trans. "Lucha Corpi." In *Fireflight: Three Latin American Poets, Bilingual Anthology*, pp. 43–83. Berkeley: Oyez, 1976.

Rodríguez Valdés, María J. *La mujer azteca*. Mexico City: UNAM, 1988.

Sahagún, Bernardino de. *Florentine Codex: General History of the Things of New Spain*. Ed. and trans. Arthur J. O. Anderson and Charles E. Dibble. 12 vols. Santa Fe: School of American Research, and Salt Lake City: University of Utah, 1950–1969.

———. *Historia general de las cosas de Nueva España*. Ed. Angel María Garibay K. 4 vols. Mexico City: Editorial Porrúa, 1956.

Saldívar, Samuel G. *Evolución del personaje femenino en la novela mexicana*. Lanham, Md.: University Press of America, 1985.

Sánchez, José. *Hispanic Heroes of Discovery and Conquest of Spanish America in European Drama*. Estudios de Hispanófila. Chapel Hill, N.C.: Editorial Castalia Madrid, 1978.

Sánchez, Marta E. *Contemporary Chicana Poetry: A Critical Approach to an Emerging Literature*. Berkeley and Los Angeles: University of California Press, 1985.

Sánchez Albornoz, Nicolás. *The Population of Latin America*. Berkeley: University of California Press, 1974.

Santley, Robert S. "Recent Works on Aztec History." *Latin American Research Review* 19.1 (1984): 261–269.

Sapir, J. David. "The Anatomy of Metaphor." In *The Social Use of Metaphor*, ed. J. David Sapir and J. Christopher Crocker, pp. 3–32. Philadelphia: University of Pennsylvania Press, 1977.

Scholes, Walter V. *Mexican Politics during the Juárez Regime*. Columbia: University of Missouri Press, 1957.

Schweickart, Patrocinio P., and Elizabeth A. Flynn. "Introduction." In Gender and Reading: Essays on Readers, Texts, and Contexts, ed. Elizabeth Flynn and Patrocinio Schweickart, pp. ix–xxx. Baltimore: Johns Hopkins University Press, 1986.

Sierra, Justo. *Evolución política del pueblo mexicano*. Vol. 12 of *Obras completas del maestro Justo Sierra*, ed. Edmundo O'Gorman. Mexico City: UNAM, 1957.

———. *The Political Evolution of the Mexican People*. Intro. Edmundo O'Gorman. Trans. Charles Ramsdell. Austin: University of Texas Press, 1969.

Simmons, Merle E. *The Mexican Corrido as a Source of Interpretive Study of Modern Mexico, 1870–1950*. Bloomington: Indiana University Press, 1957.

Solís, Antonio de. *Historia de la conquista de México*. Prol. Edmundo O'Gorman. Mexico City: Editorial Porrúa, 1968.

———. *The History of the Conquest of Mexico by the Spaniards*. 2 vols. 1753. Trans. Thomas Townsend. Rev. Nathanael Hooke. New York: AMS Press, 1973.

Sommer, Doris. "Not Just Any Narrative: How Romance Can Love Us to Death." In *The Historical Novel in Latin America*, ed. Donald Balderston, pp. 47–73. Gaithersburg, Md.: Ediciones Hispamérica, 1986.

Sommers, Joseph. "Critical Approaches to Chicano Literature." In *Modern Chicano Writers*, ed. Joseph Sommers and Tomás Ybarra-Frausto, pp. 31–40. Englewood Cliffs, N.J.: Prentice-Hall, 1979.

———. "Interpreting Tomás Rivera." In *Modern Chicano Writers*, ed. Joseph Sommers and Tomás Ybarra-Frausto, pp. 94–107. Englewood Cliffs, N.J.: Prentice-Hall, 1979.

Somonte, Mariano G. *Doña Marina, "La Malinche."* Mexico City: Edimex, 1969.

Sonntag, Iliana. "Hacia una bibliografía de poesía femenina chicana." *La palabra* 2.2 (1980): 91–109.

Soto, Shirlene A. *The Mexican Woman: A Study of Her Participation in the Revolution, 1910–1940*. Palo Alto: R and E Pubs., 1979.

———. "Tres modelos culturales: La Virgen de Guadalupe, la Malinche y la Llorona." *Fem* 10.48 (1986): 13–16.

Stabb, Martin B. "Indigenism and Racism in Mexican Thought, 1857–1911." *Journal of Interamerican Studies* 1 (1959): 405–423.

Sullivan, Constance. "*Macho* and *Machismo* as Loan Words to American English." *Ideologies and Literature* 4.17 second cycle (1983): 46–62.

Sweeney, Judith. "Chicana History: A Review of the Literature." In *Essays on La Mujer*, ed. Rosaura Sanchez and Rosa Martinez Cruz, pp. 99–123. Los Angeles: Chicano Studies Center, 1977.

Taggart, James M. *Nahuat Myths and Social Structures*. Austin: University of Texas Press, 1983.

Teja Zabre, Alfonso. *Historia de México: Una moderna interpretación*. 4th ed. Mexico City: Juan Pablos, 1961.

Tibón, Gutierre. *Historia del nombre y de la fundación de México*. Mexico City: Fondo de Cultura Económica, 1975.

Todorov, Tzvetan. *The Conquest of America*. Trans. Richard Howard. New York: Harper and Row, 1985.

Tompkins, Jane. *Sensational Designs: The Cultural Work of American Fiction (1790–1860)*. New York: Oxford University Press, 1985.

Turner, Victor. *Dramas, Fields, and Metaphors: Symbolic Action in Human Society*. Ithaca: Cornell University Press, 1974.

Urrutia, Elena, ed. *Imagen y realidad de la mujer*. Mexico City: SepSetentas, 1975.

Vidal, Hernán. *Literatura hispanoamericana e ideología liberal: Surgimiento y crisis*. Buenos Aires: Ediciones Hispamérica, 1976.

Warner, Ralph E. *Historia de la novela mexicana en el siglo XIX*. Mexico City: Antigua Librería Robredo, 1953.

Whitaker, Arthur P. "The Dual Role of Latin America in the Enlightenment." In *Latin America and the Enlightenment*, ed. Arthur P. Whitaker, pp. 3–21. 2d ed. Ithaca: Cornell University Press, 1961.

White, Hayden. *Metahistory: The Historical Imagination in Nineteenth Century Europe*. Baltimore: Johns Hopkins University Press, 1973.

———. *Tropics of Discourse: Essays in Cultural Criticism*. Baltimore: Johns Hopkins University Press, 1978.

White, John Manchip. *Cortés and the Downfall of the Aztec Empire: A Study in a Conflict of Cultures*. London: Hamish Hamilton, 1971.

Wogan, Daniel. "The Indian in Mexican Dramatic Poetry." *Bulletin of Hispanic Studies* 27 (1950): 163–171.

Yarbro-Bejarano, Yvonne. "Chicana Literature from a Chicana Feminist Perspective." In *Chicana Creativity and Criticism: Charting New Frontiers in American Literature*, ed. María Herrera-Sobek and Helena Viramontes, pp. 139–145. Houston: Arte Público Press, 1988.

———. "The Female Subject in Chicano Theatre: Sexuality, 'Race,' and Class." *Theatre Journal* 38 (1986): 389–407.

Young, Dolly J. "Mexican Literary Reactions to Tlatelolco 1968." *Latin American Research Review* 20.2 (1985): 71–85.

Zantwijk, Rudolph van. *The Aztec Arrangement*. Norman: University of Oklahoma Press, 1985.

Zendejas, Adelina. *La mujer en la intervención francesa*. Mexico City: Sociedad Mexicana de Geografía y Estadística, 1962.

Index

Lightning Source UK Ltd.
Milton Keynes UK
UKHW041006171122
412280UK00017B/168